Better Homes and Gardens

ENCYCLOPEDIA
of
COOKING

Volume 13

Turn twice-baked potatoes into dinner's main attraction by serving Ham-Stuffed Potatoes. Bits of green pepper and pimiento and cheese over the top make this a colorful entrée.

On the cover: Meatball Pie for supper. Cereal and sesame seeds coat refrigerated biscuits for the topper, while canned meatballs and carrots combine in the mixture underneath.

BETTER HOMES AND GARDENS BOOKS
NEW YORK   DES MOINES

© Meredith Corporation, 1971. All Rights Reserved.
Printed in the United States of America.
First Printing.
Library of Congress Catalog Card Number: 73-129265
SNB 696-02013-0

POPOVER—A big, puffy, steam-raised quick bread with a crusty outer shell and a hollow interior. The crisp, golden brown shell has a tender, moist lining.

Before the advent of a reliable baking powder in the mid-1800s, popovers were one of the few quick bread alternatives the homemaker had to the time-consuming yeast-raised breads. It seems likely that the name popover came about because the batter "popped over" the edge of the pan in which it was baked. In fact, cast iron pans resembling muffin pans, but with straighter sides, were manufactured specifically as popover pans.

The Englishman's beloved Yorkshire pudding is actually popover batter made with drippings from roast beef and baked in a large pan rather than as individual popovers. The popover is also a first cousin of the cream puff, as they both contain the same basic ingredients, only in different proportions. Popover batter is quite thin; cream puff dough is very stiff. Both are leavened by the steam that forms during the first few minutes of baking at a very high temperature. However, the steam would be useless if it were not for the physical properties of the ingredients used in popovers, particularly those of the flour and of the whole eggs.

When making popovers, all-purpose flour or bread flour is essential because it contains a large amount of hard-wheat protein, which forms gluten when mixed with a liquid. As the batter is beaten, the gluten develops an elastic quality that later allows the gluten to stretch to form the shell around the expanding steam. (Do not use cake flour since the gluten-producing protein, unnecessary in cake baking, is present in only a very small amount.) At the same time the gluten is stretching, the starch in the flour swells to produce the moist, tender lining.

The amount of egg in popovers has a great effect on the final volume. Two eggs per cup of flour is the standard proportion, but three eggs are sometimes used. The beaten egg stretches along with the starch during the high temperature baking, then it begins to coagulate so that the walls of the shell will not collapse before baking of the popover is completed.

Other ingredients are also important in popovers. Milk is the liquid and salt adds flavor. Although popovers could be made without shortening or oil, these ingredients contribute greatly to the tenderness of the final popover product.

In years gone by, two steps were considered important in making popovers—although neither is now necessary. One was lengthy beating. The other was preheating the popover pan or custard cups before pouring in the batter. Test kitchen experience has shown that you need not beat the batter for more than two minutes, pro-

Add the amount of curry to suit your taste for Curried Ham in Popovers. Then, spoon the flavorful meat mixture over Popovers.

Serve crisp and crusty Popovers hot from the oven. For elegant entertaining, accompany with butter curls and sweet-tart jelly.

viding the beating is done with a rotary beater or an electric mixer. Beating is even easier and quicker with a blender. And since there is no appreciable difference between popovers from preheated pans and those from pans not preheated, you do not have to preheat the pan or cups.

As the popovers complete the last few minutes of baking, prick them with a fork to prevent sogginess. Since the structure of the popovers has already been set, the popovers will not collapse when this is done. Then, when the baking time is up, if you prefer dry, crisp popovers, turn off the oven and leave them in the oven 30 minutes longer with the oven door ajar.

Popovers are easy to make and a delight to serve. In addition to being crusty and delicious, they are bound to generate conversation. Popovers are equally at home with butter and jam for breakfast or as a piping-hot partner for a luncheon salad or a bowl of soup. Split lengthwise, popovers steal the spotlight when the hollow is filled with a creamed mixture. And who can pass them by when they are served with a beef dinner. (See also *Bread*.)

A few minutes before baking time is up, prick Popovers with a fork to let the steam escape. This helps to make Popovers crisp.

Toasted with butter and Parmesan cheese, Poppy Seed Rolls are easy-to-fix grillmates for steak or chicken cooked over the coals.

Popovers

      2 eggs
      1 cup milk
      1 cup sifted all-purpose flour
    ½ teaspoon salt
      1 tablespoon salad oil

Place eggs in mixing bowl; add milk, flour, and salt. Beat 1½ minutes with rotary or electric beater. Add oil and beat 30 seconds longer. Pour batter into 6 to 8 greased custard cups, filling them only half full.

Bake at 475° for 15 minutes. Reduce oven temperature to 350° and bake till browned and firm, 25 to 30 minutes longer. (Do not open oven door to peek until total baking time is almost completed.) A few minutes before removing from oven, prick with a fork to let the steam escape. Serve hot. Makes 6 to 8 popovers.

Note: If you like popovers dry and crisp, turn off oven after popovers are baked and leave them in oven 30 minutes with oven door ajar.

Pecan Popovers

Follow recipe for Popovers. Stir ¼ cup finely chopped pecans into batter before filling the custard cups. Bake as directed above.

Curried Ham in Popovers

      2 tablespoons chopped green
          pepper
      1 tablespoon chopped onion
      1 tablespoon butter or margarine
          •   •   •
      1 10½-ounce can condensed cream
          of celery soup
    ⅓ cup mayonnaise or salad
          dressing
    ⅓ cup milk
    ¼ to ½ teaspoon curry powder
      2 cups cubed fully cooked ham
      6 popovers

In medium saucepan cook green pepper and onion in butter or margarine till tender but not brown. Stir in celery soup, mayonnaise or salad dressing, milk, curry powder, and cubed ham. Cook and stir till heated through. Split hot popovers lengthwise. Spoon creamed ham mixture into popover halves. Makes 6 servings.

POPPY SEED—The tiny, slate blue seeds of an annual poppy plant. Poppy seeds are so small that it takes about 900,000 to make a pound. Although they appear to be round, these tiny seeds are actually kidney-shaped.

Although the poppy from which poppy seeds come is thought to be native to Asia, most of the seeds imported today come from Holland. Some come from France, Poland, Germany, and England, too. These seeds come from the same poppy plant that gives opium; however, because of the plant structure, the ripe, dried seeds have no narcotic properties and are perfectly safe to eat as a food.

Poppy seeds have been enjoyed as a food for hundreds of years in Greece, India, and Europe. And they are still in wide use today. Occasionally, the seeds are crushed for the oil that they contain, which is used in the production of some margarines. Most often, however, poppy seeds are used as toppers for breads, mixed with noodles, or ground or crushed and sweetened for use as filling for rolls, sweet breads, and desserts. When the seeds are toasted, the nutty flavor is enhanced, as the heat brings out the flavor of the oil. Because of their oil content, poppy seeds that are not used right away should be stored in the refrigerator to prevent rancidity from developing at a rapid rate.

In addition to the whole seeds, prepared poppy seed fillings are available on the market. These fillings are ready to use in cakes, coffee cakes, and sweet breads.

Poppy Seed-Lime Dressing

⅓ cup vinegar
¼ cup lime juice

. . .

¾ cup sugar
1 teaspoon salt
1 teaspoon dry mustard
1 teaspoon poppy seed
1 teaspoon paprika
1 cup salad oil
½ teaspoon onion juice

In saucepan heat vinegar and lime juice to boiling. Combine sugar, salt, dry mustard, poppy seed, and paprika. Add to hot mixture in saucepan. Stir to dissolve sugar. Add salad oil and onion juice. Beat with rotary beater till thoroughly mixed and slightly thickened. Chill thoroughly. Spoon the salad dressing over fresh or canned fruit. Makes 1¾ cups dressing.

Stroganoff with Poppy Seed Noodles

1 pound beef sirloin, cut in
   ¼-inch strips
1 tablespoon shortening or oil
1 medium onion, sliced
1 clove garlic, crushed
1 10½-ounce can condensed cream
   of mushroom soup
1 cup dairy sour cream
1 3-ounce can broiled sliced
   mushrooms, undrained (⅔ cup)
2 tablespoons catsup
2 teaspoons Worcestershire sauce
4 ounces medium noodles, cooked
1 tablespoon butter or margarine
1 teaspoon poppy seed

In skillet brown meat in hot shortening. Add onion and garlic; cook till onion is crisp-tender. Blend next 5 ingredients. Pour over meat. Cook and stir over low heat till hot. Drain noodles; toss with butter and poppy seed. Serve sauce over noodles. Makes 4 servings.

Poppy Seed Torte

⅓ cup poppy seed
¾ cup milk
¾ cup butter or margarine
1½ cups sugar
1½ teaspoons vanilla
2 cups sifted cake flour
2½ teaspoons baking powder
¼ teaspoon salt
4 stiffly beaten egg whites
   Filling

Soak poppy seed in milk for 1 hour. Cream butter and sugar till fluffy. Mix in vanilla and milk with seed. Sift together dry ingredients; stir into creamed mixture. Fold in egg whites. Bake in 2 well-greased and lightly floured 8x1½-inch round pans at 375° till cake tests done, about 20 to 25 minutes. Cool 10 minutes; remove from pans. Cool. Split layers. Spread Filling between layers; chill. Sift confectioners' sugar atop the torte.

Filling: In saucepan mix ½ cup sugar and 1 tablespoon cornstarch. Combine 1½ cups milk and 4 slightly beaten egg yolks. Stir into sugar. Cook and stir till bubbly; cool. Add 1 teaspoon vanilla and ¼ cup chopped walnuts.

Poppy Seed Swirled Bread

    2 **packages active dry yeast**
    5 **to 6 cups sifted all-purpose**
          flour
1½ **cups milk**
⅓ **cup sugar**
⅓ **cup shortening**
    1 **teaspoon salt**
    3 **eggs**
        Poppy Seed Filling

In large mixer bowl combine yeast with *2 cups* of the flour. Heat together milk, sugar, shortening, and salt just till warm, stirring to melt shortening. Add to dry ingredients. Add eggs. Beat at low speed ½ minute, scraping bowl constantly. Beat 3 minutes at high speed. By hand, stir in enough of the remaining flour to make a moderately stiff dough.

Turn out onto lightly floured surface; knead till smooth and satiny, 5 to 10 minutes. Shape into ball. Place in lightly greased bowl, turning once to grease surface. Cover; let rise in warm place till double, 1 to 1¾ hours.

Meanwhile, prepare *Poppy Seed Filling;* Pour 1 cup boiling water over ¾ cup poppy seed (4 ounces); drain. Cover with 1 cup lukewarm water and let stand 30 minutes. Drain thoroughly. Grind the poppy seed in blender, or use the finest blade of food grinder. Stir in ½ cup chopped nuts, ⅓ cup honey, and 1 teaspoon grated lemon peel. Fold in 1 stiffly beaten egg white.

Punch down bread dough. Divide dough in 2 parts. Cover and let rest 10 minutes. On lightly floured board, roll one part of dough to a 24x 8-inch rectangle; spread with *half* the filling. Roll up, starting on 8-inch side; seal long ends. Place, seam side down, in greased 9x5x3-inch loaf pan. Repeat with second part of dough and filling. Cover loaves with cloth. Let rise till double, 30 to 45 minutes. Bake at 350° for 35 to 40 minutes. Remove from pans and cool on rack. Makes 2 loaves.

Poppy Seed Rolls

    3 **tablespoons butter or margarine**
    1 **teaspoon poppy seed**
    2 **tablespoons grated Parmesan**
          cheese
    6 **brown-and-serve cloverleaf rolls**

In foilware pan melt the butter or margarine on the grill. Add poppy seed and grated Parmesan cheese. Separate the sections of cloverleaf rolls and arrange in butter mixture in pan. Brown the pieces of rolls on grill, turning rolls until all sides are toasted.

PORCUPINE MEATBALL—A type of meatball containing rice, which, when cooked, protrudes from the meat in such a way as to resemble the quills of a porcupine. The rice is uncooked when the balls are shaped but swells during cooking in a sauce.

Porcupine Meatballs

    1 **slightly beaten egg**
    1 **10¾-ounce can condensed tomato**
          soup
  ¼ **cup uncooked long-grain rice**
    2 **tablespoons finely chopped onion**
    1 **tablespoon snipped parsley**
  ½ **teaspoon salt**
      Dash pepper
    1 **pound ground beef**

        • • •

  ½ **cup water**
    1 **teaspoon Worcestershire sauce**

Combine beaten egg, ¼ *cup* of the tomato soup, uncooked rice, onion, parsley, salt, and pepper. Add ground beef; mix well. Shape the mixture into 20 meatballs; place in skillet. Mix remaining soup, water, and Worcestershire sauce. Pour over meatballs. Bring to boiling; reduce heat and simmer, covered, for 40 minutes, stirring often. Makes 4 to 5 servings.

PORGY (*pôr'gē*) A lean, saltwater fish that is found in warm, coastal waters throughout the world. One type of porgy, the scup, inhabits the waters along the east coast of North America.

The porgy is a good-eating fish that attains a length of 12 to 18 inches and can weigh up to four pounds. Those sold in markets average two pounds. Fish markets near the coast sell fresh, dressed porgy. They are seldom cut into fillets or shipped inland. Fry, broil, or bake the porgy in a sauce. (See also *Fish.*)

# PORK

Leaner breeds of pork produce a wide selection
of tender, meaty cuts for recipe preparation.

When a juicy, tender pork chop is placed before you on the dinner table, you may well say, "That's a nice piece of pork," and you'd be right. But did you know that pork chops come from lean hogs, which make them ideal for low-calorie diets?

Pork is the meat of a hog which is from 4 to 6½ months old, generally weighing 190 to 250 pounds. From this hog you get pork chops, loin cuts, ham, bacon, and a host of other meaty cuts. A pig, on the other hand, is a young animal that hasn't reached market weight—unless for use as a suckling pig. Once the animal weighs 190 pounds, it is called a hog. These hogs are bred and fed to provide lean meat with fewer calories. The too-fat pig of yesteryear is an animal of the past.

Hogs of former years were often large, corpulent beasts that were fattened up to give the appearance of health. As such, they were used by the ancient Egyptians as a sacrifice to the gods, and in later years, by other people as animals possessing magical powers. In those superstitious eras, many farmers planted pig tails or ribs to aid the growth of their crops.

These portly animals have also served as the centerpiece for many medieval feasts; the large untamed hog (or wild boar) with an apple in its mouth and surrounded by potatoes and vegetables was placed on a platter and set on the table. Lacking the social graces of today's pork eater, medieval people would yank off large sections of the meat and eat them out of hand.

Elegant way to prepare a loin roast

← Top Rio Grande Pork Roast with crushed corn chips. Accompany with Bean and Avocado Boats (see *Salad* for recipe).

Not only has the animal changed over the years—in size, leanness, and domesticity—but cooking methods have become sophisticated as is evident in this recipe:

Roast Pork Loin

> 1 3- to 4-pound boneless rolled
>   pork loin roast
> 1 12-ounce jar pineapple preserves
> ⅓ cup horseradish mustard

Place pork on rack in shallow roasting pan. Roast, uncovered, at 325° till meat thermometer registers 170°, about 2½ to 3 hours. Heat preserves and mustard. Brush small amount on meat last 15 minutes of roasting. Pass remaining sauce. Makes 3 to 4 servings per pound.

The large porker was, and still is used for entertainment. Shakespeare referred to greased pig contests where a whole village would try to catch a greased pig. Whoever caught it took it home—hence, the term "bringing home the bacon." Even today, this animal is used at county fairs in greased pig or hog calling contests.

While De Soto was the first to introduce pigs to America (he brought them from Cuba in 1539), the early colonists also included pigs on their ships as they traveled to the New World. Since this animal was well suited to the wild terrain in America, people took the hog along with them as they went westward. Thus, it became one of America's first farm animals.

By the mid-1800s, hog production was important to the economy of the Midwest. So much so, in fact, that canals were built primarily for transporting these animals to the packing plants. Frequently, this was to Cincinnati. In the 1850s, Cincinnati packed or "salted down" so much pork that it became known as "Porkopolis." Fortunately, with the development of the refrigerated railroad car, fresh pork was shipped across the country for all to enjoy so that today, you don't have to live by one of these waterways to enjoy it.

Nutritional value: With the new lean breeds of hogs and the closer trimming of the meat by packers, the fat content of pork is often low, depending on the cut of pork. Consequently, meat from these leaner hogs is good for weight-control diets. A 3½-ounce serving of roasted tenderloin has 240 calories, meat from six roasted, medium-sized spareribs has 246 calories, and one 6-ounce (uncooked weight) loin chop, cooked, has 314 calories. One 2½x2x2½-inch slice of roasted picnic shoulder has about 116 calories, and one 3x2x½-inch slice of roasted Boston shoulder (butt) has 164 calories.

Pork is also noted for its vitamin B content—thiamine, riboflavin, and niacin. In fact, pork has more thiamine than any other single food source. As you know, thiamine is an essential part of the diet for normal functioning of the nervous system, and it helps prevent beriberi.

As with other meats, pork also contains high-quality protein. The meat is 96 to 98 percent digestible, so it should be included in the diet often. Pork also contains minerals such as iron, potassium, phosphorus, and magnesium.

Forms of Pork

It's not only humorous, but true, to say that one can eat just about all of the pig except the squeal. Pork is available in many different cuts as fresh, cured, and cured and smoked. Familiarizing yourself with the portions of the hog from which the different cuts come will help you in identifying the common cuts.

Starting at the front of the animal, shoulder cuts include the Boston shoulder (sometimes referred to as butt) and blade steaks; the picnics and arm cuts are from the upper part of the front legs. The loin area on the top side of the midsection includes the blade loin, rib, center loin, and sirloin cuts. The expression "eating high off the hog" refers to this area, and it probably originated some years ago to signify that when a person changed from his diet of salt pork to eating the meaty loin parts, he was thought to be well-off.

The lower portion, the breast of the hog, produces spareribs and bacon, and the hind legs yield cured and smoked hams and pork leg roasts, also called fresh hams. Even the hocks and feet can be cooked.

Fresh pork: At the packing plant, the carcasses are dressed, chilled, then cut and trimmed into the various market cuts. Trimmed-off fat is used to make lard and other shortenings. Some of the fresh pork cuts are chopped, seasoned, and stuffed into casings for fresh sausage (see also *Sausage*), while some cuts are ground for use in patties and meat loaves.

Occasionally, shoulder cuts are marketed as porklets. This boneless cut has been processed through a machine that scores the surface, breaking muscle fibers.

Even the hog's ears and tail, cooked crisp or used in a sauce, are favorites in some households. Other fresh pork products include liver, heart, chitterlings, pig's feet, and tongue.

Although the majority of pork is sold in cuts, with roasts and chops being the most popular, you can special-order a whole suckling pig (a very young pig that is still nursing, weighing 10 to 12 pounds dressed) or a larger, whole dressed pig.

Cured, and cured and smoked pork: Because of the popular flavor that curing and smoking impart, a large portion of the pork available today is processed in this manner. First, the meat is cured with brine. A limited amount of pork, including some picnics and hams, is cured but not smoked. These cured cuts are often referred to as pickled. Pickled pig's feet have a slightly different pickling cure and are also marketed without being smoked. The majority of the cured cuts, however, are smoked as well as cured. Some of these need additional cooking, such as bacon, while others are ready to eat, as is the case with fully cooked and canned hams. (See *Bacon, Ham* for additional information.)

Tenderloin (left) is the small, tapering, round muscle that lies on one side of the T-bone, about one-third the length of the loin. Since this is a boneless, very tender and lean cut, it can be roasted or braised. Slices from the tenderloin can be panfried. *Sirloin Roast* (upper right) comes from the loin section and contains the hip bone. The largest muscle in this cut is referred to as the loin eye, while the smaller muscle is called the tenderloin and becomes larger as it approaches the hip. Roast this cut. *Loin Chop* (lower right) contains a T-bone and is cut from the center of the loin. The T-bone separates the larger loin eye muscle from the smaller tenderloin muscle. Braise, broil, or panfry this cut of pork.

Fresh Boston Shoulder Roast (top) is occasionally referred to as Boston Butt. It contains a part of the blade bone and comes from the shoulder area of the animal. Roast this cut. *Smoked Shoulder Roll* (or *Butt*) (left) comes from the largest muscle of the Fresh Boston Shoulder Roast. This boneless cut is cured, smoked, and rolled. Roast or simmer this cut in liquid. Slices can be panfried or broiled. *Blade Steak* (right) is a fresh pork cut from the Fresh Boston Shoulder Roast. It can be identified by the blade bone. Braise, broil, or panfry the steaks.

Crown Roast (upper left) is made from the rib sections of two pork loins with six to ten center ribs in each. The ends of the ribs are "frenched" (meat is removed, leaving about 1 inch of each bone exposed) and the backbone is removed. Then, the two sections of pork (with ribs to the outside) are tied together forming a crown. Roast. Center may be filled. *Center Loin Roast* (upper right) is cut from the middle section of the loin. The larger muscle is the loin eye, and the smaller muscle is the tenderloin. The T-bone separates the two muscles and is used for identification. Roast. *Rib Chops* (bottom) are identified by the rib bone. Chops are cut from the rib section of the loin. Muscle present is the loin eye. Extra-thick or two-rib chops are used for stuffed pork chops. Have pockets cut parallel to rib and on rib side of chop. Roast or braise.

Canadian-Style Bacon (left) is made from the boneless loin eye. This formed cut is cured and smoked and is usually available fully cooked. Canadian-style bacon is long and usually round with the characteristic pinkish color of cured and smoked pork. Roast the whole piece or slice and broil, panbroil, or panfry. *Boneless Center Loin Roast* (upper right) is the loin eye, the largest muscle in the loin section, and is cut from the Center Loin Roast. Roast this cut. *Butterfly Chop* (lower right) is made from a boned, thick chop or a boneless loin piece. A slice is made through the fat surface almost all the way through the meat, then it is spread flat, making a butterfly-shaped chop, which appears larger and cooks in less time. Braise or broil this cut of pork.

Back Ribs (left) are also called Country-Style Back Ribs. These meaty ribs contain the rib bones cut from the rib area of the loin. The thicker layer of meat covering the ribs comes from the loin eye muscle. Roast or braise these ribs. *Blade Loin Roast* (upper right) comes from the rib section of the loin next to the shoulder. This roast contains the rib bones on one side and the blade bones at one end. The loin eye is the predominant muscle. Roast this cut. *Rib Chop* (lower right) is identified by the rib bone. It is cut from the rib section of the loin; consequently, it has no tenderloin muscle. The loin eye is the only muscle. Braise, broil, or panfry rib chops.

Spareribs (left) come from the side of pork and contain the breastbone, rib bones, and rib cartilage. Roast, braise, or cook the spareribs in liquid. *Salt Side* (top right), also available as fresh, comes from the side of pork. This cut is characterized by layers of fat and lean and by a salt deposit on the outer surface because of its dry salt cure. It is used primarily for seasoning and can be cooked in liquid, panbroiled, or panfried. *Bacon* (bottom right) is available in a slab, or sliced thin or thick. Bacon comes from the cured and smoked side of pork. Broil, panbroil, or panfry slices. Bacon Squares (not shown) are cured and smoked pieces of pork from the jowl.

Smoked Picnic Shoulders (halves at bottom) are sometimes called callie hams or incorrectly referred to as picnic hams because of their resemblance in flavor to ham. The picnic is cut from the lower shoulder and arm section of the front legs, while a ham is a cured and smoked cut from the hind legs. The picnic contains the shank, arm, and blade bones. The shoulder muscles are interspersed with fat, and skin covers the shank end. Picnics are cured and smoked and can be purchased fully cooked or cook-before-eating. The smoked shoulders are available either as whole or half pieces of the shoulder. A Fresh Picnic Shoulder is the same cut, except that it has not been cured or smoked. Roast or cook these cuts in liquid. *Canned Smoked Picnic Shoulder* (top) is a boneless cut that is fully cooked. These canned picnics come in square or pear-shaped cans and generally weigh three to five pounds. Heat meat or serve it cold.

Smoked Center Loin Roast (center) is cut from the middle section of the loin. It contains the larger loin eye muscle and the smaller tenderloin muscle, and it can be identified by the T-bone. It is the same cut as the fresh cut, except that it is cured and smoked. Generally, this roast is fully cooked and needs only to be heated before serving. *Smoked Loin Chops* are cut from the Smoked Center Loin Roast and also contain the T-bone. The smaller bone separates the loin eye muscle from the tenderloin. Broil or panfry these smoked chops.

Smoked Spareribs (lower left) come from the side of pork and are similar to fresh spareribs, except that smoked ribs are first cured, then smoked. They contain the breastbone, rib bones, and rib cartilage with a thin covering of meat over the ribs. Roast, braise, or cook the smoked spareribs in liquid. *Smoked Hocks* (upper right) are cut from just above the pig's feet. They are then cured and smoked. This bony, shank cut can be identified by the round bone. Fresh hocks are also available and are similar to the smoked hocks, except that the fresh ones are not cured or smoked. To cook fresh or smoked hocks, braise or cook them in liquid.

How to select

Today, with modern breeding techniques, hogs are marketed regularly, making pork available year-round. When selecting from the abundant supply of pork available in the meat counter, there are some hints to keep in mind to ensure that you are buying the quality you expect to get.

Although federal grades have been set up for pork, they are not widely used. Some packers, however, particularly those that pack smoked pork products, often indicate the quality of pork on their packaging by means of different brand names. Even though pork is not usually federally graded, all of the meat that is sold to homemakers has been inspected.

How much pork to buy

Because of the varying amounts of fat and bone in the different pork cuts, the following list is a guide to the average number of servings per pound of pork as purchased. Be sure to allow for hearty appetites.

Cut	Servings per pound
Fresh roast—bone-in sirloin, blade loin, center loin, Boston shoulder, picnic shoulder, leg (fresh ham)	2 to 3
Fresh roast—without bone tenderloin, center loin, rolled shoulder, rolled leg (fresh ham)	3 to 4
Smoked roast—bone-in picnic shoulder, center loin, ham—butt and shank	2 to 3
Smoked roast—without bone shoulder roll (butt), picnic shoulder, ham roll	3 to 4
Fully cooked smoked ham—bone-in	3 to 4
Spareribs	1 to 2

When choosing fresh pork cuts, look for fine-grained meat that is marbled with flecks of white, firm fat. There should also be a uniform covering of firm, white fat on the outside surfaces. The lean portion of the pork cut should be firm and have a light, grayish pink color, and the bones should have a slight pink tint.

You will find that the cuts of pork in greatest demand, such as the center ham slice, spareribs, bacon, and loin chops, tend to have the highest price tags, and often they will be the cuts that are the quickest to cook. However, these select cuts make up only about a third of the animal, so there are many additional cuts that are good for stretching the budget, such as the shoulder and picnic cuts and the shank and butt cuts of ham.

In addition to the fresh, cured, cured and smoked, and canned cuts, there are several other pork products including sausages, made solely with pork or in combination with other meats and spices, canned luncheon meats, packaged sliced meats, and combination dishes. With the increased demand and widespread enjoyment of pork today, there is a greater number of specialty canned and frozen products on the market.

Besides the meat products that come from the hog, there are also some other products that should be mentioned. Lard is one of the most important of these. And one should not forget that gelatin and the casings used in sausages come from the hog as do some pharmaceuticals.

How to store

Fresh, cured, cured and smoked, and cooked pork should be promptly stored in the refrigerator to maintain the best possible quality. When longer storage is desired, use your freezer, following the recommended time limits that are listed.

Fresh pork: Prepackaged meat from the supermarket should be stored in the coldest part of the refrigerator in the original wrapping. Use fresh cuts of pork, ground pork, and variety meats within a day or two after purchase, and fresh sausage within one week of purchase.

Freeze fresh pork quickly in tightly wrapped and sealed, conveniently sized packages. Store at 0° or less. Ground pork can be frozen for up to three months, while other fresh pork cuts can be kept for up to six months. Thaw meat in the refrigerator or during cooking. Allow additional time when cooking a frozen roast.

Cured, and cured and smoked pork: Pork products processed in this manner are perishable, but they keep slightly longer than do the fresh cuts. Refrigerate cured, and cured and smoked pork in the original wrapper no longer than one week. Ham slices should be kept only three to four days. Bacon will keep slightly longer.

Canned hams should be refrigerated unless the label reads otherwise. Unopened, the canned hams will keep several months in the refrigerator. However, check the label directions for suggested storage.

Some cured and smoked cuts, such as shoulder rolls, can be frozen for up to 60 days. If necessary, bacon can be frozen up to one month. Canned hams and other canned meats should not be frozen.

Cooked pork: Cool cooked pork and gravies quickly, then cover or wrap and store in the coldest part of the refrigerator. Leave the cooked meat in pieces as large as possible, although the bones may be removed first. Use within a few days.

Pork Roasting Chart			
Cut	Approximate Weight (Pounds)	Internal Temp. on Removal from Oven	Approximate Cooking Time (Total Time)
Roast meat at constant oven temperature of 325°.			
FRESH PORK			
Boston Shoulder Roast	4 to 6	170°	3 to 4 hrs.
Picnic Shoulder	5 to 8	170°	3 to 4 hrs.
Loin, center	3 to 5	170°	2½ to 3 hrs.
Loin, center; rolled (boneless)	3 to 4	170°	2½ to 3 hrs.
Loin, half	5 to 7	170°	3½ to 4¼ hrs.
Loin, blade or sirloin	3 to 4	170°	2¼ to 2¾ hrs.
Leg (fresh ham)	10 to 16	170°	4½ to 6 hrs.
Leg, half (fresh ham)	5 to 7	170°	3½ to 4½ hrs.
CURED AND SMOKED PORK			
Ham (fully cooked)			
half, boneless	4 to 5	135° to 140°	1½ to 2 hrs.
whole, boneless	8 to 10	135° to 140°	2 to 2¼ hrs.
half	5 to 7	135° to 140°	1¾ to 2¼ hrs.
whole	10 to 14	135° to 140°	2½ to 3 hrs.
Ham (cook-before-eating)			
shank or butt	3 to 4	160°	2 to 2¼ hrs.
half	5 to 7	160°	2½ to 3 hrs.
whole	10 to 14	160°	3½ to 4 hrs.
Picnic shoulder	5 to 8	170°	3 to 4½ hrs.
Shoulder roll (boneless)	2 to 3	170°	1 to 2 hrs.
Canadian-Style bacon	2 to 4	160°	1 to 2½ hrs.

How to Prepare

Most pork cuts are tender pieces of meat, and like other types of meat, pork should be cooked at low to moderate temperatures. The type of cookery that is chosen —dry-heat or moist-heat—depends sometimes on the tenderness of the cut, but usually on the dish that is being prepared. Pork cooked using the proper method will be tender, juicy, and full-flavored.

Dry-heat cookery: Use this type of preparation for the tender cuts of pork. Dry-heat cooking methods (without added moisture) include roasting, broiling or grilling, including cooking on the rotisserie, panbroiling, and panfrying. Cuts that can be prepared by dry-heat cookery include shoulder steaks and roasts, loin cuts, cured and smoked hams, and legs (fresh hams), bacon, Canadian-style bacon, ham slices, and smoked pork chops. Although fresh, thick pork chops are tender cuts, they are frequently braised.

The best way to determine the doneness of roast pork is to use a meat thermometer. Insert it midway in the thickest portion, making sure the tip doesn't touch bone or fat. Until the completion of recent research, the recommended internal temperature for all pork roasting cuts was 185° F. Now, with the exception of smoked pork cuts, 170° F. is accepted as the temperature for optimal degree of doneness for juicy pork of top eating quality.

How to Roast a Pig

Plan on 60 to 70 servings from a pig that weighs about 60 pounds, dressed. (The pig would originally weigh 90 to 100 pounds.) Choose a grassless place for roasting. In a pit 12 inches deep and as wide and long as the pig (or at ground level), arrange charcoal the length

Meal in a dish, ready in a jiffy

←Fully cooked chops are the main feature of Smoked Pork Chop and Lima Skillet. The flavor of the chops permeates the sauce.

of the pig in two rows, about 12 to 15 inches apart. Drive notched pipes into ground to hold spit about 16 inches above the coals. Rig up a motor-driven rotisserie or provide manpower to turn the pig during roasting.

Run spit through center cavity of dressed pig; balance and secure well with wires and/or wire mesh. Tie legs together; cover tail and ears with foil. Have drip pan under pig, between the rows of hot charcoal. Tilt pan slightly to accumulate fat during roasting.

Place unstuffed pig on spit; begin roasting and turning. As it roasts, the pig will shrink— have tools handy to tighten wires. Also have a sprinkler filled with water to put out any flare-ups among coals. (Fires are more frequent during first hour or two of roasting.) Do not baste pig during roasting.

If coals are added to maintain a constant red glow, the 60-pound pig should take about 8 hours to roast. Time will vary, depending on the intensity of heat and weight of pig. The best indicator of doneness is a meat thermometer. Place thermometer in center of "ham" portion making sure thermometer is not resting against bone or on spit rod. When thermometer registers 170° to 185°, the pig is ready to carve. Have a large surface available for this process. Chances are the meat will be so thoroughly cooked it will fall off the bones.

Smoked Pork Chop and Lima Skillet

> 2 10-ounce packages frozen lima beans
> 5 or 6 smoked pork loin chops
> 1 teaspoon chicken-flavored gravy base
> 1 tablespoon all-purpose flour
> ½ teaspoon dried basil leaves, crushed
> ¾ cup water

Omitting salt in cooking water, cook lima beans according to package directions; drain. In skillet brown chops over medium heat. Remove chops. Pour off all but about 1 tablespoon drippings. Add gravy base to skillet. Blend in flour and basil. Add water; cook and stir over medium heat till thickened and bubbly. Add lima beans to skillet; stir to coat. Arrange chops over beans. Cover; cook over low heat till heated, about 5 minutes. Serves 5 or 6.

Glazed Sausage Loaf

2 slightly beaten eggs
1 cup soft rye bread crumbs
  (1¼ slices)
⅓ cup milk
2 tablespoons snipped parsley
2 pounds bulk pork sausage
1 12-ounce package frozen rice
  pilaf, thawed

. . .

1 8-ounce jar strained plums
  (baby food)
2 tablespoons sugar
2 tablespoons lemon juice

Combine eggs, rye bread crumbs, milk, and
parsley. Add sausage and rice; mix well. Shape
into loaf in shallow baking pan. Bake at 350°
for 1 hour. Remove from oven. Spoon off fat.

Combine strained plums, sugar, and lemon
juice. Heat the mixture till bubbly. Brush plum
mixture on loaf. Bake 15 minutes longer. Pass
remaining sauce. Makes 8 servings.

Kraut-Pork Pinwheel

1 pound ground fresh pork
½ cup fine dry bread crumbs
1 slightly beaten egg
1 teaspoon salt
½ teaspoon Worcestershire sauce
  Dash pepper

. . .

1 16-ounce can sauerkraut,
  drained
¼ cup chopped onion
5 bacon slices

Combine ground pork, bread crumbs, slightly
beaten egg, salt, Worcestershire sauce, and
pepper; mix thoroughly. On waxed paper pat
ground meat mixture to a 10x7-inch rectangle.

Snip drained sauerkraut. Combine sauerkraut with onion. Spread evenly over meat.
Starting at narrow end, roll up jelly-roll fashion; place seam side down in a shallow baking
dish. Arrange bacon across top. Bake at 350°
for 40 to 45 minutes. Makes 5 or 6 servings.

For a variation of Glazed Sausage Loaf, omit rice from meat
mixture. Pat meat into a 12x10-inch rectangle, then spread the
rice atop. Roll up as for jelly roll; seal. Bake as directed.

Glazed Ham Slice

1 1½-inch slice fully cooked
   ham (about 2 pounds)
½ cup brown sugar
2 tablespoons cornstarch
   Dash ground cloves
   Dash salt
1½ cups cranberry juice cocktail
½ cup orange juice
½ cup raisins

Slash fat edge of ham at 2-inch intervals. Insert whole cloves in fat, if desired. Place ham in shallow baking dish. Bake at 325° for 30 minutes. Meanwhile, mix brown sugar, cornstarch, cloves, and salt. Add fruit juices and raisins. Cook and stir till mixture thickens and bubbles. Spoon part of the sauce over the ham; bake till glazed, about 20 minutes longer. Pass remaining sauce. Makes 6 servings.

Stuffed Pork Tenderloin

2 pork tenderloins of equal size
   Salt
   Pepper
3 tablespoons chopped onion
¼ cup butter or margarine
4 cups dry bread cubes (about
   7 slices, cut in ½-inch cubes)
1 6-ounce can sliced mushrooms,
   drained
½ teaspoon poultry seasoning
½ teaspoon ground sage
¼ teaspoon salt
¼ teaspoon pepper
2 to 4 tablespoons water *or*
   chicken broth
   Salt
   Pepper
4 bacon slices

Have tenderloins split open lengthwise but do not cut through; flatten. Season with salt and pepper. Cook onion in butter. Combine with bread cubes, mushrooms, and next 4 ingredients. Toss with enough liquid to moisten. Spread mixture over one tenderloin; lay other tenderloin on top. Season with salt and pepper and top with bacon slices. Place on rack in shallow roasting pan. Roast, uncovered, at 325° for about 1½ hours. Makes 8 servings.

Choose a thick slice of ham for Glazed Ham Slice. The topper blends the flavors of cranberry juice, orange juice, and raisins.

Rio Grande Pork Roast

1 4- to 5-pound boneless rolled
   pork loin roast
½ teaspoon salt
½ teaspoon garlic salt
½ teaspoon chili powder

   . . .

½ cup apple jelly
½ cup catsup
1 tablespoon vinegar
½ teaspoon chili powder
1 cup crushed corn chips
   Water

Place pork, fat side up, on rack in shallow roasting pan. Combine the salt, garlic salt, and the ½ teaspoon chili powder; rub into roast. Insert meat thermometer. Roast, uncovered, at 325° till meat thermometer registers 165°, about 2½ to 3 hours.

In small saucepan combine jelly, catsup, vinegar, and ½ teaspoon chili powder. Bring to boiling; reduce heat and simmer, uncovered, for 2 minutes. Brush roast with glaze. Sprinkle top with corn chips. Continue roasting till thermometer registers 170°, about 10 to 15 minutes longer. Remove roast from oven. Let stand 10 minutes. Meanwhile, measure pan drippings including any corn chips. Add water to drippings to make 1 cup. Heat to boiling and pass the sauce with the meat. Makes 3 to 4 servings per pound.

Apple-Buttered Pork Loin

1 5- to 6-pound pork loin,
 boned, rolled, and tied
½ cup apple butter
2 tablespoons peanut butter
¼ teaspoon grated orange peel
2 tablespoons orange juice

Balance roast on spit. Roast over *medium* coals till meat thermometer registers 170°, about 3 hours. Gradually stir apple butter into peanut butter; add orange peel and juice. Brush over entire surface of roast; continue cooking 15 to 20 minutes. Makes 12 to 16 servings.

Ribs with Onion Sauce

4 pounds pork spareribs, cut
 in serving-sized pieces
2 cups sliced onion
2 cloves garlic, minced
1 tablespoon salad oil
½ cup water
¼ cup vinegar
¼ cup chili sauce
3 tablespoons brown sugar
2 tablespoons lemon juice
2 tablespoons Worcestershire sauce
1½ teaspoons salt
1 teaspoon dry mustard

Roast ribs, meaty side down, in shallow roasting pan at 450° for 30 minutes. Drain off excess fat. Turn ribs meaty side up. Cook onion and garlic in hot oil till tender; add remaining ingredients. Simmer 10 minutes. Pour sauce over ribs. Reduce oven temperature to 350°; bake ribs till tender, about 1½ hours, basting occasionally with sauce. If sauce gets too thick, add more water. Makes 4 to 6 servings.

Moist-heat cookery: This type of cookery is used for very lean cuts, less-tender cuts, or cuts that would be improved with the addition of moisture. Braising and cooking in liquid are methods of moist-heat cookery. Pork cuts that often are braised include chops, ribs, tenderloins, and shoulder or blade steaks. Cuts cooked in liquid include spareribs, hocks, pig's feet, and smoked shoulder cuts.

Glazed Smoked Shoulder

1 2- to 3-pound smoked pork
 shoulder roll (boneless)
 Water
1 medium onion, sliced
3 whole cloves
1 bay leaf
1 3-inch stick cinnamon
½ teaspoon celery seed
 • • •
½ cup brown sugar
1 tablespoon all-purpose flour
½ teaspoon dry mustard
⅛ teaspoon ground cloves
2 tablespoons water

Place pork in large Dutch oven; cover with water. Add onion, whole cloves, bay leaf, cinnamon stick, and celery seed. Cover tightly; simmer 2 hours. Remove meat from liquid. Place meat on rack in shallow roasting pan. Combine remaining ingredients. Brush on meat. Bake at 350° for 20 to 30 minutes. Serves 6 to 8.

Best Barbecued Ribs

Cut 2 pounds pork spareribs or back ribs in 2 large pieces. Simmer the ribs, covered, in enough salted water to cover till tender, about 45 to 60 minutes; drain.

 Meanwhile, prepare sauce: In saucepan combine ¼ cup catsup, 2 tablespoons chili sauce, 1 tablespoon brown sugar, 1 tablespoon butter or margarine, and 1 tablespoon chopped onion. Add 2 teaspoons prepared mustard, 1 teaspoon Worcestershire sauce, dash garlic salt, and 2 thin lemon slices. Bring the mixture to boiling; remove the mixture from heat.

 Grill hot ribs over slow to medium coals about 10 to 15 minutes on each side, brushing often with sauce. (Or place hot ribs in shallow roasting pan; pour sauce over. Bake at 350° about 20 to 25 minutes, basting with sauce occasionally. Makes 2 servings.

Ribs for a barbecue treat

When you can't prepare Best Barbecued →
Ribs outdoors on the grill, put them in a pan, pour sauce over, and bake in oven.

Braised Pork Chops

Brown ¾- to 1-inch thick pork chops slowly on both sides in small amount hot shortening; pour off excess fat. Season; add a little hot water, if desired. Cover tightly; cook over low heat till tender, about 45 to 60 minutes. Make gravy from pan juices, if desired.

Pork Chops in Sour Cream

   6 loin pork chops, ½ inch thick
   ¾ teaspoon dried sage leaves,
        crushed
   ½ teaspoon salt
     Dash pepper
   2 tablespoons shortening
   2 medium onions, sliced
   1 beef bouillon cube
   ¼ cup boiling water
   ½ cup dairy sour cream
   1 tablespoon all-purpose flour
   2 tablespoons snipped parsley

Rub chops with mixture of sage, salt, and pepper. Brown lightly on both sides in hot shortening. Drain off excess fat. Add onions. Dissolve bouillon cube in water. Pour over chops. Cover and simmer till tender, 30 minutes. Remove meat. Combine sour cream and flour in bowl. Slowly stir in meat drippings. Return mixture to skillet; cook and stir just till boiling. Add water till gravy is desired consistency. Serve over chops. Trim with parsley. Serves 6.

Orange-Glazed Pork Chops

   4 pork chops, ¾ inch thick
   1 tablespoon shortening
     Salt and pepper
   ½ cup orange juice
   2 tablespoons brown sugar
   2 tablespoons orange marmalade
   1 tablespoon vinegar

In skillet brown chops on both sides in hot shortening. Season with salt and pepper. Drain off excess fat. Combine orange juice, brown sugar, marmalade, and vinegar; pour over chops. Cover and simmer till chops are tender, about 45 minutes. Remove chops to warm platter. Spoon sauce over the chops. Makes 4 servings.

Cheese-Noodle Casserole

   1 pound diced uncooked pork
   1 tablespoon shortening
   1 10½-ounce can condensed
        chicken-rice soup
   ½ cup chopped green pepper
   ¼ cup chopped canned pimiento
   1 17-ounce can cream-style corn
   8 ounces sharp process American
        cheese, shredded (2 cups)
   4 ounces medium noodles

In skillet brown pork in hot shortening. Stir in soup; cover and simmer till tender, about 45 to 60 minutes. Stir in remaining ingredients *except* noodles. Cook noodles according to package directions; drain. Stir into pork mixture. Turn into a 2-quart casserole. Bake, covered, at 350° for 45 minutes. Makes 6 servings.

How to serve

Carving some of the pork roasts can be a real challenge unless you are familiar with the proper techniques. (For carving ham, crown roast, and blade loin roast, see *Carving*.) To carve the picnic shoulder, remove a slice from the bottom surface (parallel to the large bone) so that the shoulder will sit flat as it is carved. Then, find where the elbow (smaller bone) and arm bone (larger bone) are joined together. Make a cut down to the larger arm bone and cut along this bone. Remove the entire piece of meat. Slice this section. Then, remove the meat on either side of the larger arm bone and slice.

Pork roasts are not the only cuts that make delicious entrées. Other forms of pork can be used in sandwiches, casseroles, salads, and soups. (See also *Meat*.)

Pork Salad Jamboree

A good use for leftover cooked pork roast—

Sprinkle 1 cup cubed, unpeeled apple with 1 tablespoon lemon juice. Toss with 2 cups cubed, cooked pork, 1 cup halved and seeded red grapes, ½ cup chopped celery, ½ cup mayonnaise or salad dressing, and ½ teaspoon salt. Chill thoroughly. Makes 4 or 5 servings.

Hearty Hodgepodge is remindful of an old-fashioned soup, only this version contains garbanzo beans, Polish sausage, and both a ham hock and a beef shank. Pass French bread.

Hearty Hodgepodge

6 slices bacon
1 medium onion, thinly sliced
1 1-pound beef shank
1 ¾-pound ham hock
6 cups water
2 teaspoons salt
2 15-ounce cans garbanzo beans
3 cups diced, peeled potatoes
1 clove garlic, minced
1 4-ounce link Polish sausage, thinly sliced
Toasted and buttered French bread

In Dutch oven cook bacon till crisp; drain, reserving 2 tablespoons drippings. Crumble bacon and set aside. Add sliced onion to reserved drippings in pan. Cook till tender but not brown. Add beef shank, ham hock, water, and salt. Cover and simmer for 1½ hours.

Remove meat from beef shank and ham hock; dice meat and discard bones. Carefully skim fat from broth. Return diced meat to soup. Add undrained garbanzo beans, potatoes, and garlic. Simmer, covered, 30 minutes longer.

Add sliced Polish sausage and the crumbled bacon. Continue simmering, covered, for 15 minutes. Spoon into soup bowls and serve with toasted French bread. Makes 8 to 10 servings.

Chopped Meat Suey

    1 pound ground pork
    1 chicken bouillon cube
    1 cup boiling water
    2 cups celery, cut in 1-inch
        pieces
    1/3 cup green onions (with tops),
        cut in 1/2-inch pieces
    2 tablespoons cornstarch
    1/3 cup cold water
    1 tablespoon molasses
    1 tablespoon soy sauce
    1 16-ounce can chop suey vegetables,
        drained
      Hot cooked rice

In skillet brown pork; spoon off excess fat. Dissolve bouillon cube in boiling water; add to meat. Stir in celery and onions. Cook, covered, over medium-low heat till vegetables are almost crisp-tender, about 10 minutes.

Mix cornstarch with cold water; add molasses and soy sauce. Stir into meat mixture. Cook and stir till mixture is thickened and bubbly. Add drained vegetables; cook till heated through. Serve over rice. Pass additional soy sauce, if desired. Makes 4 servings.

Sausage and Muffin Bake

    3 English muffins, split and
        toasted
    1/2 pound bulk pork sausage
    1/2 pound ground beef
    1/2 teaspoon salt
    4 ounces sharp process American
        cheese, shredded (1 cup)
          . . .
    1 envelope onion sauce mix
    1 1/2 cups milk
    2 beaten eggs
    1 large tomato, cut in 6 slices

Place an English muffin half in each of 6 buttered 1-cup casseroles. In medium skillet combine meats and salt. Brown meat; drain off excess fat. Divide meat mixture between casseroles; sprinkle with the cheese.

Combine onion sauce mix and milk; stir in eggs. Pour about 1/3 cup egg mixture into each casserole. Top each with a tomato slice. Bake at 350° for 15 to 20 minutes. Serves 6.

Barbecued Pork

    3 tablespoons chopped onion
    1 tablespoon butter or margarine
    1 8-ounce can tomato sauce
    2 tablespoons brown sugar
    1 to 2 teaspoons Worcestershire
        sauce
    1 teaspoon lemon juice
    1 teaspoon prepared mustard
          . . .
    1 cup cubed, cooked pork
    2 hamburger buns, toasted

In saucepan cook onion in butter till tender but not brown. Stir in tomato sauce, brown sugar, Worcestershire sauce, lemon juice, and prepared mustard. Simmer about 20 minutes. Add cooked pork. Heat 10 minutes. Spoon sauce over toasted bun halves. Makes 2 servings.

Minestrone Bake

    1 pound ground pork
    1/2 cup chopped onion
          . . .
    1 10¾-ounce can condensed
        minestrone soup
    1 10½-ounce can condensed cream
        of mushroom soup
    1 8-ounce can cut green beans,
        drained
    3 medium raw potatoes, peeled
        and cubed (3 cups)
    1 cup milk

In skillet brown ground pork and chopped onion. Drain off excess fat. Stir in minestrone soup, mushroom soup, drained beans, cubed potatoes, and milk. Turn mixture into 2-quart casserole. Bake, covered, at 350° for 1 hour. Uncover; bake till potatoes are done, about 30 to 45 minutes longer. Makes 6 servings.

PORRIDGE—The British name for cooked oatmeal. Other meal may be substituted for the oatmeal. (See also *Oatmeal.*)

PORRINGER—A small metal bowl with one handle. Originally designed for eating porridge, it is now also used for serving items such as nuts, candies, and sauces.

PORT—A sweet, dessert wine. Port was originally named after Oporto, Portugal, a city at the mouth of the Douro River. The original port was made in the Douro Valley in northern Portugal. However, several other countries, including the United States, produce a similar wine. If the port is not a Portuguese wine, the label must indicate where the port is made. Familiar designations are California Port, New York Port, or American Port.

The early Portuguese port wines were rough and harsh tasting. However, the Portuguese in the Douro Valley experimented with port until they came up with a wine that was much more appealing to their English customers who preferred a sweeter, smoother wine. The wines they developed were mostly sweet-tasting, to which brandy was added during production.

How port is produced: This wine is made from several grape varieties, all of which grow on the steep slopes in northern Portugal. Two types of grapes are important in the making of port: one type, which lacks color and body, gives the wine its character, and the other contributes color. Some of the grape varieties used include the Tintas, Tourigas, and Mouriscos.

The grapes are harvested in late September or early October after which there is usually a festival. The grapes are placed in large troughs where the traditional method is to trample the grapes by foot. However, mechanical crushers have replaced the foot. The juice starts to ferment and is allowed to continue fermenting for a short time until the desired amount of grape sugar remains in the juice. At this point brandy is added, which immediately stops the fermentation process. The juice that remains in the skins is pressed out and made into the brandy that is used to stop fermentation.

Kinds of port: Top-quality port is called vintage port. It is made only in certain years from a select variety of grapes. Most generally, vintage port is bottled at its destination because of the heavy sediment it produces. The longer that vintage port ages in the bottle, the better it becomes and the more costly it is.

Another type of Portuguese port wine, crusted port, is similar to vintage port, except that it is a blend of several vintages rather than from a single vintage. It gets its name from the heavy crust or sediment that forms as the wine is aged for a long period of time.

Wood ports include both the tawny and ruby port and are so named because they are aged in wooden casks. Ruby is aged in wooden casks about three to four years; tawny, about five to six years. Tawny port changes color from the original purple to red with a brown tinge, while ruby port retains its dark red color. The additional aging of the wine causes the color change of tawny port.

White port from Portugal is produced from white grapes, using the same techniques as are used to make the red wines.

Most of the port consumed in the United States is produced either in this country, primarily in California and New York, or imported from Portugal. The imported Portuguese wines are usually those that have been aged in wooden casks.

Although some of the Tinta grapes, which are used in Portuguese wines, have been planted in California, the majority of the American ports are made from grapes other than those used in the ports made in Portugal. Look for the word Tinta on the label of a California port for a wine that most resembles the Portuguese type. Like some Portuguese wines, many American ports are also aged in wood before bottling.

How to use: Port served with cheese and nuts is delightful at the end of a meal. Remember, however, that because the vintage, crusted, and aged ports have a sediment, they should be carefully decanted so that the sediment remains in the bottle. Serve port at a cool room temperature in a regular 8- to 10-ounce wineglass, filling it only part way so that the delightful bouquet of the wine, entrapped in the glass, can be enjoyed. Or serve port in a 5-ounce dessert wineglass.

In addition to being enjoyed as a beverage, port is also used in the preparation of some cheeses, sauces, fruit cups and compotes, jellies, desserts, and salads. (See also *Wines and Spirits.*)

Cranberry-Wine Salad

   2 3-ounce packages raspberry-
     flavored gelatin
   2 cups boiling water
   1 16-ounce can whole cranberry
     sauce
   1 8¾-ounce can crushed pineapple,
     undrained
   ¾ cup port
   ¼ cup chopped walnuts

Dissolve gelatin in boiling water. Stir in the cranberry sauce, *undrained* pineapple, and port. Chill till partially set. Fold in the nuts. Pour gelatin mixture into a 6½-cup mold. Chill till firm. Makes 10 to 12 servings.

Hot Fruit Medley

A dessert specialty made in a chafing dish—

   1 13½-ounce can pineapple chunks
   1 16-ounce can apricot halves
   1 16-ounce can peach halves
   1 16-ounce can pitted dark sweet
     cherries
   ¼ cup brown sugar
   ¼ teaspoon ground cinnamon
   ⅓ cup port
   1 tablespoon lemon juice

Drain pineapple and apricots, reserving *all* of pineapple syrup and ½ *cup* of apricot syrup. Drain other fruits well; set aside. In blazer pan of chafing dish, blend together sugar and cinnamon; add reserved syrups, port, and lemon juice. Heat over direct heat till bubbly. Add pineapple, apricots, and peaches; heat through. Add cherries. Makes 8 servings.

Port du Salut is great for desserts or appetizers.

PORT DU SALUT CHEESE *(port' duh suh loo')*—A semisoft, ripened, creamy, mild- to strong-flavored cheese made from cow's milk. It is also referred to as Port Salut.

Originally, it was made at the abbey of the Trappist monks in Port du Salut, France, after which this cheese is named. However, it is now also made in other parts of Europe, in Canada, and in the United States. (See also *Cheese*.)

PORTER—A dark, heavy beer that contains browned malt. (See also *Beer*.)

PORTERHOUSE STEAK—A tender beef steak that is cut from the center loin. It is the largest of the steaks having a T-shaped bone and is easily identified by its large tenderloin muscle. (See also *Beef*.)

Swank Porterhouse Steak

   ½ cup finely chopped onion
   1 tablespoon butter or margarine
   1 clove garlic, minced
     Dash salt
     Dash pepper
     Dash celery salt
   1 2½- to 3-pound Porterhouse
     steak, cut 2 inches thick
   ¼ cup dry red wine
   2 tablespoons soy sauce
   ½ teaspoon cornstarch
   1 tablespoon cold water
   2 tablespoons butter, melted
   1 3-ounce can sliced mushrooms,
     drained

In small saucepan cook onion in 1 tablespoon butter till tender. Combine with garlic, salt, pepper, and celery salt. Slash fat along edges of steak. Slitting from fat side, cut pocket in each side of lean meat, almost to bone. Fill pockets with onion mixture. Combine wine and soy sauce; brush some on steak. Grill over *hot* coals or broil till desired doneness, about 25 to 30 minutes for medium-rare. Turn once. Brush occasionally with soy mixture. Blend cornstarch with the cold water. Combine with remaining soy mixture (about 3 tablespoons), 2 tablespoons butter, and mushrooms. Heat and stir till bubbly. Serve with steak. Slice meat across grain. Makes 4 servings.

PORTUGUESE COOKERY—A type of cooking done in Portugal that blends a variety of ingredients into tasty and appealing foods and individual dishes.

Foods commonly used in Portuguese recipes, many of which are flavored with herbs and spices, include olive oil, garlic, figs, eggs, seafood, rice, and nuts (almonds and walnuts). The variety of dishes and flavorings that make up this cuisine are partially attributed to the famous explorers who set out from Portugal and brought back their finds from far-off lands. For example, curry, used primarily as a flavoring in peasant cooking, is one of the spices brought from India by Vasco da Gama in the late fifteenth century.

Portugal has some dishes that are considered to be national favorites. Soups include a chicken broth called *canja* and dry bread soups called *açorda,* which are made with soaked bread and garlic. Vegetables, meat, poultry, or seafood is added, depending on what is available. The soup is often seasoned with fresh coriander and topped with a raw egg that cooks as it is stirred into the hot mixture.

Because of Portugal's seaboard location, main dishes often consist of fish and shellfish. A seafood stew called *caldeirada* is a mingling of both freshwater and saltwater varieties flavored with cumin and parsley. Although cod is not caught in the waters bordering Portugal, it is considered the national fish. Each year Portuguese fishermen travel to Newfoundland to fish for cod. The catch, which is salt-cured and dried, is used extensively throughout the country. While the preparation of cod varies, a popular method of serving the cooked salt fish is in codfish cakes, which are topped with poached eggs.

A wide variety of meats are eaten in Portugal, including poultry and game. Some people enjoy tripe, which is often prepared with beans. Occasionally, the

Choose a thick cut of meat for preparing Swank Porterhouse Steak. Fill pockets in steak with a seasoned onion-garlic mixture. Then, brush with a sauce of wine and soy as it cooks.

meats are cooked with wine, or the cooked meat is drizzled with lemon juice.

Desserts sometimes consist of cheese, fruit, and nuts, or perhaps a caramel custard, called *pudim flan,* another national dish. Many of the sweets served for dessert are rich with eggs and are often accompanied by port or coffee.

Nogados (Portuguese Christmas Log)

Deep-fat fried pastry strips with a honey glaze—

    1¼ cups sifted all-purpose flour
     1 tablespoon sugar
     ¼ teaspoon salt
     2 tablespoons shortening
     2 beaten eggs
     ½ teaspoon grated lemon peel
     ½ cup sugar
     ½ cup honey
     ½ teaspoon vanilla

In large bowl sift together flour, the 1 tablespoon sugar, and the salt. Cut in shortening till mixture resembles coarse crumbs. Add eggs and lemon peel; mix well. Turn out onto lightly floured surface. Roll dough to 15x12-inch rectangle, ⅛ inch thick. Cut crosswise into five 3-inch wide pieces; cut each piece into strips ¼ inch wide and 3 inches long. Fry a few at a time in deep, hot fat (375°) for about 4 minutes, turning once or twice. Remove with a slotted spoon and drain on paper toweling.

When all the strips have been fried, prepare glaze: Combine the ½ cup sugar and the honey in a small saucepan. Cook and stir till mixture is boiling; continue cooking to hard-ball stage (255°). Stir in vanilla. On well-greased baking sheet, drizzle half the honey-sugar glaze over strips, tossing them to coat all sides. With moistened hands, shape strips quickly into a round log, about 10 inches long and 3 inches wide. Drizzle remaining glaze over top and sides of log. Slice the log thinly to serve.

A trio of Portuguese sweets

← Prepare a Portuguese-inspired dessert—nut-topped Rabanados, sugar-coated Dreams, or Portuguese Christmas Log.

Rabanados

Ladyfingers laced with wine syrup and nuts—

     1 3-ounce package ladyfingers
         (7), split
     2 well-beaten eggs
         •   •   •
     ½ cup sugar
     ½ cup water
       Dash ground cinnamon
     1 tablespoon port
       Pine nuts

Dip ladyfinger halves into beaten eggs, coating each completely. Fry ladyfingers in deep, hot fat (375°), about 2 minutes on each side, turning once. Drain on paper toweling.

Place ladyfingers in ovenproof serving dish; keep warm in oven. To make syrup, in a saucepan combine sugar, water, and cinnamon. Bring to boiling; boil till slightly thickened, about 10 minutes. Stir in wine. Simmer 3 to 4 minutes more. Pour some of the hot syrup over ladyfingers in dish. Sprinkle with additional ground cinnamon and a few pine nuts. Pass remaining syrup. Makes 8 to 10 servings.

Sonhos (Dreams)

     ½ cup water
     ¼ cup butter or margarine
     2 teaspoons sugar
       Dash salt
     ½ cup sifted all-purpose flour
     2 eggs
     ½ cup sugar
     1 teaspoon ground cinnamon

In saucepan combine water, butter or margarine, the 2 teaspoons sugar, and the salt. Bring to boiling, stirring till butter melts. Add flour all at once. Cook and stir over low heat till mixture forms a ball that does not separate. Remove from heat and vigorously beat in eggs, one at a time, till mixture is smooth and shiny. Drop by rounded teaspoonfuls into deep, hot fat (375°); fry till golden brown, about 4 minutes, turning once. Remove with slotted spoon and drain on paper toweling.

Combine the ½ cup sugar and the cinnamon. Shake puffs in sugar mixture till thoroughly coated. Makes about 2½ dozen.

POSSET *(pos' it)*—A beverage that is made by curdling milk with ale or wine. It is often sweetened and spiced.

POTAGE *(pô tazh')*—The French word for soup. A good example, Potage Saint Germain, a dish that often appears on restaurant menus, is made with fresh peas.

POTATO—An edible, white tuber used as a vegetable. The word potato has been adapted from the Spanish word *potata*. The hard, white interior of a raw potato is encased by a skin that is off-white, brown, or red in color and paper-thin or moderately thick. Although white potatoes seem similar to sweet potatoes and yams in appearance and use, they are not related.

Now one of the world's most important foods, potatoes first grew in the Andes Mountains of Peru and Chile. Dried potatoes and potato motifs found in second-century South American remains indicate that Indian tribes of that time used potatoes for food. However, not until Spanish explorers arrived in that area 14 centuries later were people from other continents introduced to potatoes.

Before long, the people of many countries were eating this staple food. The Spanish introduced potatoes into Europe, and shortly thereafter potatoes were a dietary staple throughout Europe, Asia, and North America. The Irish quickly incorporated potatoes into their diets. In fact, they became so dependent on this vegetable that the potato famine of 1846 forced thousands of them to flee to Europe and the United States. A French scientist, Antoine-Auguste Parmentier, promoted the use of potatoes in his country in the 1770s as did Frederick the Great of Prussia (now Germany). The influx of potatoes into China began during the seventeenth century. A group of Irishmen in New Hampshire in 1719 are credited with establishing potatoes as a major crop in the United States.

At the same time that potato use was expanding, folklore linked with potato cultivation (some of which is still followed today) had its beginnings. For example, according to superstition, a potato crop should be planted at night during a new moon so that the plants will thrive. If planted on Good Friday, however, the resulting crop will supposedly be poor. And once pulled from the ground, potato storage stability is thought to be ensured only if the entire family eats the first ones harvested.

Potatoes have played various roles in the treatment of certain disorders, too. Many people have carried them in their pockets as a means of warding off rheumatism and sciatica. But in Holland, it is believed that only a stolen potato brings about such a cure. In the United States, potatoes have been used for the cure and prevention of warts and for the treatment of black eyes. Newfoundlanders have tied sliced baked potatoes around their necks to alleviate sore throats, and the Irish have rubbed boiled potato water on aches, sprains, and broken bones.

How potatoes are produced: The major United States commercial production of potatoes is carried on in Idaho, Maine, California, and New York, although many other states produce potatoes on a smaller scale. Growing conditions are controlled as closely as is humanly possible.

For optimum tuber formation, potato plants require a certain number of daylight hours, sufficient moisture to prevent the plants from drying out but not too much moisture to cause rotting (irrigation is sometimes necessary), rich silty soil, and temperatures from 50° to 60°.

Propagation involves planting the "eyes" or cut-up tubers of potatoes rather than seeds. At maturity, the tubers are mechanically dug out of the ground.

The largest percentage of the potato crop is harvested between September and November, but storage facilities enable potatoes to be marketed year-round. Cool but not refrigerated air is recirculated in storage rooms located on the individual farms or at grower association centers.

Potatoes a'plenty

Although white potatoes (center), sweet → potatoes (left), and yams (rear) have similar uses, they are not related.

Nutritional value: Potatoes have been unnecessarily maligned as starchy vegetables that are high in calories. As with so many other foods, however, it's the other foods added, such as the butter, sour cream, sauce, or cooking fat, that give the bulk of calories. In fact, one potato 2½ inches in diameter yields only 76 calories.

This same portion of potato also makes a valuable contribution of Vitamin C and the B vitamin niacin, and a fair contribution of the B vitamin thiamine. Since the major portion of the vitamins and minerals is in or just beneath the skin, eating the skin of baked potatoes provides the diner with a bonus of nutrients.

Types of potatoes: There are many varieties of potatoes. Each is developed for one of three reasons: it will grow under specific conditions, it can be used for a specific cooking purpose, or it will mature at a predetermined time. In general, the varieties range in shape from oblong to round and in skin color from creamy white to red and russet brown. Government regulations permit application of a harmless red dye or wax to red potatoes, but this addition must be labeled on the package. Some widely marketed varieties are Russet Burbank, Red Pontiac, White Rose, Cherokee, Irish Cobbler, and "new" potatoes.

Russet Burbanks, the most well-known variety, are frequently called Idaho potatoes because they are so widely produced in that state. They are oval in shape and have heavily netted, rough brown (russeted) skins and white interiors. They are best used for baking or French-frying.

Red Pontiacs may be round to oblong. Their intense red skins are smooth. The white flesh is very good when boiled.

White Roses are large and elliptical in shape. They have smooth, yellow white skins and a white flesh that makes them especially suitable for boiling.

Cherokees have a round to elliptical shape that is quite often flattened toward the stem end. These potatoes are used for both boiling and baking.

Irish Cobblers are round with white, smooth skins. They are used for boiling.

"New" potatoes are not a specific potato variety. They may be one of several varieties that are harvested while still immature. Their sizes and shapes are determined by the variety of the potato. The thin, delicate skins often appear to have been feathered (an effect of mechanical harvesting). New potatoes are used primarily for boiling.

How to select: Although the development of potato varieties that possess all-purpose cooking characteristics is a recent trend, many still are best used for a specific cooking purpose. In general, round-shaped potatoes have firm, waxy interiors that are best suited for boiling. The interiors of long, oval potatoes are characterized as being mealy and make the best baked, fried, or mashed products.

Look for fresh potatoes that are sound and smooth, that have shallow eyes, and that are free of blemishes. There should be no large cuts or bruises. Avoid those with patches of green on the skin, as they have been subjected to light and are bitter and inedible. Do not choose potatoes that are sprouting or appear shriveled. Select uniform-sized potatoes so that all will cook in about the same time.

In addition to fresh potatoes, there are an increasing number of convenience forms that eliminate cooking steps.

How to store: Store all potatoes in a cool (about 55°), dark place. Under these conditions, mature varieties will keep several months. New potatoes do not keep well and should be stored for only a few days.

Potatoes are very sensitive to other storage temperatures. If the storage area is too cold (29° or less), the potatoes will freeze. Even 35° to 40° temperatures cause the starch in the potatoes to convert to sugar more quickly. This results in a dark, fried product and gives the potatoes an astringent flavor.

How to prepare: Prior to cooking, scrub the potato surfaces thoroughly with a vegetable brush. Remove any sprouts or green areas. Personal preference and ultimate use largely determine whether the potatoes are cooked with skins on or off.

The skins can be left on for baking or boiling. To bake potatoes, select uniform-sized baking varieties. After scrubbing, rub the skins with shortening if a soft skin is desired. Prick the potatoes with a fork to allow steam that forms during baking to escape. Bake at 425° for 40 to 60 minutes. If the potatoes are cooked with other foods, bake at 350° to 375° for 70 to 80 minutes. When done, roll the potatoes gently with the palm of your hand to make them mealy. Cut crisscrosses in the tops with a fork. Press the ends to push up the centers slightly, then top with butter or other topping. To foil bake, scrub, prick, and wrap in foil. Bake at 350° for 1½ hours.

Baked Potato Toppers

Whip 1 cup shredded sharp process cheese and ¼ cup soft butter till these ingredients are fluffy. Add ½ cup dairy sour cream and 2 tablespoons snipped green onion; whip.

Soften one 8-ounce package cream cheese. Add ⅓ cup light cream; beat till fluffy. Add 1 tablespoon snipped chives, 1½ teaspoons lemon juice, and ½ teaspoon garlic salt; blend the ingredients together well.

Whole potatoes boiled in skins should be cooked, covered, in boiling, salted water. The potatoes may be scored around the center prior to cooking to facilitate skin removal later. Cooking time varies from 25 to 40 minutes, depending on the potato size. The smaller new potatoes require only 15 to 20 minutes of cooking.

To prepare potatoes for cooking with the skins off, immerse the peeled potatoes or potato pieces in cold water until all the potatoes have been prepared. This prevents the cut surfaces from darkening.

Peeled potatoes may be boiled whole, quartered, or cubed, depending on the final use. Cook the potato pieces, tightly covered, in a small amount of boiling, salted water. Cooking time varies with the piece size: whole potatoes require from 25 to 40 minutes; quarters, from 20 to 25 minutes; and cubes, from 10 to 15 minutes.

Peeled raw potatoes may also be prepared for roasting or frying. Roasted potatoes must be parboiled to speed cooking time. Fried potatoes, raw or precooked, may be pan- or deep-fat fried.

Oven-Browned Potatoes

Peel medium potatoes; cook in boiling, salted water for 15 minutes. Drain. About 45 minutes before meat roast is done (oven temperature 325°), place hot potatoes in drippings around roast, turning potatoes to coat. Roast till done.

How to use: It's hard to beat the versatility of potatoes. Their mild flavor combines well with so many other seasonings and foods that it is possible to serve them several times a day without monotony. Popular herbs and spices that are often used in combination with potatoes include basil leaf, bay leaf, caraway seed, celery seed, dill, mace, marjoram, mustard, nutmeg, oregano, poppy seed, rosemary, savory, cinnamon, sage, and thyme.

As a vegetable side dish, potatoes taste good by themselves, in combination with other vegetables, or in seasoned sauces. Baked potatoes and French fries are probably the most popular serving versions, but other well-known and well-liked concoctions include mashed potatoes, creamed potatoes, hashbrowns, cottage-fries, twice-baked potatoes, duchess potatoes, and scalloped potatoes.

Hashed Browns

Boil 3 medium potatoes in jackets; chill. Peel and shred to make 3 cups. Add 1 to 2 tablespoons grated onion, 1 teaspoon salt, and dash pepper. Melt ¼ cup butter or margarine in 10-inch skillet. Pat potatoes into pan, leaving ½-inch space around edge. Brown about 9 minutes. Reduce heat, if necessary. Cut with spatula to make 4 wedges; turn. Brown till golden, about 7 minutes longer. Makes 4 servings.

Mashed Potatoes

Peel potatoes. Cook in boiling, salted water till tender. Drain; shake over low heat to dry. Remove pan from heat. Mash with potato masher or electric mixer, using lowest speed. Gradually add hot milk as needed and continue beating till light and fluffy. Add salt, pepper, and butter or margarine, as desired.

Crisscross Potatoes

Scrub 3 medium baking potatoes; halve the potatoes lengthwise. Make diagonal slashes, about 1/8 inch deep, in cut surfaces of potatoes, forming a crisscross pattern. Brush the cut surfaces with 2 tablespoons melted butter; season the potatoes with salt and pepper. Arrange them in a baking dish. Bake at 350° for 1 hour. Sprinkle potatoes with paprika; continue baking 15 minutes more. Makes 6 servings.

Scalloped Potato Bake

    8 cups thinly sliced, peeled
        potatoes
    1/4 cup finely chopped onion
    1 10½-ounce can condensed
        cream of mushroom soup
    1 10½-ounce can condensed
        cream of celery soup
    1 cup milk
    3/4 teaspoon salt

Spread *4 cups* sliced potatoes in bottom of a greased 11¾x7½x1¾-inch baking dish. Combine the next 5 ingredients and dash pepper; pour *half* of the mixture over the potatoes. Repeat layers. Cover; bake in a 350° oven for approximately 1 hour. Uncover and bake 30 to 45 minutes longer. Makes 8 servings.

Score raw potato around center, then boil. Hold potato with a fork speared into the scored area and peel from center out.

Blue Cheese-Bacon Potatoes

    4 medium baking potatoes
    1/2 cup dairy sour cream
    1 ounce blue cheese, crumbled
        (1/4 cup)
    1/4 cup milk
    1/4 cup butter or margarine
    3/4 teaspoon salt
        Dash pepper
    4 slices bacon, crisp-cooked,
        drained, and crumbled

Scrub potatoes; rub with shortening. Bake at 400° till potatoes are done, about 1 hour. Remove from oven; cut a lengthwise slice from top of each potato. Scoop out inside of each; mash. Add sour cream, blue cheese, milk, butter or margarine, salt, and pepper to mashed potatoes; beat with electric mixer till fluffy.

Spoon mixture lightly into potato shells. Place on baking sheet; return to oven till heated through, about 15 minutes. Sprinkle each with crumbled bacon. Makes 4 servings.

Quick Dill Potatoes

Add 2½ cups cubed, peeled potatoes, 2 tablespoons finely chopped onion, and 1 teaspoon salt to 1/3 cup boiling water. Cover and cook for about 15 minutes. Add 1/2 cup light cream; simmer the mixture for about 5 minutes, stirring occasionally. Sprinkle with dried dillweed and pepper. Makes 4 servings.

Potatoes in Lemon Sauce

    2 pounds potatoes
    1/4 cup butter or margarine
    1 tablespoon lemon juice
    1 tablespoon snipped green
        onion tops
        Dash pepper
        Dash ground nutmeg
    1 teaspoon grated lemon peel

Peel potatoes; cook, covered, in boiling, salted water till done, about 30 minutes. Drain and set aside. In small saucepan heat butter with next 4 ingredients. Pour over potatoes, coating each potato well. Sprinkle with grated lemon peel. Makes 6 servings.

As an ingredient in recipes, potatoes can be the background or major flavor of soups, stews, breads, casseroles, and salads. Favorite potato soups come in hot and cold versions. Steaming hot potato soup can serve either as an appetite booster at a first course or as the substantial main dish accompanied by a sandwich. Feature the famous cold soup, vichyssoise, at your next dinner for special guests.

Potato Soup

>   4 cups cubed, peeled potatoes
>   1 10½-ounce can condensed
>   chicken broth
>   1 cup thinly sliced celery
>   ½ cup chopped carrot
>   ½ cup chopped onion
>   2 tablespoons snipped parsley
> 1½ teaspoons salt
>   ⅛ teaspoon pepper
>   Dash dillweed
>   1 tablespoon chopped canned
>   pimiento (optional)
> 3½ cups milk
>   3 tablespoons all-purpose flour
>   ½ cup milk
>   2 tablespoons butter or margarine

In 3-quart saucepan combine first 9 ingredients. Bring to boiling; reduce heat. Cover and simmer till vegetables are tender, about 15 to 20 minutes. Add pimiento and the 3½ cups milk. Heat soup just till milk is hot. Blend flour with the ½ cup milk; stir into soup. Cook, stirring constantly, till thickened and bubbly. Add butter or margarine. Makes 6 to 8 servings.

Gourmet Potato Soup

>   3 cups diced potato
>   ½ cup diced celery
>   ½ cup diced onion
>   1 tablespoon chicken-flavored
>   gravy base *or* 2 chicken
>   boullion cubes
>   2 cups milk
>   1 8-ounce carton sour cream dip
>   with chives (1 cup)
>   1 tablespoon all-purpose flour

In large saucepan combine potato, celery, onion, 1½ cups water, gravy base, and ¼ teaspoon salt. Cover and cook till vegetables are tender, about 20 minutes. Add *1 cup* milk; heat through. In medium bowl blend sour cream dip and flour; gradually stir in remaining milk.

Pour about *one-third* of hot potato mixture into sour cream mixture; return to saucepan. Cook and stir till thickened. Garnish with parsley, if desired. Makes 6 to 8 servings.

Potato flavor can be added to various types of breads—loaves, rolls, and doughnuts—and is usually achieved by adding mashed potatoes to the recipe formula. Leftover or instant mashed potatoes are perfectly suited for this use.

Potato Rolls

Serve warm and fragrant right from the oven—

>   1 package active dry yeast
>   4 to 4½ cups sifted all-purpose
>   flour
>   • • •
> 1¼ cups milk
>   ¼ cup shortening
>   ¼ cup sugar
> 1½ teaspoons salt
>   ½ cup hot mashed potatoes
>   • • •
>   1 egg

In large mixer bowl combine yeast and *2 cups* flour. Heat milk, shortening, sugar, and salt just till warm, stirring occasionally to melt shortening; stir in the potatoes.

Add to dry mixture in mixer bowl; add egg. Beat at low speed of electric mixer for ½ minute, scraping sides of bowl constantly. Beat 3 minutes at high speed. By hand, stir in enough remaining flour to make a soft dough. Knead on lightly floured surface till smooth and elastic, about 6 to 8 minutes.

Place in lightly greased bowl, turning once to grease surface. Cover; let rise till double, about 1 hour. Punch down. Shape in ball. Cover and let rest 10 minutes. Shape in rolls; place on greased baking sheet. Let rise till almost double, about 1 hour. Bake at 400° for 10 to 12 minutes. Cool on rack. Makes 2 dozen.

Men, women, and children alike are meat-and-potato fans. Use this combination as the basis for meal-in-one casseroles, stews, and other main dish recipes.

Ham-Stuffed Potatoes

    4 large baking potatoes
    2 cups ground fully cooked ham
    1 cup mayonnaise or salad dressing
    2 ounces process Swiss cheese, shredded (1/2 cup)
    2 tablespoons chopped green pepper
    2 tablespoons chopped canned pimiento
    1 tablespoon instant minced onion
    1 ounce process American cheese, shredded (1/4 cup)

Scrub potatoes. Bake at 425° till done, about 45 to 60 minutes. Cut slice from top of each. Scoop out insides and cube. Toss with ham and next 5 ingredients; spoon into potato shells. Bake at 425° for 15 minutes. Sprinkle American cheese atop. Heat till cheese melts, about 1 to 2 minutes more. Makes 4 servings.

Sausage au Gratin

Reserve 3 links from one 12-ounce package smoked sausage links (8 links); slice remaining and set aside. Beat together one 8-ounce jar process cheese spread (1 cup) and 1 cup dairy sour cream till mixture is smooth. Add 1 tablespoon instant minced onion, 2 teaspoons dry parsley flakes, and 1/2 teaspoon salt.

Fold into 6 cups sliced, peeled, cooked potatoes (about 6 medium) with sliced sausages. Turn into a 1 1/2-quart casserole. Bake the mixture at 350° for 40 minutes. Cut reserved sausages in half; arrange them atop the casserole in pinwheel-fashion. Bake till the sausages are heated through and the mixture is hot, about 10 minutes more. Makes 6 servings.

Hale and hearty

← Ladle liberal helpings of this vegetable-laden Potato Soup. Vibrant carrots, celery, and a hint of dillweed flatter each serving.

Lamb-Vegetable Supper

    2 pounds boneless lamb, cut in cubes
    3 tablespoons all-purpose flour
    1/4 cup salad oil
    1 teaspoon salt
    1/4 teaspoon pepper
    1/4 teaspoon dried thyme leaves, crushed
    1/4 teaspoon dried basil leaves, crushed
    1 clove garlic, minced
    1 whole bay leaf
    1 cup water
    1/3 cup dry white wine
    • • •
    4 medium potatoes, peeled and cut up (3 cups)
    2 onions, quartered
    2 tomatoes, quartered

Coat lamb with flour; brown in hot oil. Sprinkle with salt and pepper. Add thyme, basil, garlic, bay leaf, water, and wine. Cover; simmer 30 minutes. Add the potato and onion. Sprinkle lightly with additional salt.

Cover; cook till vegetables are tender, about 30 minutes more. Add tomatoes. Cover; cook till heated through, 2 to 3 minutes. Remove bay leaf before serving. Makes 6 servings.

Turkey-Potato Pancakes

Make after the holidays with leftover turkey—

    3 beaten eggs
    3 cups shredded raw potato, drained (about 3 potatoes)
    1 1/2 cups finely chopped turkey
    1 1/2 teaspoons grated onion
    Dash pepper
    1 tablespoon all-purpose flour
    1 1/2 teaspoons salt

In mixing bowl combine eggs, potato, turkey, onion, and pepper. Add flour and salt; mix well. Using about 1/4 cup batter for each pancake, drop batter onto hot, greased griddle, spreading to about 4 inches in diameter. Cook over medium-low heat for 3 to 4 minutes on each side. Serve the pancakes with cranberry sauce, if desired. Makes about 15 pancakes.

Potato shells hold a fluffy potato, blue cheese, and sour cream combo. Garnish Blue Cheese-Bacon Potatoes with bacon.

Chuck Wagon Stew

Cut 2 pounds lean beef chuck in 1½-inch cubes. In Dutch oven brown the meat slowly in 2 tablespoons hot shortening. Add 2 cups water;* 1 medium onion, sliced; 1 clove garlic, minced; 1 tablespoon salt; 1 teaspoon sugar; ¼ teaspoon dried thyme leaves, crushed; and 1 teaspoon Worcestershire sauce. Cover the mixture; simmer about 1½ hours, stirring occasionally to prevent the meat from sticking.

Add ½ cup celery, sliced in ½-inch pieces; 6 carrots, cut in 1-inch slices; ½ pound small white onions *or* one 16-ounce can onions, drained; and 3 potatoes, peeled and quartered. Cook, covered, for 20 minutes. Add 2 or 3 tomatoes, cut in wedges *or* one 16-ounce can tomatoes, drained (reserve liquid). Cook till the meat and the vegetables are tender, about 15 minutes. Skim fat from the stew. Thicken liquid with flour, if desired. Makes 6 to 8 servings. *If canned tomatoes are used, use the drained juice as part of the liquid.

Monday Meat Pie

½ cup chopped onion
1 tablespoon shortening
2 to 3 cups cooked beef, cut in ½-inch cubes
2 cups cubed, peeled, cooked potatoes
2 medium carrots, cooked and sliced (1 cup)
4 ounces sharp process American cheese, shredded (1 cup)
½ cup mayonnaise or salad dressing
1 10¾-ounce can beef gravy (1¼ cups)
1 14-ounce package corn bread mix

Cook the ½ cup chopped onion in hot shortening till tender but not brown. Add beef, potatoes, carrots, *half* the cheese, mayonnaise, and gravy. Heat to boiling; pour into a 9x9x2-inch baking dish. Prepare corn bread mix according to package directions, adding remaining cheese. Spoon over meat mixture. Bake at 400° for 25 minutes. Makes 6 to 8 servings.

Meat and Potato Balls

1 beaten egg
2 tablespoons milk
¼ cup fine dry bread crumbs
1 cup finely shredded, peeled, raw potato, drained (1 large)
¼ cup chopped green onion with tops
1 teaspoon prepared mustard
1 pound ground pork
2 tablespoons shortening
1 chicken bouillon cube
2 tablespoons all-purpose flour

Combine first 6 ingredients, ¾ teaspoon salt, and ⅛ teaspoon pepper. Add pork; mix well. Shape into 24 meatballs. In skillet brown meatballs in hot shortening; drain off fat. Dissolve bouillon cube in 1 cup boiling water; add to meatballs. Cover and cook over low heat for 20 minutes, turning occasionally.

Remove meatballs to serving bowl; reserve pan drippings. Blend flour with ⅓ cup cold water; stir into reserved drippings. Cook and stir till thick and bubbly. Serve with meatballs. Makes 4 to 6 servings.

The summer picnic favorite, potato salad, has been adapted to fit many different tastes. Hot or cold, cubed or mashed, potatoes are accompanied by vegetables varying in texture, flavor, and color. Coat with a creamy mayonnaise dressing, piquant sour cream blend, or tangy vinegar-oil mixture according to preference.

Potluck Potato Salad

    ¼ cup clear French salad dressing
        with spices and herbs
    4 to 5 medium potatoes, cooked,
        peeled, and cubed (4 cups)
    1 cup chopped celery
    ¼ cup chopped onion
    4 hard-cooked eggs, sliced
    1 teaspoon salt
    ½ cup mayonnaise

Pour French dressing over warm potatoes; chill 2 hours. Add celery, onion, eggs, and salt. Add mayonnaise to the mixture and mix carefully. Stir in 1 teaspoon celery seed, if desired. Chill about 4 hours. Makes 8 servings.

Calico Potato Salad

    6 cups diced, peeled, cooked
        potatoes
    ½ cup diced cucumber
    ½ cup chopped onion
    ¼ cup chopped green pepper
    3 tablespoons chopped canned
        pimiento
    1½ teaspoons salt
    ¾ teaspoon celery seed
    ¼ teaspoon pepper
    2 hard-cooked eggs
    ½ cup whipping cream, whipped
    ½ cup mayonnaise
    2 tablespoons vinegar
    1 tablespoon prepared mustard

Combine first 8 ingredients. Coarsely chop eggs, reserving 1 whole egg yolk. Add chopped eggs to potato mixture. Chill. Combine remaining ingredients, *except* yolk; toss with potato mixture ½ hour before serving. To serve, spoon into lettuce-lined bowl. Sieve reserved yolk over. Makes 10 to 12 servings.

Peppy Potato Salad

    ¼ teaspoon mustard seed
    ¼ teaspoon dillseed
    1 tablespoon water
    1½ cups diced, peeled, cooked
        potatoes
    1 tablespoon sliced green onion
    2 tablespoons thinly sliced celery
    1 hard-cooked egg, chopped
    ¼ cup Zippy Cooked Dressing

Soak mustard seed and dillseed in water several hours or overnight. Combine seed-water mixture and ½ teaspoon salt. Add potatoes, onion, and celery; mix lightly. Add egg and ¼ cup Zippy Cooked Dressing; toss to coat. Chill thoroughly. Garnish with radish roses, if desired. Serves 2.

Zippy Cooked Dressing: In a small saucepan mix together 1 tablespoon all-purpose flour, 1 tablespoon sugar, ½ teaspoon salt, ½ teaspoon dry mustard, and dash cayenne. Gradually stir in 1 slightly beaten egg yolk and ⅓ cup milk. Cook and stir over medium heat till mixture is thickened and bubbly. Remove from heat; stir in 2 tablespoons vinegar and 1 teaspoon butter. Cover; cool. Makes ½ cup.

Note: Make Thousand Island dressing from remaining cooked dressing, stirring in 1 tablespoon chili sauce and 1 teaspoon pickle relish; serve over lettuce another time.

Hot Dill-Potato Salad

    1 tablespoon butter or margarine
    1 tablespoon all-purpose flour
    1 teaspoon salt
    ¼ teaspoon dried dillweed
    ⅛ teaspoon pepper
    1 cup milk
    ½ cup mayonnaise or salad
        dressing
    2 tablespoons finely chopped onion
    4 cups diced, peeled, cooked
        potatoes
    Paprika

In saucepan melt butter over low heat. Stir in flour, salt, dillweed, and pepper. Add milk; cook and stir till thickened and bubbly. Blend in mayonnaise and onion; fold in potatoes. Heat through. Spoon into serving dish; sprinkle with paprika. Serve at once. Serves 4 to 6.

German Potato Salad

½ pound bacon (10 to 12 slices)
½ cup chopped onion
2 tablespoons all-purpose flour
2 tablespoons sugar
1½ teaspoons salt
1 teaspoon celery seed
Dash pepper
1 cup water
½ cup vinegar
. . .
6 cups sliced, peeled,
cooked potatoes
2 hard-cooked eggs, sliced
(optional)
Parsley
Chopped canned pimiento
Bacon curls

Cook bacon till it is crisp; drain and crumble the bacon, reserving ¼ cup fat. Cook onion in the reserved fat till the onion is tender. Blend in flour, sugar, salt, celery seed, and pepper. Add water and vinegar; cook and stir till the mixture is thickened and bubbly. Add bacon, potatoes, and eggs; heat thoroughly, tossing lightly. Garnish with parsley, pimiento, and bacon curls. Makes 8 to 10 servings.

Ham and Potato Salad

2 cups cubed, peeled, cooked
potatoes
1 tablespoon Italian salad
dressing
1½ cups cubed fully cooked ham
2 hard-cooked eggs, chopped
½ cup diced unpeeled cucumber
¼ cup sliced radishes
¼ cup chopped celery
2 tablespoons chopped onion
2 tablespoons chopped green
pepper
¼ teaspoon salt
⅛ teaspoon paprika
½ cup mayonnaise

Sprinkle cubed potatoes with Italian dressing. Let stand for ½ hour. Add the remaining ingredients, *except* mayonnaise, to the potatoes. Chill the mixture thoroughly. Before serving, gently fold in mayonnaise. Makes 5 servings.

Potato products: Supermarket shelves and freezer cases are lined with various prepared potato products to tempt you into enjoying potatoes with time saving ease. Their increasing popularity has reduced the cost per serving, making them almost comparable in cost to fresh potatoes.

Potato chips are very thin slices of potato that are fried to crisp goodness, then salted. Seventy percent of all processed potatoes are utilized in this manner. Their popularity as a snack, appetizer, or sandwich accompaniment is a well recognized fact. Crushed potato chips also serve occasionally as a recipe ingredient.

Crunchy Ham Sandwiches

Add sliced cheese and tomato, coat with crushed potato chips, and grill—

8 slices white bread
Butter or margarine, softened
Prepared mustard
4 slices boiled ham
4 slices process American cheese
1 tomato, thinly sliced
. . .
2 slightly beaten eggs
2 tablespoons milk
Dash onion salt
1¼ cups crushed potato chips

Spread 4 slices bread on one side with butter; spread remaining bread slices on one side with mustard. Top each mustard-spread slice with 1 slice ham, 1 slice cheese, and 1 or 2 slices tomato, then with second slice of bread.

Combine eggs, milk, and onion salt. Dip sandwiches in egg mixture, then in crushed potato chips. Pat to secure chips to bread, turning to coat both sides. Brown the sandwiches on both sides in a buttered skillet or on a lightly greased griddle till crisp, about 8 minutes. Serve the sandwiches hot. Serves 4.

For a potluck supper

Bring a bowlful of Calico Potato Salad garnished with sieved egg yolk and lined with green onion, ham, and cheese roll-ups.

Canned potatoes include small, whole potatoes as well as sliced potatoes and plain as well as dressed-up versions. Shoestring potatoes are short potato strips that have been crisp-fried and salted like potato chips. They have the advantage over potato chips of being shelf stable. Canned potato salads are also produced.

Hot Potato Salad Fix-Up

Brings out the best in canned potato salad—

        2 16-ounce cans German–style
            potato salad
        8 slices bacon, crisp-cooked,
            drained, and coarsely crumbled
        4 ounces sharp process American
            cheese, diced (1 cup)

Combine all of the ingredients in a 1½-quart casserole. Bake the mixture, uncovered, in a 300° oven for about 25 to 30 minutes. Serve the potato salad hot. Makes 6 servings.

Dehydrated potatoes permit the jiffy preparation of some of the most popular potato dishes using instant mashed potato granules and flakes, hashed brown potato mixes, and potato casserole mixes.

Creamy Potato Bake

Omitting the butter, prepare 6 servings instant mashed potatoes according to package directions. Add one 4-ounce carton whipped cream cheese; beat well. Stir in 1 beaten egg, 2 tablespoons finely chopped green onion, and 1 tablespoon finely snipped parsley; blend well.

Transfer the mixture to a well-greased 1-quart baking dish. Dot with 1 tablespoon butter. Sprinkle with paprika. Bake at 400° for about 40 minutes. Makes 6 servings.

Just for two

Peppy Potato Salad is a scaled-down salad for the twosome to enjoy. Colorful radish roses and romaine leaves crown the salad.

Potato Clouds

> Packaged instant mashed potatoes
>   (enough for 4 servings)
> 2 slightly beaten egg yolks
> 2 teaspoons snipped parsley
> 2 teaspoons instant minced onion
> 1/4 cup sifted all-purpose flour
> 1 teaspoon baking powder
> 2 stiff-beaten egg whites

Prepare instant mashed potatoes according to package directions; cool. Stir in egg yolks, parsley, and onion. Sift together flour, baking powder, and 1/2 teaspoon salt. Add to potato mixture; mix well. Fold in egg whites.

Drop by rounded tablespoons into deep hot fat (385°). Cook till puffs of potato are brown, turning once. Drain on absorbent towels. Keep hot in 300° oven while frying the remainder of the puffs. Makes about 2 1/2 dozen.

Golden Potato Bake

Adding 1 teaspoon instant minced onion to cooking water, prepare enough packaged instant mashed potatoes to make 4 servings, according to package directions. Fold in 1 cup cubed cooked carrots. Spoon the mixture into 4 individual casserole dishes. Top each casserole dish with 1 tablespoon grated Parmesan cheese. Bake the casseroles at 350° till they are golden brown, about 25 minutes. Makes 4 servings.

Double Potato Bake

> Packaged dry hashed brown
>   potatoes (enough for 4 servings)
> 1 10 1/4-ounce can frozen condensed
>   cream of potato soup
> 1 soup can milk
> 1 tablespoon instant minced onion
> 1 tablespoon snipped parsley
> 1/3 cup grated Parmesan cheese

Prepare potatoes according to package directions, reducing cooking time to 11 or 12 minutes; drain. Combine soup, milk, onion, parsley, and dash pepper. Heat till soup thaws. Add to potatoes; mix lightly. Turn into a 10x6x1 3/4-inch baking dish. Sprinkle with cheese. Bake at 350° for 35 minutes. Serves 6.

Frozen potatoes also come in a wide variety of shapes and styles. Many-shaped French fries, hashed browns, nuggets, and puffs are only a few of the products. These require only minimal heating in an oven or skillet. (See also *Sweet Potato, Vegetable, Yam* for additional information.)

Creamy Hashed Brown Bake

So quick, yet so good—

> 1 10 1/2-ounce can condensed cream
>   of celery soup
> 1/3 cup milk
> 1 3-ounce package cream cheese
>
> • • •
>
> 4 cups loose-pack, frozen hashed
>   brown potatoes
> 1 8-ounce can small whole onions,
>   drained and cut in pieces
>
> • • •
>
> 2 ounces sharp process American
>   cheese, shredded (1/2 cup)

In saucepan combine celery soup, milk, and cream cheese; cook and stir over medium heat till ingredients are smooth. Combine frozen hashed brown potatoes and canned onions; stir in soup mixture. Pour into a 10x6x1 3/4-inch baking dish; cover with foil. Bake at 350° till the potatoes are tender, about 1 1/4 hours. Remove foil; top with shredded process cheese. Return to oven until the cheese melts. Serves 6.

POTATO FLOUR or STARCH—Dried and ground potato used by itself as a thickener or in combination with wheat flour for breads and baked goods. When used for thickening, one-half tablespoon potato flour produces the same thickness as one tablespoon of wheat flour. (See also *Flour*.)

POTATO PANCAKE—The English translation of the German phrase *Kartoffel Pfannkuchen*, a dish made with grated raw potato. (See also *Kartoffel Pfannkuchen*.)

POT-AU-FEU (*pô tō foe'*)—A French phrase that literally means "pot on the fire," but which traditionally refers to a rich soup or stew made with meat and vegetables.

POT CHEESE—A soft, unripened cheese that is similar to cottage cheese. In fact, cottage cheese is sometimes called pot cheese, although real pot cheese is drier.

POTHERB—1. An herb or plant cooked like a vegetable. 2. An herb used as a seasoning. Thyme, spinach, and wild greens are herbs and plants used as potherbs.

POT LIQUOR, POTLIKKER, or POTLICKER—The liquid that remains after meat, such as salt pork or bacon, and/or vegetables, such as greens, have been cooked in a large amount of water.

Pot liquor is mainly associated with southern and Afro-American cookery. Corn bread is a favorite combination with this broth. (See also *Regional Cookery.*)

POTPIE—A deep-dish pie or stew made with meat or poultry, vegetables, and a biscuit, dumpling, or pastry topping. The Pennsylvania Dutch also use noodles in potpies.

Potpies are a favorite with homemakers because all kinds of leftovers as well as newly purchased ingredients can be used in them. Just save those dabs of cooked vegetables and combine all of them with chunks of cooked meat to create a new dish. Make the topping from scratch if you like, or use mixes or refrigerated biscuits.

There is also a large selection of frozen potpies in the supermarkets that you can keep on hand for quick meals.

Chicken Potpie

  1 3-pound ready-to-cook stewing chicken, cut up
  1 medium onion, quartered
  3 celery leaves
  3 sprigs parsley
  1 bay leaf
 10 whole black peppercorns
 ¼ teaspoon dried rosemary leaves, crushed
  1 10-ounce package frozen peas
  7 carrots, peeled and cut up
 ¼ cup all-purpose flour
 ½ cup milk
     Plain Pastry (See *Pastry*) for 1-crust pie

In large kettle combine chicken, onion, celery leaves, parsley, bay leaf, peppercorns, and rosemary. Add 2 quarts water and 2 teaspoons salt. Bring to boiling; simmer, covered, till chicken is tender, about 2 hours. Meanwhile, thaw peas. Remove chicken from broth. Strain stock. In 2 cups of the stock, cook carrots, covered, till tender. Remove chicken from bones; cube. Turn into 2-quart casserole.

Blend flour, 1 teaspoon salt, and dash pepper with milk. Stir quickly into stock with carrots. Add thawed peas. Bring to boiling, stirring constantly. Simmer till peas are tender. Pour over chicken in casserole; toss.

Roll pastry to fit top of casserole with ½-inch overhang. Turn edge under; seal and crimp. Slash vents in top. Bake at 425° for about 20 minutes. Makes 6 to 8 servings.

Meatball Pie

 ½ cup chopped onion
  1 tablespoon butter or margarine
  2 12-ounce cans meatballs and gravy
  1 16-ounce can sliced carrots, drained
  2 tablespoons snipped parsley
  2 teaspoons Worcestershire sauce
 ¼ cup crisp rice cereal, crushed
 ½ teaspoon sesame seed
 ⅛ teaspoon salt
  1 package refrigerated biscuits (10 biscuits)
     Milk

Cook onion in butter till tender but not brown. Add meatballs and gravy, carrots, parsley, and Worcestershire sauce. Heat till bubbling. Pour meatball mixture into a 2-quart casserole.

Mix cereal, sesame seed, and salt. Brush tops of biscuits with milk; then dip in cereal mixture. Arrange biscuits atop *hot* meatball mixture. Bake at 425° till biscuits are done, 10 to 12 minutes. Makes 6 servings.

Speedy family supper

Begin Meatball Pie with canned meatballs →
and carrots. Then, top with refrigerated biscuits dipped in a cereal-sesame mixture.

POT ROAST–1. A large piece of meat, usually beef, that is cooked by braising. **2.** A term meaning to braise meat or poultry in a "pot" with a cover, which includes a Dutch oven, covered skillet, or a foil wrap.

Any type of meat or poultry can be pot roasted (braised). The less-tender beef cuts, such as chuck, blade, and arm pot roasts, are well suited to this method of cooking. Occasionally, lamb, pork, veal, variety meats, and poultry are braised, too.

The procedure for pot-roasting begins with browning the meat in fat. This develops the brown color and the flavor that appeal to many people. The meat may or may not be coated with flour for browning. Water, tomato juice, diluted soy sauce, broth, cider, or wine is added for the long, slow cooking, which tenderizes the meat. The pot roast is simmered, tightly covered, in this liquid for several hours.

During the last hour of cooking, vegetables are quite often added. This is sometimes referred to as a Yankee pot roast. Onions, carrots, potatoes, tomatoes, and turnips are among the vegetables that are used alone or in combinations. Once the meat and vegetables are tender, the juices are made into a gravy that is served with the roast. (See also *Beef*.)

Beef Pot Roast

Coat one 3- to 4-pound beef pot roast with flour. In Dutch oven, large skillet, or roasting pan, brown slowly on all sides in 2 tablespoons hot shortening or salad oil. Season with salt and pepper. Remove from heat; add ½ cup water *or* beef broth. Cover; simmer till tender, 2½ hours. Add water, if needed.

If desired, add small potatoes, peeled and halved; small whole onions; and medium carrots, peeled and cut in 1-inch pieces, the last 45 to 60 minutes. Using pan juices, prepare Pot Roast Gravy (See *Gravy*). Serves 6 to 8.

All-American favorites

← Simmering the meat and vegetables together makes Yankee Pot Roast what it is — a hearty, wholesome dish with great flavor.

Pot Roast Variations

Use tomato juice instead of the ½ cup water for the cooking liquid in Beef Pot Roast. Thicken the juices for Pot Roast Gravy (See *Gravy*), *except* use tomato juice instead of water and use only 3 tablespoons all-purpose flour. Season the pot roast with salt, pepper, and ½ teaspoon Worcestershire sauce.

Cook Beef Pot Roast, slicing 2 small onions over meat after browning. Add 2 bay leaves and 5 whole cloves. Use ¼ cup vinegar and ¼ cup water as the cooking liquid for the roast.

After browning, season Beef Pot Roast with salt, pepper, and 1 tablespoon dillseed. Top meat with 2 medium onions, sliced. Serve roast with Sour Cream Gravy (See *Gravy*).

Mix one 8-ounce can tomato sauce, 1 cup water, 1 envelope *dry* onion soup mix, 1 teaspoon caraway seed, and 2 bay leaves. Pour the mixture over Beef Pot Roast after browning. Thicken liquid as for Pot Roast Gravy, *using only* 2 tablespoons all-purpose flour.

Yankee Pot Roast

Select a 3- to 4-pound chuck roast. Trim off excess fat; heat trimmings in Dutch oven or large skillet. When there are about 2 tablespoons melted fat, remove trimmings. Coat pot roast with flour; brown slowly on both sides in hot fat. Season with salt and pepper.

Add ½ cup water. Cover tightly and cook over low heat till tender, 2½ to 3 hours. Add more water, if needed. The last hour of cooking, add small whole onions, peeled carrots, and peeled small potatoes. Place meat on platter; surround with vegetables. Garnish with fresh celery leaves. Make Yankee Pot Roast Gravy, if desired. Makes 6 to 8 servings.

Yankee Pot Roast Gravy: Skim most of fat from pan juices. Reserve 1½ to 2 cups stock. Put ½ cup cold water into a shaker or small screw-top jar, and then add ¼ cup all-purpose flour. Shake to mix thoroughly.

Remove stock from heat and slowly stir in flour mixture. Return to heat and cook, stirring constantly, till gravy is bubbling vigorously. Season to taste with salt and pepper. Cook about 5 minutes more, stirring constantly.

Savory Blade Pot Roast

Simmering meat in an herb-seasoned liquid tenderizes and flavors the roast—

        1 **3-pound blade-bone pot roast**
           Salad oil
           Salt
      ¼ **cup wine vinegar**
      ¼ **cup salad oil**
      ¼ **cup catsup**
        2 **tablespoons soy sauce**
        2 **tablespoons Worcestershire sauce**
        1 **teaspoon dried rosemary leaves,**
           crushed
      ½ **teaspoon garlic powder**
      ½ **teaspoon dry mustard**

In skillet or Dutch oven brown meat slowly in a small amount of hot salad oil. Sprinkle meat with salt. Combine wine vinegar, the ¼ cup salad oil, catsup, soy sauce, Worcestershire sauce, dried rosemary, garlic powder, and dry mustard. Pour mixture over meat. Cover tightly and simmer till tender, about 2 hours.

Remove pot roast to a heated platter. Skim excess fat from pan juices; spoon juices over meat, Or, if desired, make Pot Roast Gravy to serve with roast (see *Gravy*). Serves 6 to 8.

POTS AND PANS—Containers that hold food during cooking. The category of pots and pans ranges from skillets and saucepans to baking pans and pressure cookers. The distinction between the two is that pans are used on top of the range and almost always have one handle, while pots have two handles. Many pots and pans are available in two forms—as a standard utensil and as a small electrical appliance.

Pots and pans were one of the earliest inventions of man. Needing something in which to cook food, he fashioned crude pots out of clay, reeds, and mud.

Once man learned how to work metal, he used this skill not only to make weapons but also to make utensils in which to cook his food. By the beginning of the Christian Era, the Romans, as surviving records show, had an amazing number of cooking utensils. In addition to the many earthenware vessels, they had a type of saucepan, kettles that could be suspended over a fire,

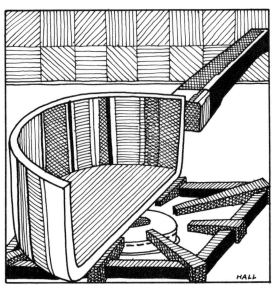

Selecting a good pot or pan will make cooking easier. Be sure the pan is balanced, has a flat bottom, and has straight sides.

a grill-like unit for broiling meat, a handled frying pan, and a double-bowled utensil that served the purpose a double boiler does today.

The settlers in America didn't fare so well. Although they had come from Europe where there were many cooking utensils, many pioneers had only a spit and an iron kettle suspended over the fire, and perhaps, a long-handled iron frypan called a spider with legs that sat over coals.

Today, however, the number and variety of pots and pans on the market dazzle the imagination. Some of these utensils are large; others are small. Some have multipurpose uses, while others fill specific needs. Therefore, you must choose pots and pans so that you will have the right utensil for the cooking job you want to do without taxing your budget or overloading the kitchen cabinets.

How to select: Whether you are a bride setting up your first kitchen, a career girl settling into an apartment, or an experienced homemaker replacing or adding to your basic kitchen equipment, consider these things when buying pots and pans: use, material, size, and design.

How the pot or pan is to be used is the first thing to consider when buying new equipment. Today, you can buy a pot or pan—from a common frypan and saucepan to the specialized springform pan and poele—to fill every basic and specialty cooking purpose. If possible, choose a pot or pan that can serve many purposes in the home. For instance, an attractive casserole acts as a baking and serving dish, a double boiler divides into two saucepans, and a Dutch oven substitutes for a large saucepan when equipment is limited.

Then, consider the type of material used in making the pot or pan, for each metal affects cooking performance, ease of cleaning, and appearance differently.

Aluminum is a good conductor of heat. Thus, foods cook evenly in aluminum pots and pans. These utensils will not rust, but they do turn dark when alkaline foods are cooked in them or when they are washed in dishwashers. This reaction is not harmful and can be removed by boiling a solution of water and vinegar or water and cream of tartar in the pot or pan or by polishing with a commercial polish.

Stainless steel is usually combined with another metal in pots and pans. A copper or aluminum layer over the bottom or sandwiched between two layers of stainless steel makes heat conduction even and prevents hot spots. Stainless steel maintains its beauty due to its high polish and its stain and scratch resistance.

Copper utensils are attractive and are excellent heat conductors. Because copper darkens with exposure to heat and air, it requires frequent polishing. It is used in combination with other metals.

Glass and glass ceramic react differently than do many other materials. They heat slowly but hold the heat well. Some glass utensils, such as baking dishes, are intended for cooking in the oven; others are intended for the top of the range. But some can go from the freezer to the oven. Read the label so that you will get the type that you need, and then use it only for the type of cooking that is specified by the manufacturer. Glass is not affected by food acids or alkalies. It is not hard to clean, but care must be taken in handling glass utensils so as not to scratch or break them.

Guide for buying pans

- Choose the size of pan that you need to hold the amount of food you usually cook.
- Avoid buying pans that duplicate jobs. One pan may perform the tasks of several.
- You don't necessarily need a set of pans. Choose only the pieces you need and coordinate the colors and designs yourself.
- Choose the best quality you can afford.

Iron pots and pans, especially cast iron, are old favorites. These heavy utensils conduct and hold heat well. However, they will rust if not dried thoroughly.

Porcelain enamel and porcelain clad utensils are metal coated with a glass material. Not all of these conduct heat evenly. However, they do resist acids, alkalies, and rust. They're fairly easy to keep clean and are quite colorful, too.

Tin pots and pans are made by placing a tin coating over another metal such as steel. These utensils are lightweight and shiny when new. They can scratch, pit, and rust easily, though. Many of the small, light pots and pans such as egg poachers, pie pans, and bread pans are made of tin.

Many of the metal pans have a nonstick coating. This coating does not affect the taste of the food, but it does make the pan quite a bit easier to clean.

After you have decided on the use for the pot or pan and on which material you want, consider the size. Most pots and pans are a standard size, which the manufacturer marks on the bottom for easy reference. Saucepans are measured by volume; for example, one quart. Baking pans are grouped by dimensional measure. Baking pan sizes are measured across the top from one inside edge to the other.

Finally, consider the design. Good pots and pans have straight sides, a flat bottom for good contact with the heat, secure handles for convenience and safety, and tight-fitting lids. The handles and knobs on the lids are made of a heat-resistant material, so you can touch them without being burned and use them in the oven as well as on the top of the range.

Today, there is an abundance of attractive, gaily colored pots and pans on the market. Choose these for their charm as well as their serviceability, and they will not only help in cooking delicious foods easily, but they will also decorate the kitchen and brighten your tasks.

How to clean: Cleaning pots and pans correctly keeps them attractive and in good functioning condition. Always clean them thoroughly after each use. Any bits of stain or burned-on food will just be harder to remove the next time, so it's better to clean the pan completely the first time. Baking pans that are not completely clean bake less efficiently than those that are shiny and may make removal of the cooked food from them more difficult.

If you want to soak a pot or pan to loosen any stain or food, always wait until the pan has had a chance to cool before adding water. Putting cold water into a hot pan can cause warping. This damages the future performance of the pan—a warped pan will not heat evenly.

Soaking is especially good for cleaning glass and porcelain enamel, which can scratch if scoured. Metals can be scoured if you note the manufacturer's directions and use mild products when specified. There are special cleaners and polishes sold for some metals, which make the pots and pans sparkle with less work.

How to store: Storing pots and pans correctly will make them easier to reach and will also prevent denting or breaking.

Treat everyone to a dessert that looks as enchanting as it tastes. The tiny cups not only look attractive, but they also keep servings of rich Pots de Crème Chocolate small.

Stack pie plates, cake pans, and muffin tins in graduating sizes to conserve space. Lay cookie sheets flat or stand them on end. Large, bulky items that are not used frequently, such as tube pans, should be stored out of the way so that most-used pots and pans are easier to get out and won't be scraped and dented in the shuffle.

Pots and pans that have a nonstick coating should be handled with care so that the finish is not scarred. Protect them from sharp corners or edges that might scratch the surface and damage the finish.

Taking care of pots and pans serves two purposes: it adds years of use, and it is economical. (See *Equipment,* individual metals for additional information.)

POTS DE CRÈME (*pō duh krem'*)— A custardlike dessert served in small cups. Pots de crème is rich and is usually chocolate-but sometimes vanilla- or caramel-flavored. The pudding is served cold, with or without a dollop of whipped cream.

Pots de crème is traditionally served in small cups made especially for this dessert. However, if you do not have a pots de crème set, you can serve the smooth pudding in sherbet glasses or in tiny bowls. The dessert is very rich, so only a small amount of it should be served to each person. (See also *Dessert.*)

Pots de Crème Chocolate

Make this creamy dessert in a jiffy by using a combination of convenience products—

> 2¼ cups milk
> 1 4-ounce package *regular* chocolate pudding mix
> 1 6-ounce package semisweet chocolate pieces (1 cup)
> 1 teaspoon vanilla
> Pressurized dessert topping

Using the 2¼ cups milk, prepare pudding mix according to package directions. While pudding is hot, add semisweet chocolate pieces. Stir till melted; cool. Add vanilla and beat till smooth. Spoon into pot de crème cups and chill. Before serving, garnish with swirl of pressurized dessert topping. Makes 6 servings.

Pots de Crème

A classic chocolate dessert—

> 1 6-ounce package semisweet chocolate pieces
> 1¼ cups light cream
> 2 egg yolks
> Dash salt

In heavy saucepan combine chocolate pieces and light cream. Stir over low heat till blended and satin-smooth. Mixture should be *slightly thick but not boiling.* Beat egg yolks and salt till airy and thick. Gradually stir in hot chocolate mixture. Spoon into 6 or 7 pot de crème cups or small sherbets. Cover; chill till of pudding consistency, about 3 hours.

POTTED CHEESE—A mixture of finely grated cheese and seasonings. Cheddar cheese usually forms the foundation, with butter, condiments, spirits, vinegar, salt, and coloring added in various combinations. Sometimes a smoke flavor is added. These flavors go well with toast or crackers.

Commercial potted cheese comes in glass jars or in small crocks with tight-fitting lids. Either the commercial or the homemade cheese makes a nice gift, especially around the Christmas season.

POTTED MEAT—Meat ground to a paste and mixed with seasonings. Potted meats are available in small cans, or you can make your own by using a food grinder or an electric blender. The meat makes good sandwich fillings and appetizer spreads.

POUCHONG TEA (*pōō' chong'*)—A type of oolong tea that usually comes from Formosa. The tea is scented with blossoms of jasmine or gardenia (See also *Tea.*)

POULET (*pōō lā'*)—A French word for chicken, especially a young chicken.

POULETTE SAUCE (*pōō let'*)—A velouté sauce with meat or fish stock, egg yolk, onion, lemon juice, and occasionally mushrooms added for additional flavor. This velvety sauce goes with chicken, fish, eggs, and various kinds of vegetables.

POULTRY

Make every week seem like the holidays by using these modern techniques for cooking poultry.

At one time, poultry flew free as wild game. When man domesticated this wild game, he provided himself with an abundant supply of meat and eggs: chicken, turkey, duck, goose, and guinea fowl.

The first "breeding program" began about 4000 years ago when the jungle fowl in and around India were domesticated. Later, Greeks and Romans developed poultry farms. The birds raised in Greece and Rome furnished not only meat and eggs but also a few fringe benefits. On one occasion, geese are said to have saved Rome by warning its inhabitants of approaching enemies. Because of this, geese were rewarded with the questionable honor of being eaten only at public feasts.

Because birds were small and supplied meat and eggs, they were taken along as man roamed the world. The colonists brought poultry with them to America. The Americans also had native birds, turkeys, which were introduced to Europe.

Man continued to raise poultry in much the same way as the Romans had first begun their poultry farms. The birds ran in a barnyard eating grain, scraps from the family meals, and anything else they could find. These birds were somewhat more tender and meatier than the wild ones because they didn't have to fly and hunt for food.

Few breeding improvements occurred until after World War II when great changes came about in poultry farming. The family-style barnyard operation grad-

ually disappeared and was replaced by the giant, highly mechanized enterprise of to-day. Breeds were improved to produce uniform birds that were meaty and tender.

Even the function of the bird was changed. No longer were birds used for both egg laying and meat. They were developed for one or the other. No longer were chickens kept for their eggs and eaten when they were old and tough. Instead, the new breeds of chickens were ready for market in 9 weeks; turkeys, in 5 months.

Now, poultry is widely available and economical, so there can be "a chicken in every pot," as King Henry IV of France, President Herbert Hoover, and Huey Long had promised. A chicken dinner isn't just a Sunday treat, and turkey isn't only for the Thanksgiving and Christmas holidays.

Turkey-Noodle Bake

1½ cups milk
1 10½-ounce can condensed cream of mushroom soup
3 beaten eggs
3 ounces fine noodles, cooked and drained (2 cups)
2 cups cubed, cooked turkey
1 cup soft bread crumbs (1½ slices)
4 ounces sharp process American cheese, shredded (1 cup)
¼ cup chopped green pepper
¼ cup butter or margarine, melted
2 tablespoons chopped, canned pimiento

Blend milk and soup; stir in eggs. Add remaining ingredients. Turn into 11¾x7½x1¾-inch baking dish. Bake at 350° till knife inserted off-center comes out clean, 30 to 40 minutes. Cut into squares. Makes 6 to 8 servings.

Year-round barbecue

← Move barbecuing indoors when it gets cold and cook pineapple-stuffed Cornish Game Hens on a Spit on an electric rotisserie.

As an example of the growing use and popularity of poultry in menus, Americans are eating more than three times as much chicken and turkey as they did in 1940. This makes poultry third to beef and pork in per capita consumption.

Nutritional value: Poultry is an excellent nutritional meat. Just as with red meats, it supplies high-quality protein, yet poultry is often lower in calories than are the red meats. Younger birds have less fat than do the more mature birds, and geese and ducks are higher in fat than chickens and turkeys. Dark meat has slightly more calories than light meat. You can reduce the calorie count of any type of poultry by removing the skin (where the fat is stored) before cooking.

Poultry also contains iron and the B vitamins thiamine, riboflavin, and niacin. As is the case with calories, the dark meat will contain more of these important nutrients than the light meat.

How to select

Choosing the right bird for a meal and preserving its top quality is important to the consumer. Not only is this necessary for good flavor and nutrition, but it is also more economical for you.

Types of poultry: First, you must decide which type of poultry to serve—chicken, turkey, duck, goose, or guinea fowl. Chicken is readily available year-round fresh, frozen, and canned. Turkey is most often marketed frozen and is available throughout the year, too. However, during the holiday season, there is such a large demand for turkeys that it is wise to make an advance order to be assured you will have one of the desired size. Duck, goose, and guinea fowl are not readily available, but most supermarkets and meat markets do carry them at times and often will special-order them for you upon request.

Next, decide how the poultry will be cooked for this will determine the class (mature or young) that you want. If you plan on stewing or braising it, then a more mature bird will do. The slow cooking with moisture will tenderize the meat. These may be labeled mature. Mature chickens are called hen or stewing chickens. Turkeys may be labeled yearlings. If you intend to fry, broil, or roast the bird, you will want a young one. These may be labeled young, rooster, or broiler-fryer. Young turkeys are called young hen or tom; young ducks are called ducklings.

Forms of poultry: Poultry may be selected in a variety of forms—fresh, frozen, smoked, and canned. Fresh and frozen poultry is ready-to-cook. It has been completely cleaned and is ready for use.

Fresh and frozen birds are sold whole and cut into pieces. You usually save money by buying whole poultry and cutting it up yourself. There is an increase in price for the cut-up birds, but there is also an advantage of work saved and the choice of buying all pieces alike. There are also boneless roasts or rolls on the market.

Plum-Glazed Turkey Roasts

Cook turkey on the patio or with a battery-operated rotisserie at the picnic site—

> 2 3- to 4-pound rolled turkey roasts, thawed
> 1 30-ounce can purple plums
> ¼ cup frozen orange juice concentrate, thawed
> ½ teaspoon Worcestershire sauce
> 8 to 10 drops red food coloring

Tie each turkey roast together securely with twine, if necessary. Insert a spit rod through the center of each roast; attach holding forks and test balance. Wrap turkey roasts tightly in foil, crimping the ends of the foil tightly against spit rod close to the roasts. Attach the spit to the rotisserie; roast over *medium-hot* coals for about 3 hours.

Prepare glaze by sieving the plums. Add orange concentrate, Worcestershire sauce, and food coloring. Mix the ingredients well. Bring to boiling; boil about 15 minutes. Remove foil from the roasts; brush the roasts with glaze. Insert meat thermometer. Roast till thermometer registers 185°, about 15 minutes more. Brush occasionally with glaze. Let stand 10 minutes; slice. Makes 9 to 12 servings.

Smoked poultry has a unique flavor and an added advantage of longer refrigerator storage than the fresh poultry. Canned poultry products range from whole birds to pieces of meat to prepared entrées.

Grades: When you are selecting any poultry product, the United States Department of Agriculture inspection circle and grade shield are reliable guides. These are found on all types of poultry products.

The round inspection mark reads, "Inspected for Wholesomeness by U.S.D.A." This means that the product is wholesome for food, clean, safe, accurately labeled, and not adulterated. Federal law requires that all poultry pass this federal inspection or some other equivalent inspection.

The shield-shaped grade mark is an assurance of quality. Grading is a voluntary program; therefore, poultry processors must pay for federal or federal-state grading services. Poultry can be graded only if it has passed the wholesomeness test.

The top grade for poultry is U.S. Grade A. Poultry with this stamp on it has a good overall shape and appearance, and it is meaty, full fleshed, and practically free from defects. U.S. Grade B and U.S. Grade C poultry may have defects such as cuts and bruises and may be slightly less fleshy and meaty than the Grade A poultry.

Most of the poultry products (including whole poultry, parts, and roasts or rolls) that are found in the supermarkets are Grade A. The lower grades of poultry are usually used in processed products.

In addition to noting the grade, when buying frozen poultry, be sure that it is solidly frozen and the wrapping is not torn.

How to store

Poultry is quite perishable, so it's essential that proper care be exercised from the time of purchase till you are ready to eat it. Therefore, as soon as you arrive home, refrigerate fresh poultry or put frozen poultry into the freezer.

For short periods of refrigeration, you can leave poultry in the clear plastic wrap that the packer or market puts around it. However, if it's wrapped in market paper, unwrap it, take out the giblets, and wrap the poultry and giblets separately. It's a good idea to set the poultry on a platter to catch drippings.

If the fresh poultry won't be used within a day or two, cover it with moisture-vapor-proof wrapping and freeze it.

To use frozen poultry, cook it from the frozen state allowing extra time, or thaw it according to one of these procedures:

(1) Refrigerator thawing. Leave the original wrap on the bird and place it on a drip tray. Thaw in the refrigerator for one to three days, depending on the bird's size. When the bird is thawed, cook immediately or keep refrigerated for only a short period of time before cooking.

(2) Cold-water thawing. Leave the poultry in the original wrap, or put it into a plastic bag. Place in cold, *never warm or hot* water. Change the water frequently. Allow 30 minutes to 1 hour for small birds and 6 to 8 hours for large ones.

(3) Room-temperature thawing. Leave the bird in its original wrap. Place it in a paper bag, or wrap it in two or three layers of newspaper (this will keep the surface cool while the inside thaws). Thaw in a cool room away from heat. Thawing will take 6 to 8 hours for birds weighing 4 to 8

When making Plum-Glazed Turkey Roasts, baste rolled turkey roasts with sauce as they turn on the rotisserie over hot coals.

How to cut up poultry

To cut up poultry, cut skin between thighs and body. Grasping one leg in each hand, lift until hips are free from the body.

Pull the wing away from the body. Start cutting on the inside of the wing just over the joint. Cut down through the joint.

To remove the leg and thigh piece, cut between hip joint and body close to bones in back of the chicken. Repeat with other leg.

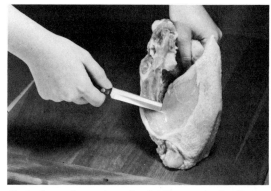

Cut along breast end of ribs to neck. Separate breast and back; cut through joints. Bend back in half to break; cut at joint.

If desired, separate the thigh and leg. Locate the knee joint by bending the thigh and leg together. Cut through this joint.

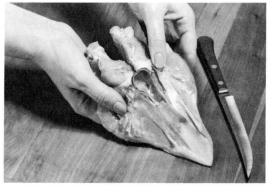

To bone breast, cut through cartilage at V of neck. Grasp small bones on each side; bend back. Push up to snap out breastbone.

pounds, and about 8 to 12 hours for those weighing between 8 and 12 pounds. Check the bird often during the last hours of thawing to prevent spoiling.

Cooked poultry must also be stored properly. Be sure to refrigerate leftovers as soon as possible. If the bird was stuffed, the stuffing *must be removed* and stored separately. Gravy should also be refrigerated separately, but if frozen, the gravy can be combined with the meat. This lengthens the storage time of the meat.

Basic preparation

Whichever method of cooking you are using for the poultry—broiling, frying, stewing, braising, or roasting—sanitary handling is important. Be sure that you clean your hands, counter top, cutting board, and knives both before and after handling. Rinse poultry with cold water and drain. Now you are ready to cook it.

Broiling: Young turkey, chicken, duck, and guinea are suitable for broiling. Small birds are split in half lengthwise or quartered, and large ones are cut into pieces. A sharp knife or poultry shears will make the job much easier. If you like, disjoint but don't separate the bones. This speeds up cooking and makes the poultry easier to handle when eating it.

Place the poultry pieces on the broiler pan or on a grill for cooking. Tuck the wings under so that they won't cook too fast. Broil with the skin side away from the heat first, then turn. Baste with melted butter, sauce, or glaze during broiling.

Poultry can also be broiled on a rotisserie over a grill or under a broiler. This is true of whole chicken, turkey, duck, and goose or large pieces of poultry.

To prepare poultry for the rotisserie, mount the whole birds or pieces on a spit following the manufacturer's instructions. Balance the spit for even rotation, and secure the birds tightly with prongs. If two birds are used, mount them with both head ends facing the center. If you have more than two birds, mount them crosswise on the spit. Tie the birds' wings and legs to the body so that they won't overcook or unbalance the spit as it turns.

Storage time for poultry

Raw poultry	Refrigerator	Freezer
Chicken	1-2 days	12 months
Turkey, Duck, Goose	1-2 days	6 months
Giblets	1-2 days	3 months
Cooked poultry		
Slices or pieces	1-2 days	1 month
Slices or pieces in gravy	Refrigerate separately	6 months
Casseroles or creamed dishes	1-2 days	2-4 months

Island Broiled Chicken

> ½ cup salad oil
> 3 tablespoons lemon juice
> 1½ tablespoons soy sauce
> 1 small clove garlic, minced
> ½ teaspoon dried oregano leaves, crushed
> 2 2-pound ready-to-cook broiler-fryer chickens, cut in half

Combine first 5 ingredients, ¼ teaspoon salt, and ⅛ teaspoon pepper for marinating sauce. Seal chickens and sauce in plastic bag. Marinate in refrigerator 4 to 5 hours, turning often. Drain chickens, reserving marinade.

Place, skin side down, in broiler pan (without rack). Broil the chickens 5 to 7 inches from heat till lightly browned, about 25 minutes. Brush occasionally with sauce. Turn; broil 15 to 20 minutes longer. Makes 4 servings.

Cornish Game Hens on a Spit

Rinse four 1-pound Cornish game hens; pat dry with paper toweling. Lightly salt cavities. Stuff with one 20½-ounce can pineapple chunks, drained. Truss birds and tie cavity closed. Mount crosswise on spit, alternating front-back, front-back. Do not have birds touching. Secure with extra-long holding forks. Combine 1 teaspoon salt; ½ cup butter, melted; and 2 tablespoons lemon juice. Brush some of this mixture on the birds. Place on rotisserie over *medium* coals. Broil 1 to 1¼ hours, brushing with sauce every 15 minutes. Makes 4 servings.

Turkey-Pineapple Grill

     1 13-ounce can pineapple chunks
    1/3 cup extra-hot catsup
    1/4 cup soy sauce
     3 tablespoons salad oil
     2 tablespoons vinegar
     2 tablespoons brown sugar
     2 tablespoons finely chopped onion

· · ·

    2 1/2 to 3 cups cooked boneless turkey
         roast, cut in 1/2-inch cubes

Drain pineapple, reserving 1/4 cup syrup. Combine the reserved syrup with catsup and the next 5 ingredients. Marinate turkey cubes for several hours in the mixture. Turn the cubes occasionally. Drain and reserve the marinade. Alternately thread turkey cubes and pineapple chunks on short skewers. Brush generously with marinade. Grill on hibachi till lightly browned, turning and brushing often with the marinade. Makes 16 appetizers.

Frying: This method of preparation is very popular, especially for chicken. However, other types of young poultry can be fried, too. The pieces of poultry are dipped in a batter, then in flour or crumbs before frying in shortening. An alternate method is oven-frying. The pieces are rolled in a commercial or homemade crumb mixture and then baked in a hot oven. This eliminates adding extra calories and frees you from watching closely.

Chicken Parmesan

     1 cup crushed, packaged, herb-
         seasoned stuffing mix
    2/3 cup grated Parmesan cheese
    1/4 cup snipped parsley
     1 2 1/2- or 3-pound ready-to-cook
         broiler-fryer chicken, cut up
    1/2 cup butter or margarine, melted

Combine stuffing mix, Parmesan, and parsley. Dip chicken in butter; roll in crumb mixture. Place pieces, skin side up and not touching, in a greased, shallow baking pan. Sprinkle with remaining butter and crumbs. Bake at 375° till done, about 1 hour. Do not turn. Serves 4.

Stewing and braising: These methods of cooking are similar in that both involve cooking in a liquid. With stewing, the poultry simmers in water or broth. This technique is often used for older birds. The long, slow cooking helps to tenderize and bring out the flavor of the meat.

Braising involves two steps. First, the meat is browned for an attractive appearance. Then, the poultry simmers in a small amount of broth or sauce. This helps to tenderize mature poultry, and it also imparts the flavor from the liquid into both older and younger poultry.

Spanish-Style Chicken

     1 2 1/2- to 3-pound ready-to-cook
         broiler-fryer chicken, cut up
     3 tablespoons shortening
    1/2 cup chopped onion
     1 clove garlic, minced
     1 cup tomato juice
     2 cups chicken broth
     1 cup uncooked long-grain rice
     1 10-ounce package frozen peas,
         broken apart
    1/4 cup chopped, canned pimiento

Season chicken with 1 teaspoon salt and 1/4 teaspoon pepper. In skillet brown chicken in hot shortening. Add 1/2 cup chopped onion and minced garlic; cook till onion is tender but not brown. Add tomato juice and 1/2 *cup* chicken broth. Cover; simmer for about 20 minutes.

Add rice and remaining broth. Simmer, covered, for 20 minutes. Add peas and pimiento. Simmer till peas are tender, about 5 minutes longer, stirring once or twice. Makes 4 servings.

Roasting: Roasting is one of the most popular ways to cook poultry. This method leaves the bird in an attractive shape and able to hold a stuffing.

With a Spanish flair

Set the theme for a foreign menu with → Spanish-Style Chicken and avocado halves. Then, add bread sticks and a crisp salad.

Poultry roasting chart

General Roasting: Stuff, if desired. Truss. Place, breast side up, on rack in shallow roasting pan. Rub skin with salad oil. If meat thermometer is used, insert without touching bone in center of inside thigh muscle. Roast, uncovered, according to chart. When bird is 2/3 done, cut band of skin or string between legs and tail. Continue roasting till done.

Test for Doneness: The thickest part of the drumstick should feel very soft when pressed between fingers protected with paper towels. The drumstick should move up and down and twists easily in socket. Meat thermometer should register 185°. Remove bird from oven; let stand 15 minutes so that meat can firm up before carving. (See Carving.)

Poultry	Ready-To-Cook Weight	Oven Temp.	Roasting Time Stuffed and Unstuffed	Special Instructions
Chicken	1½-2 pounds	375°	¾-1 hr.	Brush dry areas of skin occasionally with pan drippings. Cover loosely with foil.
	2-2½ pounds	375°	1-1¼ hrs.	
	2½-3 pounds	375°	1¼-1½ hrs.	
	3-4 pounds	375°	1½-2 hrs.	
	4-5 pounds	375°	2-2½ hrs.	
Capon	4-7 pounds	375°	1½-2 hrs.	Same as above.
Turkey	6-8 pounds	325°	3½-4 hrs.	Top loosely with foil. Press lightly at end of drumsticks and neck, leaving air space between bird and foil. Last 45 minutes, cut band between legs and tail; continue roasting, uncovering, till done.
	8-12 pounds	325°	4-4½ hrs.	
	12-16 pounds	325°	4½-5½ hrs.	
	16-20 pounds	325°	5½-6½ hrs.	
	20-24 pounds	325°	6½-7½ hrs.	
Foil-wrapped Turkey	8-10 pounds	450°	2¼-2½ hrs.	Place trussed turkey, breast up, in center of greased, wide heavy foil. Bring ends of foil up over breast; overlap fold and press up against ends of turkey. Place bird in shallow pan (no rack). Open foil last 20 minutes to brown turkey.
	10-12 pounds	450°	2½-3 hrs.	
	14-16 pounds	450°	3-3¼ hrs.	
	18-20 pounds	450°	3¼-3½ hrs.	
	22-24 pounds	450°	3½-3¾ hrs.	
Domestic Duck	3-5 pounds	375° then 425°	1½-2 hrs. 15 minutes	Prick skin well all over to allow fat to escape. Do not rub with oil.
Domestic Goose	4-6 pounds	325°	2¾-3 hrs.	Prick legs and wings with fork so fat will escape. During roasting, spoon off fat in pan. Do not rub with oil.
	6-8 pounds	325°	3-3½ hrs.	
	8-10 pounds	325°	3½-3¾ hrs.	
	10-12 pounds	325°	3¾-4¼ hrs.	
	12-14 pounds	325°	4¼-4¾ hrs.	
Cornish Game Hen	1-1½ pounds	375°	1½ hrs.	Roast, loosely covered, for 30 minutes, then 60 minutes uncovered or till done. If desired, occasionally baste with melted butter or glaze the last hour.
Guinea Hen	1½-2 pounds	375°	¾-1 hr.	Lay bacon over breast. Roast loosely covered. Uncover last 20 minutes.
	2-2½ pounds	375°	1-1½ hrs.	

To prepare the bird for roasting, rinse and drain it. Then, rub the inside with salt, if desired. The salt is usually omitted if a stuffing is to be added. If you are preparing a stuffed bird, mix the stuffing but *do not stuff the poultry until just before cooking.* Put some stuffing loosely into the wishbone cavity. You probably won't be able to do this on a duck or goose because of the small opening. Pull the neck skin to the back and fasten with a skewer. Then, spoon stuffing into the tail cavity, being careful not to pack it because the stuffing will expand during cooking.

The next step is to push the drumsticks under the piece of skin or a wire clamp, if provided, across the tail. If there is no band, close the opening by using wooden picks or skewers to hold the sides together. Lace the cavity shut and tie the drumsticks to the tail. Tuck the wings behind the shoulders and tie them, if necessary.

Secure the drumsticks and wings of the poultry. This keeps the bird in an attractive shape. If you desire, fill the cavity with celery and quartered onions. Discard these vegetables before serving, or save them for use in soup or gravy.

Cook the bird on a rack, breast side up, in a shallow baking pan. Rub chickens and turkeys with salad oil and baste with but-

ter, margarine, or drippings. Cover loosely with a tent of foil, or cover the breast with a foil tent or a piece of cheesecloth that has been dipped in butter.

Ducks, geese, and guinea fowl do not require basting. Geese and large ducks have more fat than other poultry. Therefore, they are pricked before cooking around the breast, tail, wings, legs, and back so that the fat drains away.

Always cook poultry completely at one time. Never cook it partially, store it, and finish cooking it later. Partial cooking of poultry very often promotes the growth of food poisoning bacteria.

Fruit-Stuffed Goose

Make stuffing by tossing together $3\frac{1}{2}$ cups soft bread cubes (4 slices); $1\frac{1}{2}$ cups diced peeled apple; $\frac{1}{2}$ cup chopped onion; $\frac{1}{2}$ cup raisins; $\frac{1}{2}$ cup melted butter; $\frac{3}{4}$ teaspoon salt; $\frac{1}{4}$ teaspoon rubbed sage; $\frac{1}{4}$ teaspoon dried rosemary leaves, crushed; and $\frac{1}{8}$ teaspoon pepper. Stuff goose with fruit mixture. Truss the goose.

Place goose, breast side up, on rack in shallow roasting pan. Prick the legs and the wings of one 4- to 6-pound ready-to-cook goose with a fork. Roast, uncovered, at 325° for $2\frac{3}{4}$ to 3 hours, spooning off fat occasionally during cooking. Makes 4 servings.

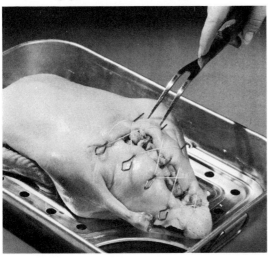

Lace cord or twine across skewers like on a boot to truss a stuffed bird. Prick the fat areas deeply, and duck is ready to roast.

Roast Duckling with Cranberry Sauce

Place one $3\frac{1}{2}$- to 5-pound ready-to-cook duckling, breast up, on rack in shallow pan. Roast, uncovered, at 375° for $1\frac{1}{2}$ hours, then at 425° till tender, 15 minutes. Place neck and giblets in saucepan. Add one $10\frac{1}{2}$-ounce can condensed beef broth. Simmer, covered, for 1 hour. Strain.

To strained broth, add $\frac{3}{4}$ cup cranberry juice cocktail; cook till reduced to 1 cup. In saucepan melt 2 tablespoons butter or margarine; blend in 2 tablespoons sugar. Cook and stir till brown. Add 2 tablespoons vinegar and cranberry mixture. Remove duckling from pan. Skim fat from meat juices; add juices to cranberry mixture. Stir in 1 tablespoon cornstarch blended with 1 tablespoon cranberry juice cocktail. Cook and stir till bubbly; simmer 1 to 2 minutes. Serve giblets with the duckling and pass cranberry sauce. Makes 4 servings.

Substitute chicken for turkey sometimes to vary Swiss Turkey-Ham Bake. Either way, an artichoke-grapefruit salad, hot poppy seed rolls, and cherry parfaits complement the main dish.

Roasting or stewing poultry has a double advantage. After the whole bird appears as a main course, the leftovers can be used in casseroles, soups, salads, and sandwiches. This saves the homemaker time, and it disguises the food so the family doesn't become bored with repetition.

Turkey-Crab Sauce

Prepare rich biscuit dough or puff pastry shells. *Or* halve and seed 3 medium acorn squash; cook till tender. Dot with butter.

In saucepan combine 2 cups dairy sour cream; one 7½-ounce can crab meat, drained, flaked, and cartilage removed; 2 cups diced, cooked turkey *or* chicken; and 2 tablespoons sauterne. Place the mixture over low heat just till serving temperature. Spoon mixture over biscuits, puff pastry shells, or squash halves. Sprinkle ¼ cup shredded process Swiss cheese over top. Serve at once. Makes 6 servings.

Swiss Turkey-Ham Bake

Convert leftovers into an elegant dish by adding water chestnuts, wine, and cheese—

In skillet cook ½ cup chopped onion in 2 tablespoons butter or margarine till onion is tender but not brown. Blend in 3 tablespoons all-purpose flour, ½ teaspoon salt, and ¼ teaspoon pepper. Add one 3-ounce can sliced mushrooms, undrained, 1 cup light cream, and 2 tablespoons dry sherry; cook and stir till the mixture is thickened and bubbly.

Add 2 cups cubed cooked turkey, 1 cup cubed, fully cooked ham, and one 5-ounce can water chestnuts, drained and sliced.

Pour into a 1½-quart casserole; top with 2 ounces process Swiss cheese, shredded (½ cup). Mix 1½ cups soft bread crumbs and 3 tablespoons butter or margarine, melted; sprinkle bread crumb mixture around edge of casserole. Bake at 400° till lightly browned, about 25 minutes. Makes 6 servings.

POULTRY SEASONING—A commercial mixture of ground herbs and spices used primarily to season poultry stuffings and poultry dishes. A typical blend includes thyme, sage, pepper, marjoram, and nutmeg. Savory, ginger, allspice, cloves, and mace may also be used.

Its use is not limited to poultry stuffings, casseroles, and giblet gravies. Poultry seasoning also highlights the flavor of stuffings for veal, pork, and fish and accents meat loaves, biscuits, gravies, and dumplings. (See also *Herb.*)

Chicken à la France

- ¼ cup all-purpose flour
- ½ teaspoon salt
  Dash pepper
- 1 2½- to 3-pound ready-to-cook broiler-fryer chicken, cut up
- 2 tablespoons chopped onion
- 2 tablespoons butter or margarine

• • •

- 1 11-ounce can condensed Cheddar cheese soup
- ½ cup canned tomatoes
- ¼ cup sauterne
- ¼ teaspoon poultry seasoning
- ⅛ teaspoon garlic powder

Combine flour, salt, and pepper in paper or plastic bag; add 2 or 3 pieces chicken at a time; shake to coat. Brown chicken and onion in butter in a skillet.

Combine soup and remaining ingredients. Blend well. Pour over browned chicken. Cook, covered, over low heat till chicken is tender, about 40 minutes; stir often. Serves 4.

POULTRY SHEARS—A heavy-duty instrument that resembles scissors or wire clippers. Poultry shears are especially useful in the kitchen for cutting through the flesh and bones of all types of poultry.

POUND CAKE—A rich, moist, compact cake that is usually baked in a loaf. Pound cake was once made with a pound each of butter, sugar, eggs, and flour; hence, the name pound cake. This scrumptious dessert cake now has different proportions and includes baking powder as a leavening agent. Lemon or spices are sometimes included to enhance the flavor of the cake.

Never before has it been easier to make pound cake than it is today. You can make the cake from basic ingredients, using tested recipes, or from cake mixes. If you decide not to make the cakes yourself, good packaged bakery cakes and frozen ones are available in the supermarkets.

There are a few techniques to follow when making your own pound cake. First, have all the ingredients at room temperature before you begin. Then, be sure to beat the batter sufficiently—this is the key to a good pound cake. Always follow the recipe directions or package instructions for length of beating time, especially for beating the batter thoroughly after adding each egg. Today, with the aid of electric mixers, it is much easier and quicker to beat batters than it was in years past when homemakers spent as long as an hour beating cake batters by hand.

Swirl chocolate- and lemon-flavored batters together for the marbled effect found in the flavor and color of Marble Pound Cake.

Freshly baked pound cake makes a delicious dessert by itself, or with butter or a fruit sauce. The cake has other uses, too. Cubes or fingers are excellent topped with a pudding or arranged around the edges of a bowl before adding a creamy filling. The slices substitute for bread when making party or tea sandwiches. If the cake becomes stale, it can be salvaged by toasting or soaking in wine.

Pound cake that is not used immediately will store well. It should be wrapped tightly. The cake will keep well in the refrigerator or in the freezer for as long as six months. (See also *Cake.*)

Marble Pound Cake

  1¼ **cups sugar**
   ¾ **cup butter or margarine,**
      softened
   ½ **cup milk**
   1 **teaspoon grated lemon peel**
   1 **tablespoon lemon juice**
  2¼ **cups sifted cake flour**
  1¼ **teaspoons salt**
   1 **teaspoon baking powder**
   3 **eggs**

       • • •

   2 **tablespoons boiling water**
   1 **tablespoon sugar**
   1 **1-ounce square unsweetened**
      chocolate, melted
     Confectioners' sugar

In large mixer bowl gradually beat the 1¼ cups sugar into the butter or margarine. Cream till light and fluffy, 8 to 10 minutes at medium speed on electric mixer. Beat in milk, lemon peel, and juice. Sift together flour, salt, and baking powder. Add to creamed mixture and mix on low speed till smooth, about 2 minutes. Add eggs, one at a time, beating 1 minute after each; beat for 1 minute more, scraping sides of bowl often. Combine the boiling water, the 1 tablespoon sugar, and the melted chocolate; stir into *half* the batter. In greased 9x5x3-inch loaf pan, alternate light and dark batters by spoonfuls. With narrow spatula, gently stir through batter to marble. Bake at 300° about 1 hour and 20 minutes. Cool 10 minutes before removing from pan. When completely cool, sift confectioners' sugar over top of cake.

Loaf Pound Cake

   ¾ **cup butter or margarine**
   ½ **teaspoon grated lemon peel**
   ¾ **cup sugar**
   1 **teaspoon vanilla**
   3 **eggs**
  1¼ **cups sifted all-purpose flour**
   ½ **teaspoon baking powder**

Cream butter and lemon peel; gradually add sugar, creaming till light, about 6 minutes at medium speed on electric mixer. Add vanilla, then eggs, one at a time, beating well after each. Sift together flour, baking powder, and ¼ teaspoon salt; stir in. Grease *bottom* only of 9x5x3-inch pan; turn in batter. Bake at 350° till done, about 50 minutes. Cool in pan. Sift confectioners' sugar on top, if desired.

POUSSE CAFÉ *(pōos' ka fā')*— **1.** Any liqueur served in a cordial glass with coffee after dinner. **2.** An after-dinner drink made by layering from two to seven liqueurs of different colors, flavors, and densities in a cordial glass. This rainbow-colored drink is spectacular and impressive.

Experimentation with various combinations and brands of liqueurs is necessary to perfect your technique in making a pousse café. Start with a narrow cordial glass and from two to seven liqueurs. To keep the layers separate, you must put the heaviest liqueur on the bottom and graduate up to the lightest on the top. A typical combination includes, from bottom to top, green crème de menthe, yellow chartreuse, cherry-flavored liqueur, and cognac.

Layering the liqueurs in the glass requires a steady hand. Use one teaspoon to one tablespoon of each liqueur, depending on the number of layers. Pour each layer gently down the side of the glass or over the back of a demitasse spoon that is placed in the glass upside down.

POWDERED SUGAR—Term for confectioners' sugar. (See also *Confectioners' Sugar.*)

PRALINE *(prä' lēn, prā' lin, prä lēn')*—A rich, creamy, patty-shaped candy. Pralines are usually made with granulated sugar, brown sugar, corn syrup, milk or cream,

Satisfy that sweet tooth with rich pralines chock-full of pecan halves. One of these Creamy Pralines makes a good snack or a perfect dessert after a spicy meal, such as a Mexican dinner.

Stir carefully when making pralines to keep sugar crystals in the lower part of pan. Crystals should be dissolved when the candy boils. This helps to make it smooth.

When mixture starts to boil, reduce heat and continue stirring with a wooden spoon to keep it from boiling over. Remove pan from heat before adding butter and pecans.

butter, and pecans. However, this is not the way the original pralines were made. The first ones were delicious sugar-coated almond confections made by the French chef of Marshal César du Plessis Praslin. The name, praline, is said to have been derived from the marshal's last name.

Pralines were brought to America by New Orleans travelers who visited France. The renowned Creole cooks adapted the recipe by adding brown sugar and changing the nuts to pecans. Since that time, New Orleans and the South have become quite famous for their smooth praline candies and praline-flavored toppings for desserts and as after-dinner confections.

Homemakers who want to make these nutty, rich candies can do so easily. Simply follow the recipe directions carefully and use the basic principles of making crystalline candy. (See also *Candy*.)

Creamy Pralines

> 2 cups sugar
> ¾ teaspoon baking soda
> 1 cup light cream
> . . .
> 1½ tablespoons butter or margarine
> 2 cups pecan halves

Combine sugar and baking soda in 3½-quart saucepan; mix well. Stir in cream. Bring to boiling over medium heat, stirring constantly. Reduce heat; cook and stir to soft-ball stage (234°). (Mixture caramelizes slightly.) Remove mixture from heat; add butter. Stir in pecan halves; beat till thick, about 2 to 3 minutes. Drop from tablespoon onto waxed paper-lined cookie sheet. If candy becomes too stiff, add a tablespoon hot water. Makes 30 pralines.

Pralines

> Butter or margarine
> 1½ cups brown sugar
> 1½ cups granulated sugar
> 3 tablespoons dark corn syrup
> 1 cup milk
> . . .
> 1 teaspoon vanilla
> 1½ cups pecan halves

Butter the sides of a heavy 3-quart saucepan. In it combine brown sugar, granulated sugar, dark corn syrup, and milk. Cook and stir over medium heat till the sugars dissolve and the mixture boils. Cook to soft-ball stage (234°), stirring occasionally. Cool 10 minutes.

Add vanilla to the candy mixture. Beat by hand 2 minutes. Add pecan halves; beat till the mixture loses its gloss. Drop by tablespoons onto waxed paper-lined cookie sheet. If candy becomes too stiff to drop, add a teaspoon of hot water. Makes 16 pralines.

PRAWN—A shellfish similar to the shrimp. Prawns, like shrimp, inhabit fresh and saltwaters in tropical and temperate regions. These two shellfish look alike, causing them to be confused in markets and on menus. Prawns, however, grow to a larger size than does the average shrimp.

Prawns are considered a great delicacy, especially by the Europeans who eat them more than Americans do.

Clean, cook, and serve prawns in the same way as large shrimp. (See *Shellfish, Shrimp* for additional information.)

Boiled Prawns

> 6 quarts water
> 1 tablespoon salt
> 1½ pounds frozen raw prawns,
>   in the shell
> Cocktail Sauce (See *Cocktail*)

In large kettle bring water and salt to boiling. Add frozen prawns. Return to boiling; reduce heat and boil gently for 2 minutes. Drain the prawns. Cool quickly in cold water. Peel and devein prawns. Serve with Cocktail Sauce, if desired. Makes 3 or 4 servings.

PRECOOK—To completely or partially cook a food before it's used as an ingredient in a recipe. Vegetables are often precooked. For instance, whole green peppers are boiled a few minutes before being stuffed with a meat mixture so that the peppers will be tender. Variety meats are precooked by simmering in water for 30 minutes. This improves the texture and flavor.

Commercial products are sometimes precooked for faster preparation at home. One of the most common is packaged precooked rice. You can prepare this type of rice in very little time.

PREHEAT—To bring an oven or a cooking utensil to the desired temperature before putting the food into it. Preheating is necessary to start cooking immediately and to produce uniform cooking results.

Ovens should always be preheated unless the recipe specifically directs you to begin in a cold oven. About 10 minutes are needed for most ovens to preheat. Many ovens have a signal light to show when the oven has reached the preset temperature.

Broilers are not always preheated. The manufacturer's instructions will tell you whether to preheat or not. Skillets, waffle bakers, and griddles are preheated. This sears meats, cooks foods quickly with little loss of flavor and nutrition, and prevents overcooking of the foods.

PREPARED HORSERADISH—A condiment containing ground horseradish root and white vinegar. Bottles of prepared horseradish are found in supermarket refrigerator cases. Keep it refrigerated at home to preserve flavor and quality.

Prepared horseradish loses its strength gradually. Therefore, older bottles of horseradish will not give as much hot flavor or bite as newer bottles of it will. You can compensate for this by adding a little more than usual until the flavor suits your taste. (See also *Horseradish.*)

PREPARED MUSTARD—A bright yellow condiment prepared from dry, ground mustard seeds. The dry mustard is usually mixed with wine or vinegar, but sometimes water or beer is used. Various spices and seasonings are also added by manufacturers to give a distinctive taste. Dijon-style and horseradish mustard are examples of specially flavored mustards.

Prepared mustard is one of America's favorite condiments. It's a must on hot dogs and many other sandwiches. It lends zesty flavor and color when used as an ingredient in salads, appetizers, sauces, and main dishes. (See also *Mustard.*)

Ham Salad Supreme

      2 3-ounce packages lemon-flavored
          gelatin
  ½ cup dairy sour cream
  1½ teaspoons prepared horseradish
  1½ teaspoons prepared mustard
  ¼ teaspoon salt
      2 3-ounce packages smoked sliced
          ham, snipped
  ½ cup diced celery

Dissolve gelatin in 2 cups boiling water. Stir in 1 cup cold water. To ½ *cup* gelatin, add sour cream, prepared horseradish, prepared mustard, and salt. Beat mixture just till smooth with rotary beater. Pour into 5½-cup mold. Chill the mixture till it is *almost* firm.

Meanwhile, chill remaining gelatin till partially set. Fold in ham and celery. Carefully pour over almost firm sour cream layer. Chill till firm. Makes 5 servings.

Franks in Foil

      2 cups finely chopped frankfurters
  ⅓ cup shredded sharp process
          American cheese
      2 hard-cooked eggs, chopped
      3 tablespoons chili sauce
      2 tablespoons pickle relish
      1 teaspoon prepared mustard
  ¼ teaspoon celery seed
      8 frankfurter buns, split

Combine all ingredients *except* buns. Fill buns with frankfurter mixture. Wrap each securely in foil. Place on baking sheet; bake at 400° for 15 to 18 minutes. Makes 8 sandwiches.

PRESERVATIVE—A natural or chemical substance that keeps foods from spoiling. Salt, sugar, wood smoke, spices, vinegar, alcohol, and brine have been used for centuries to preserve foods. For instance, ham is preserved with wood smoke, and anchovies are packed in a brine.

More recently, chemical compounds have been added to foods to lengthen storage time, retain flavor, and postpone fermentation or decomposition. Salad oil and shortening do not become rancid as fast as they used to because of antioxidants, and breads do not mold rapidly because of the sodium and calcium propionate added.

The additives that are used in foods are approved by the Food and Drug Administration. (See also *Food Additive*.)

PRESERVE—1. Whole fruit or large pieces of fruit in a thick syrup. **2.** To prepare foods, usually by canning or freezing, so that they will keep for later use.

Preserves are usually made with acid fruits such as peaches, pears, pineapple, raspberries, cherries, and strawberries. The fruit is cooked in sugar and water until it's tender, clear, and a bright, good color. The fruit should hold its shape and dominate the flavor of the sugar. Besides adding sweetness and acting as a preservative, the sugar syrup also penetrates and plumps the fruit.

Hot preserves are packed into hot jars and sealed. These jars store well in a cool, dark, dry place. Once the jars are opened, they should be refrigerated.

Preserves are delicious as snack spreads on breads or muffins. They are tasty and attractive served as accompaniments in a meal. Preserves also add flavor and color when used as ingredients in desserts, breads, and glazes for meats.

Winter Preserves

1½ cups prunes
1½ cups dried apricots
1 large orange
1 8¾-ounce can crushed pineapple
5 cups sugar

Rinse prunes and apricots. Cover with 5 cups water in medium saucepan. Simmer, covered, 15 minutes; drain, reserving liquid. Cool. Pit and cut up prunes. Cut up apricots. Peel orange, reserving peel. Section orange, saving juice. Dice orange sections. Scrape; discard white portion. Slice peel into *thin* slivers.

In large kettle combine prunes, apricots, reserved cooking liquid, orange peel, orange sections and juice, *undrained* pineapple, and sugar. Boil gently till desired thickness, about 20 minutes, stirring occasionally. Seal in hot, scalded jars. Makes three ½ pints.

Pineapple Drop Cookies

¾ cup butter or margarine, softened
1 cup sugar
1 egg
¼ cup pineapple preserves
2½ cups sifted all-purpose flour
1 teaspoon baking soda
½ teaspoon salt

Cream butter or margarine and sugar till light. Beat in egg and pineapple preserves. Sift together dry ingredients; add to batter, mixing thoroughly. Drop from teaspoon, 2 inches apart, on *ungreased* cookie sheet. Bake at 375° for 10 minutes. Cool 1 or 2 minutes; remove from pan. Top with preserves and a walnut half just before serving, if desired. Makes 42 cookies.

Jubilee Sauce

1 16-ounce jar dark cherry preserves
¼ cup port
¼ teaspoon almond extract

Combine dark cherry preserves, wine, and almond extract; chill. Serve sauce over ice cream or filled cream puffs. Makes 1⅔ cups.

Plum-Glazed Ribs

4 pounds pork loin back ribs, cut in serving-sized pieces
1 10-ounce jar plum preserves
¼ cup frozen orange juice concentrate, thawed
1 tablespoon vinegar
½ teaspoon Worcestershire sauce

Place ribs, meaty side down, in shallow roasting pan. Roast at 450° for 30 minutes. Remove meat from oven; drain off excess fat. Turn ribs meaty side up; season with 2 teaspoons salt. Reduce oven temperature to 350° and continue roasting for 1 hour; drain.

Meanwhile prepare plum glaze by combining preserves, orange juice concentrate, vinegar, and Worcestershire sauce; blend. Pour glaze over ribs; roast till tender, 30 minutes, basting occasionally. Makes 4 to 6 servings.

Cherry-Sauced Pork Loin

Excellent for holiday dinners—

  1 4- to 5-pound pork loin roast,
      boned, rolled, and tied
  ½ teaspoon salt
  ½ teaspoon pepper
      Dash dried thyme leaves,
      crushed
  1 cup cherry preserves
  ¼ cup red wine vinegar
  2 tablespoons light corn syrup
  ¼ teaspoon ground cinnamon
  ¼ teaspoon ground nutmeg
  ¼ teaspoon ground cloves
  ¼ teaspoon salt
  ¼ cup toasted, slivered almonds

Rub roast with a mixture of the ½ teaspoon salt, pepper, and thyme. Place the roast on rack in a 13x9x2-inch baking pan. Roast, uncovered, at 325° for about 2½ hours.

Meanwhile make cherry sauce in small saucepan by combining cherry preserves, vinegar, corn syrup, cinnamon, nutmeg, cloves, and the ¼ teaspoon salt. Heat to boiling, stirring occasionally; reduce heat and simmer 2 minutes more. Add the toasted, slivered almonds.

Spoon sauce over roast and continue roasting till meat thermometer registers 170°, about 30 minutes longer. Baste roast with cherry sauce several times. Pass sauce with the roast. Makes 10 to 12 servings.

Glazed Pork Shoulder

Glaze adds flavor plus color—

  1 4- to 6-pound fresh pork
      shoulder roast
      • • •
  ½ cup apricot preserves
  2 teaspoons vinegar
  1 teaspoon prepared mustard
  ¼ teaspoon ground ginger

Place meat on rack in shallow roasting pan. Roast at 325° till the meat thermometer registers 185°, about 4 hours. Combine preserves, vinegar, mustard, and ginger. Remove meat from the oven; spoon on sauce. Roast 15 minutes more. Makes 12 to 16 servings.

Apricot-Ham Patties)

  1½ pounds ground fully cooked ham
  ½ cup soft bread crumbs
  ½ cup milk
  2 eggs
  ¼ cup chopped onion
  1 ounce blue cheese, crumbled
      (¼ cup)
  1 tablespoon Worcestershire sauce
  1 teaspoon prepared mustard
  ¼ teaspoon ground sage
  ¼ teaspoon pepper
      • • •
  ½ cup apricot *or* peach preserves
  2 teaspoons vinegar
  1 teaspoon prepared mustard

Combine ham, bread crumbs, milk, eggs, onion, cheese, Worcestershire sauce, mustard, sage, and pepper. Shape in 6 patties. Place in a 13x9x2-inch baking dish; bake at 350° for 30 minutes. Combine preserves, vinegar, and mustard; brush mixture on the ham patties. Bake 10 minutes longer. Makes 6 servings.

Foods that are preserved for later use include fruits, vegetables, and meats. These have been preserved in various ways since the beginning of civilization. Methods used for preserving foods include drying, smoking, curing, canning, freezing, pickling, and jelly- or jam-making. The newest methods are dehydrating and freeze-drying. (See *Canning, Freezing, Jelly* for additional information.)

PRESERVED GINGER—Fresh ginger packed in a heavy syrup. Bottles of preserved ginger consist of cleaned, peeled, and boiled ginger preserved in a sugar solution. Preserved ginger is used as a sauce or an ingredient. This ginger comes from Hong Kong and Australia. (See also *Ginger.*)

PRESSED COOKIE—A rich cookie shaped by forcing the dough through a cookie press. Spritz are one of the better-known pressed cookies. These cookies make attractive gifts and party refreshments because of their shapes. Tint the dough to add a seasonal color. (See *Cookie, Spritz* for additional information.)

PRESSED DUCK—A dish consisting of sliced duck meat and a sauce made with the juices extracted from the duck carcass.

This delectable French dish is traditionally prepared at the dinner table. When the whole, roasted duck is brought to the table, the legs are removed and the breast meat is sliced. Then, the remaining duck is put into a duck press (usually an ornate piece of equipment). The juices are pressed out, cooked down, and blended with wine and brandy to make the sauce that garnishes the sliced breast meat.

PRESSURE COOKING—A method of cooking foods with pressurized steam using a specially designed pan. One of the main advantages of pressure cooking is speed, especially in high-altitude areas. In fact, pressure pans were once known as Denver cookers because they were so widely used around that area of the country.

The basic principle of pressure cooking is that steam is held in the pan under pressure so that the temperature is higher than the boiling point of water. Therefore, foods cook in about a third of the time required by normal methods. Because of the short cooking time and the small amount of water used in pressure cooking, the vitamins and minerals in food and the bright color of vegetables are preserved. Pressure cooking helps to tenderize the less-tender cuts of meat such as stewing meats, pot roasts, and older poultry.

Equipment: The pressure pan consists of several basic parts—the pan, cover, sealing gasket, pressure indicator, and safety valve or automatic air vent.

The pans are constructed of sheet or cast aluminum or of stainless steel. Saucepans come in sizes of 4, 6, and 8 quarts. The canners are larger than saucepans and range up to 21-quart capacities.

The covers are constructed so they lock tightly onto the pan. The gasket, usually rubber, helps to seal the two together. The pressure indicator shows how many pounds of pressure are inside the pan.

Air vents and safety valves in the covers are made of metal or rubber. Both types are designed to release steam if pressure is not released immediately.

Guide to pressure pans

Pressure saucepan—a deep pan shaped either like a saucepan or a more shallow skillet. These have one long handle. Some models are electric and have controlled heat.

Pressure cooker or canner—A utensil larger than the saucepan.

Cookers and saucepans can be used interchangeably: canners to cook large quantities of food as well as processing canned food; and saucepans to can small jars of food.

How to care for pressure pans: Always study the instruction booklet that comes with a pan and keep it in a convenient place. The booklet will give specific instructions for your particular utensil.

Generally, pressure pans should be handled with care. Do not drop or bang them, for this can cause cracks and chips. Clean all parts after each use, being sure the vent tube is completely clean. Avoid putting any parts of the pan into water if the instructions say "not immersible."

Store all parts of the pan together. The cover should not be fastened on the pan, so turn it upside down over the pan, or store inside or separately.

How to cook in a pressure pan: Cooking in pressure pans is simple and safe if you follow the manufacturer's directions. Be sure to keep the vent clean, use the correct amount of water, and control the heat.

Follow the recipe directions for the amount of food and water to be put into the pan, filling the pan only ½ to ⅔ full. Check to see that the vent is not clogged and then fasten the cover securely. Begin heating the pan and place the pressure indicator on as the instruction specifies. When it reaches the correct pressure, begin timing and lower the heat to keep the pressure constant. You should stay near the pan to control the heat.

Remove the pan from the heat immediately when the recommended time is up to avoid overcooking. Depending on the food, pressure is completely reduced in one of two ways: (1) removing the pan from the heat and letting the pressure drop of its own accord; or (2) *cooling* the pan quickly by placing it under running, cold water, by pouring cold water over the top, or by setting the pan in cold water. To be sure the pressure is down, test by tilting the pressure indicator slightly. If there is no steam, the pressure is down and you can remove the food safely.

How to can in a pressure pan: Processing in a pressure canner is necessary when canning many types of foods. Low-acid foods such as meats and most vegetables must have a higher temperature than boiling water to kill spoiling bacteria.

To can foods in a pressure canner or cooker, follow the directions in your instruction booklet. Put the correct amount of water in the canner. Place the jars of food on a rack in the canner so that steam can flow around each jar. Lock the cover in place and heat the canner. Let the steam escape for about seven to ten minutes so the air is removed from the utensil and jars. Then, put the pressure indicator in place and bring the pan to the pressure called for. Adjust the heat to hold this pressure. Process for the length of time specified in the recipe. When the time has elapsed, remove the pressure pan from the heat and let the pressure go down by itself. When all the pressure is gone, remove the pressure indicator and then the cover. (See also *Canning*.)

Quick Ribs and Kraut

  2 **pounds pork spareribs**
  1 **27-ounce can sauerkraut,**
     undrained
½ **cup tomato juice**
  2 **tablespoons brown sugar**

Cut ribs in serving-sized pieces. In skillet brown ribs on both sides. In 4-quart pressure pan combine sauerkraut, tomato juice, and brown sugar. Top with ribs; season with salt and pepper. Close cover securely. Cook at 15 pounds pressure for 15 minutes. Cool pan by placing under cold running water. Serves 4 or 5.

Pork Chop Supper

  2 **teaspoons shortening**
  4 **pork chops, ½ inch thick**
  1 **teaspoon salt**
    Dash pepper
½ **cup chicken broth**
  4 **small potatoes, peeled and halved**
    or quartered
  4 **medium carrots, peeled and**
    cut up
  1 **small onion, chopped**
    Salt and pepper

      • • •

  2 **tablespoons all-purpose flour**
¼ **cup cold water**

Heat shortening in a 4-quart pressure pan. Season chops with the 1 teaspoon salt and dash pepper; brown the chops on both sides in hot shortening. Add chicken broth. Place potatoes, carrots, and onion atop chops. Sprinkle with additional salt and pepper. Close cover securely. Cook 10 minutes at 15 pounds pressure. Cool quickly under cold running water.

Remove chops and vegetables to serving platter. Blend flour and cold water. Add to juices in pan. Cook and stir till thickened and bubbly. Pass gravy. Makes 4 servings.

Jiffy Spaghetti Sauce

  2 **tablespoons shortening**
    or salad oil
  1 **pound ground beef**
  2 **large onions, sliced**
½ **teaspoon garlic salt**
  2 **8-ounce cans tomato sauce**
  1 **6-ounce can tomato paste**
  1 **to 1½ teaspoons chili powder**
  1 **teaspoon sugar**
½ **teaspoon salt**
    Dash cayenne

      • • •

  8 **ounces long spaghetti, cooked**
    Grated Parmesan cheese

Combine all ingredients *except* spaghetti and cheese in 4-quart pressure pan. Cook 12 minutes at 15 pounds pressure. Reduce the pressure quickly under cold running water. Serve sauce over hot cooked spaghetti. Top with grated Parmesan cheese. Makes 6 servings.

Saucy Chicken Dinner

1 2½- to 3-pound ready-to-cook
    broiler-fryer chicken, cut up
2 tablespoons shortening
1 teaspoon salt
¼ teaspoon dried basil leaves,
    crushed
1 tablespoon instant minced onion
½ cup chopped carrot
1 8-ounce can tomatoes, cut up
        . . .
1 2-ounce can chopped mushrooms,
    drained
1 tablespoon all-purpose flour
    Hot cooked noodles

Sprinkle chicken with salt and pepper. Heat shortening in skillet. Brown chicken; place on rack in a 4-quart pressure pan. Add 1 teaspoon salt, dash pepper, basil, onion, carrot, and tomatoes with juice. Close cover securely. Cook 13 minutes at 15 pounds pressure.

Cool pan at once by placing under cold running water. Add mushrooms to saucepan; heat in open pan about 1 minute. Remove chicken to platter. Mix flour and 2 tablespoons cold water. Stir into liquid in pan and cook till thickened and bubbly. Serve over chicken and hot cooked noodles. Makes 4 servings.

PRETZEL—A crisp, biscuitlike snack shaped in a knot, stick, or circle. Originally, they were soft with a tough, chewy texture. Now, the majority are dry and hard with shiny crusts. Either type comes unsalted or studded with crystals of coarse salt.

Monks created pretzels more than fifteen hundred years ago. They were the architects of the traditional pretzel shape—a loose knot with the ends twisted in the center. Legend says that this shape was suggestive of arms crossed in prayer; therefore, priests gave pretzels to children as a reward for learning prayers.

Pretzels are now a popular snack food. They make a delicious treat eaten alone or combined with various other foods. Crisp, salty pretzels are a traditional combination with cold beer or cocktails. Pretzels also serve as good dunkers for dips and other foods. Some people are fond of them with peanut butter or mustard.

In combination with other foods, pretzels become the basis for scramble cereal mixes, another cocktail accompaniment. Crushed pretzels lend a crunchy texture and salty flavor when mixed into stuffings or sprinkled over casseroles as toppings.

Parmesan Nibble Mix

Store any leftover mix in airtight containers to serve later for snacks—

6 cups round oat cereal
3 cups pretzel sticks
3 cups beer nuts
½ cup butter or margarine,
    melted
1 envelope Parmesan salad
    dressing mix (1 tablespoon)

In a 13x9x2-inch baking pan heat cereal in 300° oven till warm, about 5 minutes. Remove from oven. Add pretzel sticks and beer nuts. Pour the melted butter or margarine over pretzel mixture; sprinkle with dry salad dressing mix. Stir well. Return pan to oven and heat 15 to 20 minutes longer. Makes 12 cups of nibble mix.

Ham-Pretzel Teasers

Eat the pretzel handle, too—

1 3-ounce package cream cheese,
    softened
1 cup ground fully cooked ham
¼ cup chopped pecans
¼ teaspoon Worcestershire sauce
    Several drops onion juice
    Thin pretzel sticks
½ cup finely snipped parsley

Blend cream cheese, ham, pecans, Worcestershire sauce, and onion juice; chill. Shape mixture into 3 dozen small balls. Chill till serving time. Insert pretzel stick into each ball. Roll sides in snipped parsley. Makes 3 dozen.

PRICKLY PEAR—A pear-shaped fruit that comes from any one of several cactus plants. The purple red flesh contains many large, hard seeds and is enclosed by a red, greenish red, or yellow skin. The fruit's shape and its spine-covered skin are the basis for its descriptive name.

Although there are over 100 species of prickly pears, only a few are used for food. The most familiar species are the Indian fig, tuna fig, and harberry fig. The first two are common in the southwestern United States; the last, in the east.

Prickly pear plants look different than other cacti. Instead of leaves, they have broad, flat stems or branches. Depending on the species, these stems are round-, oval-, cylindrical-, or club-shaped. The fruits that develop at the points where flowers have bloomed are actually swollen portions of the stems.

Prickly pears are another of the many foods indigenous to tropical America. Analysis of Mexican archaeological remains indicate that prickly pears were an important food as far back as 7000 B.C.

The Spanish explorers were the first Europeans to whom American Indians introduced prickly pears. In fact, at times prickly pears were the only food available to Cortez and his army as they marched through Mexico in 1519.

The Spanish took back samples of prickly pears to the Mediterranean countries where prickly pear cultivation was soon undertaken. The plants eventually spread throughout the world, becoming dietary mainstays in some countries, and troublesome weeds in others.

The name prickly pear aptly describes the appearance of this cactus fruit. When cut, the seed-filled, purple red flesh is exposed.

Nutritional value: A 3½-ounce portion of this fruit contains about 42 calories, most of which are contributed by carbohydrates. A fair amount of vitamin C is also available, while other vitamins and minerals are present in trace amounts.

How to select and store: Prickly pears are primarily available during fall and early winter. Ripeness is indicated by well-reddened skins. In addition, choose ones that are firm, yet not excessively hard, and that have a bright, fresh appearance. At home, prickly pears should be stored at a moderate room temperature.

How to prepare and use: The spines are usually removed from prickly pears prior to marketing. If not, singe them off, and peel the fruits before eating.

These juicy, succulent fruits, enjoyed raw or cooked, have a distinctive, mildly sweet flavor. When used in salads or desserts, prickly pears are left whole or are sliced or cut up, as desired. For dessert, use them sweetened, or serve with lemon wedges or cream. Cook prickly pears to make tasty jellies, jams, and preserves, too. (See also *Fruit.*)

PRIME—The top federal grade of beef, veal, and lamb. Meat labeled prime is juicy, tender, and flavorful. This grade will be found stamped on meat inside the familiar shield-shaped mark. (See *Meat, USDA* for additional information.)

PRIME RIB—A name sometimes given to a standing beef rib roast. "Prime" rib may or may not be graded as prime by the USDA. This cut is tender and flavorful. Allow 8 to 16 ounces of meat per person.

Prime rib is quite often advertised as the specialty of the house in restaurants. (See also *Beef.*)

PRINTANIER, PRINTANIÈRE *(pran ta nyā'-nyâr')*—A garnish of mixed fresh vegetables. Printanier usually refers to a soup garnish, while printanière refers to a meat.

The vegetables used are young carrots, peas, turnips, green beans, onions, and cauliflower. These are scooped out in tiny balls or diced, then cooked, and buttered.

Smooth, mellow process cheese is easy to melt.

PROCESS CHEESE—A blend of one or more types of natural cheese that has a texture and flavor different from any of the original cheeses. Process cheese is made from ground natural cheese that is heated and treated with an emulsifying agent. The bacteria are killed in the processing, so no more curing takes place.

This processing yields a cheese that is easy to slice and to melt. The flavors are milder than the natural cheeses from which they are made. The calorie content and nutritional value of these cheeses are not changed much during processing. Process cheese keeps well.

Process cheeses were made in Germany and Switzerland as early as 1895. By 1914, they were introduced to America. Today, a third of the cheese made in America is process cheese. American cheese, a process Cheddar, ranks as the most popular of the processed cheeses.

Process cheeses come in many shapes and flavors. They may be purchased in loaves or slices. Some slices are individually wrapped. The flavors include spices, pimiento, fruit, nuts, meats, onion, shrimp, and smoke. (See also *Cheese.*)

Process cheese spreads come plain or flavored.

Cheese-Rice Squares

      3 cups cooked rice
      4 ounces sharp process American
           cheese, shredded (1 cup)
    ½ cup snipped parsley
    ¼ cup finely chopped onion
      1 teaspoon salt
      3 beaten eggs
    1½ cups milk
      1 teaspoon Worcestershire sauce

Mix rice, cheese, parsley, onion, and salt. Combine eggs, milk, and Worcestershire; add to rice mixture and mix thoroughly. Pour into a greased 10x6x1¾-inch baking dish. Bake at 325° just till set, about 40 to 45 minutes. Cut in squares; top with your favorite creamed chicken or tuna. Makes approximately 6 to 8 servings.

Rice, Ham, and Cheese Salad

    ¾ cup uncooked long-grain rice
    1½ cups water
    ¼ cup finely chopped onion
      2 tablespoons soy sauce
      1 medium clove garlic, minced
           •   •   •
      2 cups diced fully cooked ham
    ½ cup chopped celery
    ½ cup mayonnaise
           or salad dressing
      1 tablespoon vinegar
    ⅛ teaspoon cayenne
      4 ounces process Swiss cheese,
           shredded (1 cup)

In skillet cook rice over low heat till lightly browned. Add water, onion, soy sauce, and garlic; mix well. Cover; cook till rice is tender and liquid is absorbed, about 20 minutes. Add ham and celery; heat through. Stir in mayonnaise, vinegar, cayenne, and cheese. To serve, top with additional process Swiss cheese, if desired. Makes 4 to 6 servings.

PROCESS CHEESE FOOD—A cheese product made like process cheese but containing more moisture. It has less milk fat and less cheese than the process cheese but has added nonfat dry milk or whey solids, water, and an emulsifier. By legal definition, it

Process cheese foods are similar to process cheese.

must contain at least 51 percent cheese. Process cheese food is also called pasteurized process cheese food.

Process cheese food has a softer, more spreadable texture and melts quicker than process cheese. It makes a nice snack and blends easily into sauces or vegetables.

The cheese is available in slices, rolls, links, and loaves. Some have an additional fruit, vegetable, pimiento, or smoke flavor. It will store well like the process cheese. (See also *Cheese.*)

PROCESS CHEESE SPREAD—A cheese product that has more moisture and less fat than does process cheese food. The cheese spread comes in both jars and loaves, and may have other flavors added.

Process cheese spreads are soft enough to spread easily and to melt quickly. You can use the spread in recipes or spread it on crackers or celery for a quick snack or appetizer. (See also *Cheese.*)

PROFITEROLE (*pruh fit′ uh rōl′*)—Small cream puffs with a sweet or savory filling. The sweet type has an ice cream, custard, or jam filling and a chocolate sauce topping. The savory type has a meat, poultry, fish, or cheese filling.

PROOF—1. A standard indicating the amount of alcohol present in distilled liquor. 2. To let yeast dough rise.

In liquor, half of the proof is the percent of alcohol. For example, if the liquor is 80 proof, this indicates that 40 percent of the liquor is alcohol.

The standard for proof came about many years ago, long before the process of distilling liquor and measuring alcohol were highly developed. The distiller would show "proof" of the alcohol content by burning a small amount.

The second meaning of proof is used in baking. When yeast dough has risen and been punched down, it is shaped and put into a pan. At this stage, the "rising" is called proofing. Proofing lasts until dough is double in bulk after which it is baked. (See also *Wines* and *Spirits.*)

PROSCIUTTO HAM (*prō shoo′ tō*)—A highly seasoned Italian ham that is cured by air-drying. Because of this curing process, prosciutto does not require further cooking. The dried, salted, and well-peppered meat is pressed, then sliced.

Prosciutto's most popular use is as an antipasto or appetizer served cold with melons or figs. Prosciutto also makes a delicious sandwich. (See also *Ham.*)

Prosciutto and Artichokes

Drain one can or jar of artichoke hearts packed in water or oil. Wrap a paper-thin slice of prosciutto ham around each artichoke heart. Secure with wooden picks. Serve as an appetizer.

Special processing concentrates the flavors in prosciutto ham, so slice it very thin and eat it with chilled wedges of honeydew.

PROTEIN–A group of highly complex substances that make up most body tissues and that perform various vital functions to maintain health, growth, and energy. Every living plant and animal has proteins in its physical makeup, and it needs a continuing supply to maintain life.

In order of quantity, proteins are second only to water in the composition of the human body. Their forms vary greatly from the soft, elastic material of muscles and organs to the tough material of bones and teeth. Other important members of this group are hemoglobin, which transports oxygen through the blood stream; antibodies, which fight disease; and enzymes, which trigger many body functions.

Proteins were first observed by a Dutch physician-chemist, Gerrit Jan Mulder. In 1838 he concluded that all plants and animals contain a substance essential to life. Although unable to analyze its components, he recognized the importance of this substance and named it "protein," from a Greek word meaning first place.

Since that time, research has shown that what Mulder observed was not one simple substance, but a group that includes hundreds of different proteins, each made up of amino acids. Eight amino acids are known to be essential for adults since these cannot be synthesized by the body. A ninth probably is essential for children.

Food proteins are classified into two biological groups: complete and incomplete. The animal proteins found in meat, milk, and eggs are complete or high quality because they contain all of the essential amino acids. Plant proteins are called incomplete because they either do not contain all of the essential amino acids, or they contain them in insufficient quantities.

This does not mean that incomplete food proteins are unimportant. Quite the contrary. Proteins in legumes and nuts come close to animal proteins in food value. Plant proteins are enhanced when served with foods that complement them nutritionally. For example, the protein in cereals is made useful when served with milk.

Protein requirements change with the age and condition of the individual. During childhood and adolescence, protein is needed for body building. Proteins are

Provolone has a pleasant, smoked, sharp flavor.

needed in greatest amounts for girls between ages 13 and 15 and boys between ages 16 and 19. Protein needs for women increase during pregnancy and nursing.

Eating meat and dairy products is the easiest but most expensive way to meet protein requirements. Inexpensive dry peas and beans, lentils, nuts, and peanut butter are rich nonanimal sources of protein that can be substituted for animal foods occasionally. (See also *Nutrition*.)

PROVENÇALE, À LA (*prō' vuhn säl', prov' uhn-*)–A phrase that means "in the style of Provence" (a region in southern France). In food preparation, à la Provençale means that the food is cooked with a liberal amount of garlic and often with tomatoes and oil. Classic Provençale sauce is well suited for egg, fowl, vegetable, and meat dishes. (See also *French Cookery*.)

Sauce Provençale

  4 tomatoes, peeled, each cut in 6
     wedges, and seeded
½ teaspoon sugar
  2 tablespoons butter or margarine
¼ cup chopped green onion
½ cup dry white wine
½ cup butter or margarine
  3 cloves garlic, minced
  2 tablespoons snipped parsley

Sprinkle tomatoes with sugar; set aside. Melt the 2 tablespoons butter. Add onion and heat through. Add wine; cook and stir till liquid is slightly reduced. Add tomatoes; heat through. Add remaining ingredients. Heat and stir just till butter melts. Season. Serves 6 to 8.

PROVOLONE CHEESE (*prō′ vuh lō′ nē*)—A semihard, mellow, smooth cheese that was first made in Italy but is now domestically produced, too. After it is salted and dried, this cow's milk cheese is usually smoked, then dipped in paraffin, or oiled.

Although this cheese is traditionally shaped like a pear, bound in rope baskets, and hung for curing, provolone is also formed into other shapes that range in weight from 1 to 200 pounds.

Provolone is suitable for an appetizer or dessert cheese tray or for cooking. Italian cooks use provolone in many of their food dishes. (See also *Cheese.*)

PRUNE—A dried plum. Only certain varieties of plums, descendants of the European *Prunus domestica*, can be converted to prunes. In the fresh, fully ripe state, prunes are dark blue to purple in color, firm-fleshed, oblong or oval, and high in sugar content. When dried pit and all, the flesh does not ferment or spoil as would the flesh of other types of plums.

Plums have been an extremly important food to Europeans for many centuries, although they were not always used in the dried form. According to legend, Alexander the Great brought fresh prune plums to Europe from Persia in 331 B.C. However, the Hungarians were the first people to learn how to dry them for year-round use. This drying technique spread to France where prunes became one of that country's most prized products.

The United States' cultivation and processing of prunes began in the 1850s when Louis Pellier, a French immigrant, had slips of the European prune plum trees shipped from France to California. He successfully grafted these slips from the Prune d'Agen or French prune onto wild American plum varieties. Since that time, California has become the largest prune-producing region in the world.

How prunes are produced: Like the grapes that are used for making wines, prune plums that are to be dried must be completely ripe when they are harvested so that the sugar content is at its peak. The prune plums are mechanically shaken from the trees, then dropped into canvas sheets and conveyed to large bins in which the fruits are transported to the processor.

Mechanical drying, a relatively new development, has replaced to a very large extent, the centuries-old sun-drying process. The washed prune plums are stacked on trays, then placed in temperature- and humidity-controlled dehydrators. A constant stream of warm air flows over the plums. In 18 hours the plums have become prunes containing 18 percent moisture.

Next, the prunes are graded and sized according to the number of prunes that are needed to make one pound. Placed in bulk containers, the prunes then can be stored under carefully controlled conditions until they are sold to distributors.

Just prior to packaging and shipping, the prunes are steam-treated. From 6 to 12 percent moisture is added to give the prunes more moistness and greater tenderness in the packaged state.

Nutritional value: Through the removal of water, the drying of prunes concentrates the energy and other nutrients found in the fresh prune plums. Fruit sugars present in prunes are a source of quick energy. Four medium, uncooked prunes yield 58 calories, while ½ cup prune juice provides 100 calories. Prunes are a good source of Vitamin A, iron, and potassium,

Prune-Nut Bread gets part of its moistness and chewiness from the prunes. Center butter balls on the platter of bread slices.

Ready-to-serve prunes and apricots are spruced up with cinnamon, lemon, and rum or brandy for Prune and Apricot Bowl.

yet are low in sodium. The soft bulking substance present in prunes acts as a natural regulator of the body processes.

How to select: The important point in prune selection is to determine which form concurs with your needs. Prunes come pitted and unpitted, dried and canned, puréed and diced, or as prune juice.

The most familiar form, ready-to-use prunes, are now tenderized to ensure moistness and tenderness right from the package. They may be purchased in various sizes—small or breakfast, medium, large, extra-large—and with or without pits.

Ready-to-serve prunes are cooked in liquid at the processing plant. These liquid packed fruits are sealed in cans and jars. Prune juice and puréed and diced prunes are more specialized products. Puréed and diced prunes are particularly good baby foods. They are also convenient items to purchase when recipes specify prunes prepared in these forms.

How to store: Storage techniques for prunes vary, depending on whether the package is unopened or opened. Both dried and canned prunes with containers intact are shelf stable. However, dried, uncanned prunes should be refrigerated if the weather gets excessively hot or humid. Use the fruit within six to eight months.

Opened packages of prunes require cool or refrigerated temperatures. Dried prunes should be tightly covered and stored in a cool, dry place. Cooked prunes should be covered and refrigerated.

How to prepare: The amount of pre-preparation required for prunes is determined by their ultimate use. For snacking, prunes are eaten right from the package. For cooked prunes, select the canned form or cook dried prunes as directed below.

Stewed Prunes

Rinse prunes and cover with water 1 inch above the fruit in a saucepan. Cover; simmer gently for 10 to 20 minutes. If desired, add 2 tablespoons sugar per cup uncooked prunes during the last 5 minutes of cooking.

Unless purchased in pitted or diced form, prunes used in recipes must first be pitted. If you wish to retain the shape of whole prunes, cut only one side of the prunes with kitchen shears and gently squeeze out the pits. Pitting and chopping are accomplished in one operation by snipping around the pits.

When extra-plump prunes are desired, add an equal measure of hot water or fruit juice to the prunes in a jar or bowl. Cover and let stand 24 hours. Store in refrigerator till you are ready to use them.

How to use: People who like prunes know the many types of recipes in which this fruit can be used. Served for breakfast or

---

Prune arithmetic

While prunes are cooking, they absorb enough water to double in bulk. One pound of dried prunes yields 4 cups cooked prunes with pits or 3 cups cooked, pitted prunes.

for a final meal course, stewed prunes get variation with the addition of a lemon slice, orange slice, or cinnamon stick.

Prune and Apricot Bowl

    2 16-ounce jars prunes
    1 30-ounce can whole apricots
    2 inches stick cinnamon
    3 tablespoons lemon juice
    ¼ cup rum or brandy

Drain and reserve syrups from prunes and apricots. In saucepan combine ½ cup prune syrup and ½ cup apricot syrup; add cinnamon and lemon juice. Simmer 2 to 3 minutes; add rum. Arrange fruits in bowl; pour hot syrup over. Serve warm or chilled. Serves 6 to 8.

Stuffed prunes provide interesting flavor and texture in salads. Prunes with cottage cheese is another salad favorite.

Stuffed Prune Salad

For each serving, arrange 2 orange slices on lettuce-lined plate. Stuff 2 cooked, pitted prunes with drained cream-style cottage cheese; top with walnut halves. Place atop oranges.

Nut breads, coffee cakes, pancakes, and waffles take on new dimensions with the incorporation of prunes, as do pies, cakes, whips, and cookies. (See *Dried Fruit, Plum* for additional information.)

Prune-Nut Bread

    1 cup dried prunes, chopped
    2 teaspoons shredded orange peel
    1 cup orange juice
    2 cups sifted all-purpose flour
    ¾ cup sugar
    3 teaspoons baking powder
    ½ teaspoon salt
    ½ teaspoon ground cinnamon
    2 beaten eggs
    2 tablespoons salad oil
    ½ cup chopped walnuts

Combine prunes, orange peel, and juice; let stand ½ hour. Sift together dry ingredients. Combine eggs, oil, and prune mixture; add to dry ingredients, mixing well. Add nuts. Turn into greased 9x5x3-inch loaf pan. Bake at 350° for 55 minutes. Remove from pan; cool.

Prune Spice Cake

    1 cup sifted all-purpose flour
    ⅔ cup sugar
    1 teaspoon baking powder
    ¼ teaspoon baking soda
    ¼ teaspoon salt
    ¼ teaspoon ground cinnamon
    ¼ teaspoon ground nutmeg
    ¼ cup shortening
    ½ cup prune juice
    1 egg
    ½ teaspoon vanilla
      Prune Butter Frosting

Sift together first 7 ingredients into mixer bowl. Add shortening, *half* the prune juice, and egg. Beat 2 minutes. Add remaining juice and vanilla. Beat 2 minutes. Pour into well-greased and lightly floured 8x8x2-inch baking pan. Bake at 350° for 25 to 30 minutes. Cool.

Frost with *Prune Butter Frosting:* Cream 3 tablespoons butter; gradually blend in 1½ cups sifted confectioners' sugar and dash salt. Add enough prune juice for spreading.

PRUNE PLUM—A term applied to any plum variety that can be dried for prunes. Italian prune plums are the best-known type. However, they are eaten fresh more frequently than dried. (See also *Plum.*)

PTARMIGAN *(tär′ muh guhn)*—A species of grouse that is quite common to the Northern Hemisphere. (See also *Grouse.*)

PTOMAINE *(tō′ mān, tō mān′)*—Any of several chemical substances, most of which are not poisonous, that form when animal matter decomposes. Although food poisoning is sometimes called "ptomaine poisoning," this phrase is a misnomer. Toxic ptomaines occur only in foods so badly decomposed that they are easily recognizable as unfit. (See also *Food Poisoning.*)

PUDDING—A baked, boiled, or steamed food with a soft or spongy consistency that can be served in a variety of ways—as a main dish, side dish, or dessert. This definition of pudding applies to a vast assortment of dishes such as blood pudding, corn pudding, oyster pudding, plum pudding, tapioca pudding, and cream pudding.

None of these puddings has a staple ingredient, although flour, milk, and eggs are quite often used. Before the eleventh century, the British reportedly combined these ingredients to make puddings, and three hundred years later, flour, milk, and eggs constituted the basics for the first Yorkshire pudding, which is now famous as a traditional accompaniment for roast beef. As the culinary art was developed, other ingredients were added to puddings. During the next few centuries, puddings became more than staple dishes with the addition of fruits and liquors, as in the rich, moist plum pudding.

When the Pilgrims landed at Plymouth Rock, they returned to the simple pudding recipes. Their meager supplies and limited time for the luxury of specialized cooking led them to utilize the foods that were on hand. The hasty pudding made of flour, eggs, milk, and sometimes, oatmeal or cornmeal is a good example. So, too, is Indian pudding, a dish made of cornmeal. Later Americans added raisins or fresh fruit for a simple sweet pudding. In more recent years tapioca and cornstarch puddings have been popularly served to generations of Americans. Today, many of these old-fashioned puddings still exist in the modern homemaker's pudding list.

Types of puddings: Although at first glance the word pudding seems to apply to a diverse group of dishes that bear little or no relation to each other, a closer look reveals that puddings can be classified as either savory or sweet.

A pudding fix-up

Make refreshing Peach Crumble by layering instant pudding mixed with sour cream, peaches, and a crumbled walnut mixture.

Savory puddings are used either as a main dish or as a side dish. Although the classic example of a savory pudding is the British favorite, puffy Yorkshire Pudding (see *Yorkshire Pudding* for recipe), puddings made with chicken, oysters, corn, and other meats, seafoods, or vegetables are also savory puddings. Most of these delectable dishes have a custardlike consistency and should be served while hot.

Carrot-Cheese Pudding

    3 cups shredded carrots
    2 cups cooked long-grain rice
    6 ounces process American
        cheese, shredded (1½ cups)
    1 cup milk
    2 beaten eggs
    2 tablespoons instant minced onion
    1 teaspoon salt
    ¼ teaspoon pepper
            • • •
    2 ounces process American
        cheese, shredded (½ cup)

Cook carrots, covered, in 1 cup water for 10 minutes; drain. Combine with cooked long-grain rice, the 1½ cups shredded cheese, milk, eggs, instant minced onion, salt, and pepper. Turn into a 1½ quart casserole. Top with additional ½ cup shredded cheese. Bake, uncovered, at 350° for about 1 hour. Makes 6 servings.

During the last few centuries, *sweet puddings* have come into vogue. In fact, these dessert puddings are so popular that today the word pudding almost invariably conjures up visions of creamy vanilla or chocolate pudding, or lusciously warm plum pudding.

Since this type of pudding includes a great many variations, sweet puddings are further divided into steamed, baked, boiled and convenience pudding products.

(1.) Steamed puddings are cooked by steaming them for several hours. Since these puddings have a firm, almost cakelike texture that enables them to hold a shape well, they are often cooked in an attractive mold. Frequently, a sweet sauce is served along with steamed pudding.

Steamed Brazil Nut Pudding

    1 cup chopped, peeled apple
    1¾ cups raisins
    ⅓ cup chopped candied citron
    1 tablespoon grated orange peel
    ½ cup orange juice
            • • •
    2 slightly beaten eggs
    ½ cup light molasses
    1 cup coarsely chopped
        Brazil nuts
    ¾ cup fine dry bread crumbs
    ½ cup coarsely ground suet
        (2 ounces)
    ½ cup sifted all-purpose flour
    ¼ cup sugar
    1 teaspoon baking powder
    ½ teaspoon baking soda
    ½ teaspoon salt
    ½ teaspoon ground cinnamon
    ¼ teaspoon ground allspice
    ¼ teaspoon ground cloves
        Eggnog Sauce

In mixing bowl combine apple, raisins, candied citron, and orange peel. Pour orange juice over fruits; let stand 1 hour. Combine eggs, light molasses, Brazil nuts, bread crumbs, and suet. Sift together flour, sugar, baking powder, soda, salt, cinnamon, allspice, and cloves; blend into egg mixture. Mix in fruits. Pour batter into a greased 1½-quart mold with tight cover (or cover with foil; tie tightly with string). Place on rack in deep kettle; pour boiling water in pan to depth of 1 inch. Cover; steam 3 hours, adding more water if needed. Uncover pudding; bake at 350° for 10 minutes. Cool about 30 minutes before unmolding. Serve with Eggnog Sauce. Makes 10 servings.

Eggnog Sauce: Beat 1 egg till foamy; blend in 3 tablespoons melted butter or margarine, ¾ cup sifted confectioners' sugar, ½ teaspoon vanilla, and dash ground nutmeg. Whip ½ cup whipping cream; gently fold into egg mixture. Chill till serving time.

(2.) Baked puddings, which often have a spongy or a custardlike consistency, are thickened with ingredients such as eggs, rice, or bread. This type of pudding is enjoyed by many homemakers because it doesn't require attention while it bakes.

Applesauce Pudding

       8 slices firm-textured white bread
       1 16-ounce can applesauce
       ⅓ cup raisins
       ½ teaspoon ground cinnamon
       ½ cup brown sugar
       2 eggs
      2½ cups milk
       ½ teaspoon vanilla

Spread one side of each slice bread with butter or margarine. If desired, remove crusts. Arrange 4 slices bread, buttered side up, in greased 8x8x2-inch baking dish. Mix applesauce, raisins, cinnamon, and *2 tablespoons* of the brown sugar. Spread over bread in dish.

Cut each remaining slice bread into 4 triangles; arrange on filling, covering entire surface. Beat together eggs, milk, vanilla, ¼ teaspoon salt, and remaining brown sugar. Pour over bread. Sprinkle with additional cinnamon. Bake at 350° for 50 to 55 minutes. Serves 6 to 8.

(3.) Probably the most popular type of pudding is boiled pudding. Creamy, cornstarch-thickened vanilla, chocolate, butterscotch, and coconut cream puddings as well as other puddings that are cooked on top of the range, such as quick-cooking tapioca pudding, belong to this group.

(4.) In recent years convenience pudding products have become very popular. These products include regular (require cooking to thicken) and instant (thicken without cooking) pudding mixes, which, when combined with milk and sometimes eggs, make a pudding similar to a cream pudding. Canned puddings which are ready-to-eat are also popular items.

Orange Tapioca Fluff

In a 1½-quart saucepan combine 2 tablespoons quick-cooking tapioca, 2 tablespoons sugar, and dash salt. Blend in 1 egg yolk and 1 cup orange juice; let stand 5 minutes. Bring to boil over medium heat, stirring often. Remove from heat. Beat 1 egg white till soft peaks form; gradually add 2 tablespoons sugar, beating till stiff peaks form. Fold orange mixture into egg white; chill. Serves 2 or 3.

Vanilla Pudding

Also try chocolate and butterscotch variations—

       ¾ cup sugar
       2 tablespoons cornstarch
       ¼ teaspoon salt
       2 cups milk
           . . .
       2 slightly beaten egg yolks *or*
       1 well-beaten egg
       2 tablespoons butter or margarine
       1 teaspoon vanilla

In saucepan blend sugar, cornstarch, and salt; add milk. Cook over medium heat, stirring constantly, till thickened and bubbly. Cook and stir 2 minutes more. Remove from heat.

Stir small amount of hot mixture into beaten egg yolks *or* well-beaten egg; return to hot mixture. Cook, stirring constantly, 2 minutes more. Remove the mixture from heat; add butter or margarine and vanilla. Pour pudding into sherbets; chill. Makes 4 or 5 servings.

Chocolate Pudding

Follow directions for Vanilla Pudding, increasing sugar to 1 cup. Add two 1-ounce squares unsweetened chocolate along with the milk.

Butterscotch Pudding

Follow directions for Vanilla Pudding, substituting brown sugar for the granulated sugar. Increase butter or margarine to 3 tablespoons.

How to use: Although pudding is commonly thought of as a dessert in itself, it can also be used as the basis for other desserts. Cream puddings particularly are adaptable to other uses, especially since the introduction of pudding mixes.

Pies constitute one of the most popular uses for puddings. For example, a cream pie is actually pudding in a pastry shell. Although simple vanilla, chocolate, or coconut cream pies are easy to make, elaborate cream pies present few problems. Just add fruit, nuts, sour cream, or whipped cream to the pudding mixture.

Lemon Raisin Pie

Prepare pastry for 2-crust 9-inch pie (see *Pastry*). Pour boiling water over 2 cups raisins and let stand 10 minutes; drain.

Prepare one 3⅝-ounce package *regular* lemon pudding and pie filling mix according to package directions. Stir in 1 tablespoon butter or margarine and raisins. Line 9-inch pie plate with pastry; fill with raisin mixture. Adjust top crust, cutting slits for escape of steam; seal and crimp edge. Bake at 400° till slightly browned, about 35 to 40 minutes.

1-2-3 Apple Pie

>   1 21-ounce can French apple pie
>   filling
>   1 *baked* 9-inch pastry shell
>   (See *Pastry*)
> ¾ cup milk
>   1 cup dairy sour cream
>   1 3¾- or 3⅝-ounce package
>   *instant* vanilla pudding mix
>   2 tablespoons sliced, toasted
>   almonds

Turn pie filling into pastry shell. Slowly add milk to sour cream; mix well. Add pudding mix; beat according to package directions. Pour over pie filling. Chill. Trim with almonds.

As a change from the common plain pudding or cream pie, try making pudding-based parfaits, frozen desserts, and fancy puddings. The added ingredients dress up the pudding without much extra effort.

Frozen Butterscotch Dream

Combine ⅔ cup sugar, ¼ cup water, 1 egg white, 1 teaspoon lemon juice, and 1 teaspoon vanilla. Beat with electric mixer at high speed till stiff peaks form, about 5 minutes. Whip 1 cup whipping cream; fold into mixture.

Combine one 3⅝- or 4-ounce package *instant* butterscotch pudding mix and 1 cup milk; fold into whipped cream mixture. Add ½ cup chopped walnuts; turn into 10x6x1¾-inch baking dish. Top with ¼ cup chopped walnuts. Freeze 6 to 8 hours or overnight. Serves 6 to 8.

Peach Crumble

>   1 cup sugar
>   1 beaten egg
>   1 cup chopped walnuts
>   1 3¾- or 3⅝-ounce package
>   *instant* vanilla pudding mix
>   1 cup dairy sour cream
>   1 cup milk
>   1 cup diced, peeled fresh peaches
>   treated with lemon juice

Thoroughly combine first 3 ingredients. Line 15½x10½x1-inch baking pan with foil; grease foil. Spread nut mixture in pan. Bake at 350° till golden brown, about 18 to 20 minutes. Cool; then coarsely crumble. Divide *half* the crumbs among 6 sherbet glasses.

Combine pudding mix, sour cream, and milk; beat till well blended, 1 to 2 minutes. Fold in peaches. Spoon pudding mixture over crumbs in sherbet glasses; top with remaining crumbs. Chill thoroughly. Makes 6 servings.

Lemonade Pudding

>   2 slightly beaten egg yolks
> 1½ cups milk
>   1 3- or 3¼-ounce package *regular*
>   vanilla pudding mix
>   1 3-ounce package cream cheese,
>   softened
>   1 6-ounce can frozen lemonade
>   concentrate, thawed
>   2 egg whites
> ¼ cup sugar
> ½ cup vanilla wafer crumbs
>   2 tablespoons chopped walnuts
>   2 tablespoons butter, melted

Combine egg yolks and milk. Prepare pudding according to package directions, *using the egg-milk mixture as the liquid*. Add cream cheese and beat smooth with electric or rotary beater; stir in lemonade concentrate. Cover surface with waxed paper and cool 10 minutes; beat smooth again. Beat egg whites to soft peaks; gradually add sugar, beating to stiff peaks. Fold egg whites into pudding. Combine crumbs, nuts, and butter. Sprinkle *half* the crumb mixture into 6 sherbet glasses. Spoon in pudding; top with remaining crumb mixture. Chill the pudding thoroughly. Makes 6 servings.

In the past few years, recipes that use a pudding mix as an ingredient have become popular. Although the pudding loses its identity, the pudding mix adds a delightful flavor to cookies, candies, cakes, and frostings. (See also *Dessert.*)

Unbaked Caramel Cookies

Combine 2 cups sugar, ¾ cup butter or margarine, and one 6-ounce can evaporated milk. Bring mixture to rolling boil, stirring frequently. Remove from heat. Add one 3⅝- or 4-ounce package *instant* butterscotch pudding mix and 3½ cups quick-cooking rolled oats; mix thoroughly. Cool 15 minutes; drop by teaspoonfuls onto waxed paper-lined tray. Makes 60.

Butterscotch Spice Cake

Prepare one 4-ounce package *regular* butterscotch pudding mix according to package directions, *using 2¼ cups milk*. Blend 1 package 2-layer-size spice cake mix into hot pudding (mixture will not be smooth). Pour into lightly greased and floured 13x9x2-inch baking pan. Scatter ½ cup chopped walnuts over batter. Bake at 375° for 25 to 30 minutes. Cut in squares; serve warm or cold with whipped cream or ice cream. Makes 12 to 15 servings.

Easy Chocolate Fudge

    ½ cup butter or margarine
    1 4-ounce package *regular*
        chocolate pudding mix
    1 3- or 3¼-ounce package *regular*
        vanilla pudding mix
    ½ cup milk
    1 16-ounce package sifted
        confectioners' sugar
    ½ teaspoon vanilla
    ½ cup chopped walnuts

In saucepan melt butter or margarine; stir in dry pudding mixes and milk. Bring to boiling; boil for 1 minute, stirring constantly. Remove from heat; beat in sugar. Stir in vanilla and nuts. Pour into buttered 10x6x1¾-inch baking dish. Garnish with walnut halves, if desired. Chill; cut into squares. Makes 24.

Chocolate Pudding Frosting

    1 4-ounce package dark chocolate
        pudding mix
    1¼ cups milk
    ½ cup butter or margarine
    ½ cup shortening
    1 cup sifted confectioners' sugar
    1 teaspoon vanilla
    ¼ teaspoon salt

Cook pudding according to package directions, *using 1¼ cups milk*. Cover surface of pudding with waxed paper or clear plastic wrap; cool to room temperature. Cream together butter or margarine, shortening, and confectioners' sugar till light and fluffy; stir in vanilla and salt. Gradually beat in cooled chocolate pudding. Frosts two 9-inch layers.

Generous scoops of ice cream melt atop the oven-fresh Date Pudding Cake. This delicious dessert forms two layers as it bakes.

PUDDING CAKE—A dessert that forms a pudding layer and a cake layer as it bakes.

Date Pudding Cake

1 cup pitted dates
2 tablespoons butter or margarine
1 cup boiling water
1 egg
1½ cups instant-type flour
½ cup granulated sugar
½ cup brown sugar
1 teaspoon baking soda
½ teaspoon baking powder
½ cup broken walnuts
1½ cups brown sugar
1½ cups boiling water
Vanilla ice cream

Snip dates into a 9-inch round or square baking dish; add butter or margarine. Pour the 1 cup boiling water over; stir to melt butter and soften dates. Add next 7 ingredients and ½ teaspoon salt. Beat with fork till blended, about 2 minutes. Scrape bottom and sides of dish with spatula after 1 minute of beating.

Smooth batter evenly in baking dish; sprinkle with 1½ cups brown sugar. Slowly pour the 1½ cups water over all. Bake at 375° till done, about 40 minutes. Serve warm with scoops of vanilla ice cream piled in center of cake.

Brownie Pudding Cake

1 cup sifted all-purpose flour
¾ cup granulated sugar
6 tablespoons unsweetened cocoa powder
2 teaspoons baking powder
½ cup milk
2 tablespoons salad oil
1 teaspoon vanilla
¾ cup chopped walnuts
¾ cup brown sugar

Sift together flour, granulated sugar, 2 *tablespoons* cocoa, baking powder, and ½ teaspoon salt. Add milk, oil, and vanilla; mix till smooth. Stir in nuts. Pour into greased 8x8x2-inch baking pan. Combine brown sugar, remaining cocoa, and 1¾ cups hot water; pour over batter. Bake at 350° for 45 minutes. Serves 6 to 8.

A light coating of sugar and cinnamon complements the delightful flavor of Applesauce Puffs. They are made with biscuit mix.

PUFF—A light, airy pastry, such as a cream puff, or other food, such as a potato puff.

Potato Puff

Prepare 4 servings packaged instant mashed potatoes according to package directions. Add ½ cup light cream; stir over low heat till very hot. Add 2 tablespoons grated Parmesan cheese, 1 teaspoon instant minced onion, and 1 teaspoon salt. Add 3 egg yolks, one at a time, *beating well after each addition.* Add a little of the hot mixture to 3 stiffly beaten egg whites; fold egg whites into potato mixture. Pour into an *ungreased* 1½-quart casserole. Bake at 375° till knife inserted just off-center comes out clean, about 30 minutes. Serve immediately. Makes 6 servings.

Applesauce Puffs

In mixing bowl combine 2 cups packaged biscuit mix, 1/4 cup sugar, and 1 teaspoon ground cinnamon. Add 1/2 cup applesauce, 1/4 cup milk, 1 slightly beaten egg, and 2 tablespoons salad oil. Beat vigorously for 30 seconds. Fill greased 2-inch muffin pans 2/3 full. Bake at 400° for 12 minutes. Cool slightly; remove muffins from the pans.

Mix 1/4 cup sugar and 1/4 teaspoon ground cinnamon. Melt 2 tablespoons butter or margarine. Dip muffin tops in melted butter, then in sugar-cinnamon mixture. Serve the muffins while they are still warm. Makes 24.

Ginger-Sugar Puffs

1/4 cup butter, softened
1/2 cup sugar
1 egg
1 teaspoon grated lemon peel
2 cups sifted all-purpose flour
4 teaspoons baking powder
1/2 teaspoon salt
1/4 teaspoon ground nutmeg
1 cup milk
1/2 cup butter or margarine, melted
3/4 cup sugar
2 teaspoons ground ginger

Cream 1/4 cup butter and 1/2 cup sugar till light and fluffy; beat in egg and lemon peel. Sift together flour, baking powder, salt, and nutmeg; add to creamed mixture alternately with milk, beating after each addition. Fill small, greased 2-inch muffin pans 2/3 full. Bake at 375° about 15 minutes. While hot, dip muffins quickly into melted butter, then roll in mixture of 3/4 cup sugar and ginger. Makes 36.

PUFFED CEREAL—A ready-to-eat breakfast food made by applying heat and/or pressure to cereal grains until they expand in size and become light and puffy. In 1902 Dr. Alexander P. Anderson, a Columbia University professor, originated the puffing technique by putting rice under pressure in test tubes to explode the starch granules. Puffed wheat and rice were first marketed as breakfast foods in 1909. Now, puffed wheat, rice, corn, and oats are sold.

Butterscotch Cereal Bars

Blend one 3- or 3 1/4-ounce package *regular* butterscotch pudding mix and 1/2 cup light corn syrup. Heat and stir till boiling. Boil 1/2 minute. Remove from heat; blend in 1/2 cup chunk-style peanut butter. Stir in 4 cups puffed oat cereal till coated. Turn into greased 9x9x 2-inch baking pan. Cool. Makes 18 bars.

PUFF PASTRY—A rich pastry dough that is very flaky when baked. Both the large amount of butter in the dough and the handling technique, which involves rolling butter between layers of dough, contribute to the flakiness of this pastry. Patty shells, Napoleons, fruit-filled turnovers, and Danish pastries are puff pastries.

Flaky Puff Pastry forms the basis for Swiss Cream Torte. Whipped cream, a cream filling, and an icing complete the dessert.

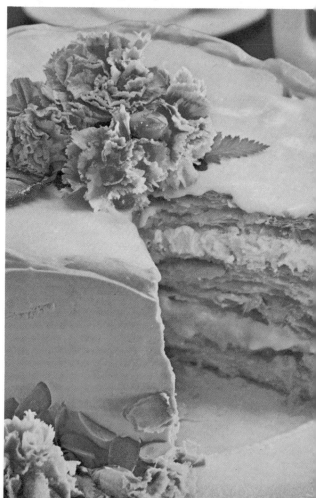

How to roll and fold puff pastry

Follow these pictures for easy Puff Pastry: Roll dough into a rectangle, place chilled butter on half, then fold over as shown.

Press with hand to seal the edge of the dough tightly on three sides. This encloses the layer of butter completely in dough.

Chill the sealed dough thoroughly, at least 1 hour, then roll out to rectangle again. Fold rolled dough evenly into thirds.

Turn the folded dough and again fold in thirds. Chill thoroughly. Repeat rolling, folding, and chilling 2 or 3 more times.

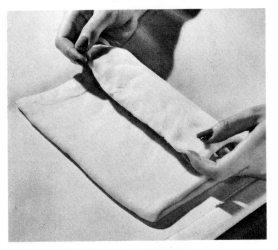

Puff Pastry

1 cup butter or margarine
1¾ cups sifted all-purpose flour
½ cup ice water

Chill butter or margarine. Reserve 2 tablespoons butter; chill. Work remaining chilled butter with back of wooden spoon just till pliable. Pat or roll between sheets of waxed paper to an 8x6-inch rectangle. Chill at least 1 hour in refrigerator or 20 minutes in freezer. (Chill utensils before each use.)

Cut reserved butter into flour till mixture resembles coarse meal. Add ice water, tossing with fork to make stiff dough. Shape into ball. Knead on *lightly* floured surface till smooth, 5 minutes. Cover; let rest 10 minutes.

On lightly floured surface, roll dough in 15x 9-inch rectangle. Peel waxed paper from one side of chilled butter or margarine; invert on half of dough. Remove remaining waxed paper. Fold dough over to cover butter. Seal edges of dough tightly. Wrap in waxed paper; chill thoroughly, at least 1 hour. Unwrap dough. On *lightly* floured surface, roll to 15x9-inch rectangle. (Roll from center just to edges.) Brush off excess flour; fold in thirds, then turn dough and fold in thirds again. Press edges to seal. Wrap; chill 1 hour. Repeat rolling, folding, and thorough chilling 2 or 3 times more.

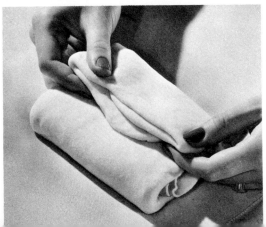

Swiss Cream Torte

> Puff Pastry (See page 1815)
> ⅔ cup sugar
> 2 tablespoons cornstarch
> ¼ teaspoon salt
> 2 cups milk
> 3 slightly beaten egg yolks
> 1 tablespoon butter or margarine
> 1½ teaspoons vanilla
>
> • • •
>
> 2 cups whipping cream
> ¼ cup sugar
> Red food coloring
> 1½ cups sifted confectioners' sugar
> 2 tablespoons water

Divide Puff Pastry dough into three parts. Roll each part to a 10-inch circle about ¼ inch thick. (Use inverted dinner plate as pattern; cut around edge with pastry wheel.) Stack circles on *ungreased* baking sheet or tray, separating and covering with waxed paper. Chill thoroughly, 2 to 3 hours or overnight. Remove top circle from refrigerator; place on *ungreased* baking sheet and prick generously. Bake at 350° till light golden brown, about 20 minutes. Repeat with remaining pastry. Cool.

To make cream filling, blend the ⅔ cup sugar, cornstarch, and salt in saucepan. Gradually stir in milk. Cook, stirring constantly, till mixture thickens and bubbles. Remove from heat. Gradually stir small amount of hot mixture into egg yolks; return to hot mixture. Cook 2 minutes more, stirring constantly. Remove the mixture from heat; add butter or margarine and *1 teaspoon* of the vanilla. Cool.

Whip cream and the ¼ cup sugar together till stiff. Add enough food coloring to *half* of whipped cream to tint pink. Set aside. For icing, blend together confectioners' sugar, water, and remaining vanilla till smooth.

To assemble torte: Place one layer of Puff Pastry on serving plate; spread evenly with cooled cream filling. Spread another layer of pastry with untinted whipped cream and gently place atop the first layer. Top with remaining layer, bottom side up. Spread icing evenly over top of torte. Frost sides with tinted whipped cream, building up a slight rim at top edge. Chill at least 2 hours before serving. If desired, garnish with a wide band of toasted, sliced almonds and sugared flowers. To serve, cut in wedges. Makes about 12 servings.

PUFFY—Light and airy. Foods such as soufflés and cream puffs become puffy as the air bubbles expand during baking.

PULLED CANDY—Noncrystalline candy, such as taffy, made from a cooled sugar syrup. At the right stage, the candy is pulled till light in color and porous. (See *Candy, Taffy* for additional information.)

Vanilla Taffy

> 3 cups sugar
> 1 cup light corn syrup
> ¾ cup boiling water
> ¼ cup vinegar
> ½ teaspoon cream of tartar
> 1 tablespoon vanilla

In large saucepan combine first 4 ingredients. Cook and stir till mixture reaches rolling boil. Stir in cream of tartar. Cook to hard-ball stage (265°). Remove from heat; stir in vanilla. Pour into buttered 15½x10½x1-inch pan. Cool till comfortable to handle. Butter hands; gather taffy into ball. Divide in half and *immediately* pull with fingertips till candy is light in color and hard to pull. Divide each piece in half. Quickly pull each piece into ½-inch thick strand and twist. With buttered scissors, quickly snip into pieces. Wrap with waxed paper.

PULLET—A young, usually under one-year-old hen. (See also *Chicken.*)

PULQUE (*pool′ ke̅*)—A Mexican alcoholic beverage made by fermenting agave juice.

PULSE—An old-fashioned name for legumes, such as beans. (See also *Legumes.*)

PUMPERNICKEL (*pum′ puhr nik′ uhl*)—A dark, heavy, European-style rye bread. Dark molasses, caraway seeds, and rye flour give pumpernickel its characteristic flavor. To give the bread structure, all-purpose white flour is added to the rye flour.

Several types of pumpernickel—medium-dark, dark, and very dark—are frequently available on the market. As a general rule, the darker the pumpernickel, the more sour the taste and chewy the texture.

Pumpernickel Bread

A favorite bread for sandwiches—

        3 packages active dry yeast
    1½ cups warm water
        ½ cup dark molasses
        1 to 2 tablespoons caraway seed
        1 tablespoon salt
        2 tablespoons shortening
    2¾ cups stirred rye flour
    2¼ to 2¾ cups sifted all–purpose
            flour

Soften active dry yeast in *warm* water (110°). Combine molasses, caraway seed, salt, shortening, rye flour, about *1 cup* of the all-purpose flour, and the softened yeast. Beat till smooth. Add enough remaining flour to make a stiff dough. Turn out on lightly floured surface and knead till smooth and elastic (8 to 10 minutes). Place dough in greased bowl, turning once to grease surface. Cover and let rise in warm place till double, about 1½ hours.

Punch down and divide dough into 2 parts. Cover and let rest 10 minutes. Round each part into a smooth ball. Place on opposite corners of a cornmeal-sprinkled baking sheet. Cover and let rise till double, about 30 minutes. Bake loaves at 375° till well browned, about 30 to 35 minutes. For a chewy crust, brush tops of the loaves with warm water several times during the baking, after the first 20 minutes. Makes 2 round loaves of bread.

Peanut Butter-Bacon Sandwich

An easy-to-make, delicious filling sandwiched between slices of pumpernickel bread—

        ½ cup peanut butter
        6 slices bacon, crisp-cooked,
            drained, and crumbled
        ⅓ cup finely chopped celery
    10 slices pumpernickel bread,
            toasted and buttered
            Lettuce

Combine peanut butter, crumbled bacon, and celery. Spread 5 slices toasted pumpernickel with peanut butter mixture, using about 3 tablespoons mixture for each; top with lettuce and remaining slices of buttered pumpernickel toast. Makes 5 sandwiches.

PUMPKIN—A large, oval to round, golden yellow to orange vegetable belonging to the gourd family and related to squash, muskmelons, and cucumbers. Pumpkins generally vary in weight from a few pounds to 30 pounds, but hundred-pound pumpkins are not at all uncommon. For many years, pumpkins were called *pompions*, an old French word derived from the Greek meaning "cooked by the sun."

Native to tropical America, pumpkins were first used by the Indians and became an integral part of the early American culture. It didn't take the Pilgrim homemakers long to learn from the Indians how to make pumpkin a good-tasting, popular food. Although it's doubtful that they served pumpkin pie at the first Thanksgiving, pumpkin in one form or another was certainly part of that well-known feast.

Pumpkins were utilized to such a great extent by these early settlers that an unknown writer in about 1630 remarked, "We have pumpkins at morning, and pumpkins at noon. If it were not for pumpkins, we should be undone." Pumpkins were often dried for year-round use.

In either form, pumpkins were used in a variety of ways. Stewed pumpkin was mixed with Indian meal for bread. A simple pumpkin pudding was made by slicing off the top of a small pumpkin, scooping out seeds and fibers, and filling the hollow with milk. With the top replaced, the pumpkin was baked in its shell until the milk was absorbed by the softened pulp. The hollowed-out pumpkin was often filled and baked with a spiced apple stuffing, too.

It is not known when the first pumpkin pie was served, although family recipes for it have been passed from mother to daughter for many generations. By the time Amelia Simmons published the first recipe for pumpkin pie in 1796, however, this dessert had become the traditional last course of a Thanksgiving dinner.

Pumpkins are not limited to America alone. In China, pumpkins were considered symbols of success and health. When introduced to Europe, pumpkins were called Turkey cucumbers because they had come by way of Turkey. The French later established a September Festival of King Pumpkin at the Paris produce market.

Two favorite pies merge into one for Two-Tone Holiday Pie.
Atop the mincemeat layer rests a velvety pumpkin custard.
A wreath of whipped cream piping decorates the pie.

Nutritional value: The greatest contribution of pumpkin to the diet is in the form of vitamin A. One-half cup of cooked pumpkin provides more than the day's recommended allowance for this vitamin as well as smaller amounts of other vitamins and minerals. Although this half-cup portion contains only about 40 calories, it is usually combined with sweet or dessert-type ingredients that increase the caloric content of the recipe.

How to select and store: The largest percentage of fresh pumpkins are marketed in October. But because of the lengthy preparation time required for fresh pumpkin, a large share of the pumpkin used today has been processed in cans.

When choosing fresh pumpkins, select small-sized, heavy ones since they have less waste and more tender flesh than do the larger pumpkins. Save the large ones for Halloween jack-o-lanterns. Also look for pumpkins that are vivid in color, firm, and have a minimum of blemishes.

Stored in a cool, dry area, pumpkins can be kept for several months. Be sure that they are never allowed to freeze.

How to prepare and use: Whether you serve fresh pumpkin as a vegetable or use it with other foods, it must always be cooked. Wash the pumpkin, cut it in half, and scrape out the seeds and fibrous material. Cut in cubes and peel. Then, cook it in boiling, salted water till tender.

As a vegetable, butter the cooked cubes and season with spices or herbs. Or mash the pumpkin and season it like squash.

Regardless of its intended use—traditional pumpkin pie, a pumpkin pie variation, pudding, custard, bread, cookie, or cake—you'll find the flavor of pumpkin pleasing. (See also *Vegetable*.)

Pumpkin Pie

A classic recipe—

1½ cups canned pumpkin
¾ cup sugar
½ teaspoon salt
1 to 1¼ teaspoons ground cinnamon
½ to 1 teaspoon ground ginger
¼ to ½ teaspoon ground nutmeg
¼ to ½ teaspoon ground cloves
. . .
3 slightly beaten eggs
1¼ cups milk
1 6-ounce can evaporated milk (⅔ cup)
1 *unbaked* 9-inch pastry shell (See *Pastry*)

Combine pumpkin, sugar, salt, cinnamon, ginger, nutmeg, and cloves. Blend in eggs, milk, and evaporated milk. Pour into pastry shell (have edges crimped high because amount of filling is generous). Bake at 400° till knife inserted halfway between center and edge comes out clean, about 50 minutes. Cool thoroughly.

Two-Tone Holiday Pie

A mincemeat-pumpkin combo—

1½ cups canned mincemeat
1 *unbaked* 9-inch pastry shell (See *Pastry*)
1 18-ounce can pumpkin pie filling
¼ cup orange juice
1 cup evaporated milk
½ teaspoon grated orange peel
. . .
Whipped cream *or* dessert topping

Spread mincemeat evenly in bottom of unbaked pastry shell. Prepare pumpkin pie filling following label directions, *substituting the orange juice and evaporated milk for the liquid called for;* stir in orange peel. Pour pumpkin mixture over mincemeat in pastry shell.

Bake the pie in a 400° oven till a knife inserted halfway between center and edge of the filling comes out clean, about 45 minutes. Cool the pie thoroughly. Serve the pie garnished with a ring of rosettes made with whipped cream or whipped dessert topping.

Pumpkin Cookies

Equally good plain or frosted—

1 cup shortening
1 cup sugar
1 egg
1 cup canned pumpkin
1 teaspoon vanilla
. . .
2 cups sifted all-purpose flour
1 teaspoon baking powder
½ teaspoon baking soda
½ teaspoon salt
1 teaspoon ground cinnamon
½ teaspoon ground nutmeg
¼ teaspoon ground allspice
. . .
1 cup raisins
½ cup chopped nuts
Butter Frosting (optional)

Thoroughly cream shortening and sugar together. Add egg, pumpkin, and vanilla; beat well. Sift together flour, baking powder, baking soda, salt, cinnamon, nutmeg, and allspice. Add to creamed mixture; blend well. Stir in raisins and nuts. Drop by rounded teaspoons, 2 inches apart, on greased cookie sheet. Bake at 350° for 12 to 15 minutes. Remove from sheet. Frost immediately with Butter Frosting, if desired. Makes about 3½ dozen cookies.

Butter Frosting: Cream 3 tablespoons butter or margarine; gradually add 1¼ cups sifted confectioners' sugar, blending well. Beat in 1 tablespoon light cream and ½ teaspoon vanilla. Gradually blend in another 1¼ cups sifted confectioners' sugar. Add enough light cream (about 1 tablespoon) to sugar mixture to make frosting of spreading consistency.

Gingersnap cookies and pumpkin-flavored ice cream alternate in layers for Pumpkin Squares. Here's a make-ahead dessert that's perfect for large-group entertaining occasions.

Pumpkin-Date Torte

Mix ½ cup chopped pitted dates, ½ cup chopped walnuts, and 2 tablespoons all-purpose flour; set aside. In a saucepan melt ¼ cup butter or margarine over low heat; blend in 1 cup brown sugar. Remove from heat; stir in ⅔ cup cooked pumpkin and 1 teaspoon vanilla. Beat 2 eggs, one at a time, into pumpkin mixture. Sift together ½ cup sifted all-purpose flour, ½ teaspoon baking powder, ½ teaspoon ground cinnamon, ½ teaspoon ground nutmeg, ¼ teaspoon baking soda, and ¼ teaspoon ground ginger. Add dry ingredients to the pumpkin mixture, blending the mixture thoroughly. Stir in floured dates and nuts. Turn the mixture into a greased 9x1½-inch round pan. Bake the mixture at 350° for 20 to 25 minutes. Serve the torte warm. Cut in wedges and top with whipped cream. Makes 8 servings.

Pumpkin Squares

  1 16-ounce can pumpkin
  1 cup sugar
  1 teaspoon ground ginger
  1 teaspoon ground cinnamon
  ½ teaspoon ground nutmeg
  1 cup chopped pecans, toasted
  ½ gallon vanilla ice cream,
      softened
36 gingersnaps

Combine first 5 ingredients and 1 teaspoon salt; add nuts. In chilled bowl fold into ice cream. Line bottom of 13x9x2-inch pan with 18 gingersnaps; top with *half* the ice cream. Cover with remaining cookies; add remaining ice cream.

Freeze till firm. Cut in squares. Garnish with whipped cream and chopped pecans. Serves 18.

Pumpkin-Raisin Loaves

> ¾ cup canned pumpkin
> ⅓ cup water
> 1 egg
> 1 teaspoon pumpkin pie spice
> 1 14-ounce package apple-cinnamon
>   muffin mix
> ½ cup raisins
>
> • • •
>
> Milk
> 2 cups sifted confectioners' sugar

In mixing bowl combine canned pumpkin, water, egg, and pumpkin pie spice. Add apple-cinnamon muffin mix and raisins; stir just till moistened. Turn batter into 3 greased 5½x3x2-inch loaf pans (or one 9x5x3-inch loaf pan). Bake at 350° for 35 to 40 minutes for small loaves or 50 minutes for large loaf. Turn bread from loaf pans; cool on rack.

To make icing, add enough milk to the sifted confectioners' sugar to make of pouring consistency. Drizzle icing over cooled loaves.

Golden Pumpkin Muffins

In mixing bowl thoroughly combine 2 cups packaged biscuit mix, ½ cup sugar, and 1½ teaspoons pumpkin pie spice. In small bowl combine ¾ cup milk, ½ cup canned pumpkin, 1 slightly beaten egg, and 2 tablespoons salad oil; stir into dry ingredients till blended. Fill greased muffin cups ⅔ full. Bake at 400° about 20 minutes. Makes 1 dozen muffins.

PUNCH—An alcoholic or nonalcoholic beverage that frequently contains fruit juice. Punch differs from most other beverages in that it has a combination of flavors rather than one predominating flavor. Punch is usually made in quantities sufficient to accommodate a large crowd.

The name punch comes from the Hindu word for "five," which originally referred to the number of ingredients in this popular beverage. A typical early punch that bore out this rule of five contained spirits, lemon juice, sugar, water, and spices. This is no longer the case, however, today, there are numerous punches that contain many more than five ingredients.

For ice ring, fill the mold half full of water. Freeze firm as quickly as possible. Arrange fruit and leaves. Anchor by pouring a small amount of water around them; freeze.

At serving time, carefully unmold the pretty ice ring by loosening bottom with hot, wet cloth or by dipping it in cold water. Float ice ring, fruit side up, atop punch.

Punch is usually served by ladling it from a large bowl into small cups. In fact, punch bowl sets, which include matching cups and a ladle, are customarily used.

If the punch is to be served cold, use cold ingredients and add a block or ring of ice to the punch bowl. Besides keeping the punch cold, the ice serves as a garnish if you place the water in a mold or ice tray and freeze flowers, fruit pieces, mint sprigs, or other decorative foods in the ice. (See also *Beverage*.)

Popfreeze Punch

    1 envelope unsweetened raspberry-
        flavored soft drink powder
 ½ cup sugar
    4 cups pineapple juice
                • • •
    4 7-ounce bottles lemon-lime
        carbonated beverage (about
        1 quart)

Combine raspberry-flavored soft drink powder, sugar, and pineapple juice. Freeze in two ice cube trays. Remove cubes and store in plastic bag in freezer.* To serve place ice cubes in glasses; fill with lemon-lime beverage; stir to blend flavors. Makes about 8 servings.

*For an outdoor meal, pack ice cubes (in plastic bag) in insulated picnic cooler—they will stay frozen for about 3 hours.

Spiced Percolator Punch

    9 cups pineapple juice
    9 cups cranberry juice cocktail
 4½ cups water
    1 cup brown sugar
                • • •
 4½ teaspoons whole cloves
    4 cinnamon sticks, broken in
        pieces
 ¼ teaspoon salt

Combine pineapple juice, cranberry juice cocktail, water, and brown sugar in 30-cup automatic coffee maker. Place cloves, cinnamon stick pieces, and salt in coffee-maker basket. Assemble coffee maker; plug in and perk. Serve piping hot. Makes about 23 cups.

Warm Cranberry Punch

 2½ quarts cranberry juice cocktail
    5 cups water
 ½ cup sugar
 ½ cup light raisins
    1 tablespoon shredded orange peel
    2 medium oranges, studded with
        whole cloves

In saucepan combine cranberry juice cocktail, water, sugar, raisins, and orange peel. Add clove-studded oranges. Cover and simmer 10 minutes. Serve warm. Makes about 25 servings.

Tropical Punch

    1 large watermelon
    1 46-ounce can red Hawaiian
        fruit punch (about 6 cups)
    1 6-ounce can frozen pink
        lemonade concentrate
    1 6-ounce can frozen orange juice
        concentrate
    1 6-ounce can frozen pineapple
        juice concentrate
    6 cups cold water
                • • •
    1 28-ounce bottle ginger ale,
        chilled (3½ cups)
    Orange and lime slices

Stand watermelon on end; cut thin slice off bottom to make it level. Cut top third off melon. Using cup as guide, trace scallops around top outside edge of melon. Carve scalloped edge, following pattern. Scoop out fruit; serve later. Chill melon shell.

Combine Hawaiian fruit punch, fruit juice concentrates, and water. Pour over ice in melon bowl. Resting bottle on rim of melon, carefully pour ginger ale down side; mix with an up-and-down motion. Float orange and lime slices. Twine melon with ivy leaves, holding with wooden picks. Makes 30 to 35 servings.

Punch for a crowd

A scalloped watermelon shell serves as a→ punch bowl for Tropical Punch made with ginger ale, Hawaiian punch, and fruit juices.

Lemon Punch

    2 cups sugar
    4 teaspoons grated lemon peel
    1 cup lemon juice
    1 to 2 pints lemon sherbet
    1 to 2 pints orange sherbet
    2 28-ounce bottles ginger ale,
        chilled

In saucepan combine sugar and 2 cups water. Heat and stir till sugar dissolves; cool. Add 2 cups water, lemon peel, and juice; chill. Pour into chilled punch bowl; add scoops of sherbet, stirring till partially melted. Pour chilled ginger ale down side of bowl, stirring with an up-and-down motion. Serve *immediately* in punch cups. Makes 4 quarts.

Lime Frosted Punch

    3½ to 4 cups pineapple-grapefruit
        drink, chilled
    ⅔ cup lemon juice
    2 quarts cold water
    3 ½-ounce envelopes unsweetened
        lemon-lime soft drink powder
    2 cups sugar
    2 pints lime sherbet
    4 7-ounce bottles lemon-lime
        carbonated beverage, chilled

In punch bowl combine fruit juices, water, soft drink powder, and sugar. Stir till soft drink powder and sugar are completely dissolved. Top with large spoonfuls of sherbet. Resting bottle on rim of bowl, carefully pour in carbonated beverage. Serve some sherbet with each cup. Makes 30 to 35 servings.

Mock Champagne Punch

In punch bowl combine one 6-ounce can frozen lemonade concentrate, one 6-ounce can frozen pineapple juice concentrate, and 2 cups cold water. Float ice ring or cubes containing fresh mint leaves and maraschino cherries on top. Carefully pour two 7-ounce bottles ginger ale, chilled; two 7-ounce bottles sparkling water, chilled; and 1 large bottle *sparkling* Catawba grape juice (white), chilled, down side of punch bowl. Makes 11 cups.

Sparkle Punch

    1 ½-ounce envelope unsweetened
        lemon-lime *or* cherry-flavored
        soft drink powder
    1 cup sugar
    2 cups cold milk
    1 quart vanilla ice cream
    1 28-ounce bottle carbonated
        water (3½ cups)

Combine soft drink powder and sugar. Dissolve in milk. Pour into 6 to 8 soda glasses. Add scoops of ice cream. Resting bottle on rim of glass, carefully pour in carbonated water to fill. Stir to muddle slightly. Serves 6 to 8.

Frosty Party Punch

    2 3-ounce packages raspberry-
        flavored gelatin
    1 3-ounce package cherry-flavored
        gelatin
    3 cups boiling water
    2 12-ounce cans pineapple juice,
        chilled
    1 12-ounce can frozen orange juice
        concentrate
    1 1-quart tray ice cubes
    2 pints pineapple *or* lemon sherbet

Dissolve raspberry- and cherry-flavored gelatins in boiling water. Add 5 cups cold water, pineapple juice, and orange juice concentrate.* Stir in ice cubes just till melted. Spoon in sherbet. Serve immediately. Serves 32.

   *If desired, prepare this mixture several hours ahead; keep at room temperature. Just before serving, add ice and sherbet.

Cranberry Punch

    1 16-ounce can jellied cranberry
        sauce
    ¾ cup orange juice
    ¼ cup lemon juice
    1 28-ounce bottle ginger ale
        (3½ cups), chilled

Beat jellied cranberry sauce till smooth. Stir in orange and lemon juice. Add ginger ale. Serve over ice. Makes 12 to 15 servings.

Quantity Fruit Punch

Makes enough for 75 people—

 3 quarts pineapple juice
1½ cups lemon juice
 3 cups orange juice
⅓ cup lime juice
2½ cups sugar
 1 cup lightly packed fresh mint
  leaves
   • • •
 4 28-ounce bottles ginger ale
 2 28-ounce bottles carbonated
  water
 1 pint fresh strawberries,
  quartered

Combine juices, sugar, and mint; chill. Just before serving, add ginger ale, carbonated water, and strawberries; pour over cake of ice in punch bowl. Makes 75 servings.

Hot Lemon Punch

 1 cup sugar
 5 cups water
 1 cup lemon juice
 1 cup gin
  Lemon slices

In saucepan combine sugar, water, and lemon juice. Cook, stirring constantly, till sugar is dissolved and mixture just begins to boil. Add gin; heat through. Pour into punch bowl. Float lemon slices on top. Makes 7½ cups.

Burgundy Punch

 2 fifths Burgundy
 2 cups port wine
 2 cups orange juice
¼ cup lemon juice
 1 cup sugar
 1 quart water
 2 quarts ice cubes

Combine Burgundy, port, orange juice, and lemon juice. Stir in sugar and water and mix well. Chill till serving time. Just before serving, pour over 2 quarts ice cubes (3 to 4 trays) in punch bowl. Makes about 4 quarts.

PUNGENT—A flavor or aroma that is so strong it causes a warm, prickly sensation in the mouth or nose. For example, limburger cheese and highly spiced Mexican foods have pungent flavors and aromas.

PUREE (*pyōō rā,'-rē', pyōōr'ā*)—**1.** To reduce a food to a smooth pulp. A cooked or a soft, raw food can be puréed by removing all seeds, then pushing the food through a sieve or whirling it in a blender. **2.** A smooth soup made from vegetable pulp.

PURI (*pû' rē*)—Small, individual breads of India that are deep-fat fried. Puris make an interesting and delicious curry accompaniment. (See also *Indian Cookery.*)

PURIS

 2 tablespoons shortening
 2 cups sifted all-purpose flour
½ teaspoon salt
 2 ounces sharp process American
  cheese, shredded (½ cup)
½ to ⅔ cup water

In mixing bowl cut shortening into flour and salt. Add cheese. Stir in water to make a soft dough. Knead and pound dough for about 10 to 15 minutes. Cover and let stand ½ hour. Roll *very thin* on lightly floured surface. Cut in 4-inch circles. Fry in deep, hot fat (400°) till puffed and golden, turning once. Drain on towels. Keep them warm in very slow oven, or warm just before serving time. Makes 12.

PURPLE BASIL—A variety of the herb basil that is characterized by dark reddish purple leaves. Like other basil, purple basil has a pleasant, spicy flavor and aroma. This herb is especially delightful in green salads since it adds color as well as flavor. (See also *Basil.*)

PURSLANE (*pûrs' lān,-lin*)—A plant characterized by thick, fleshy leaves and a reddish green stem. Although purslane can be cultivated, it more often grows wild.

  The young leaves, which can be cooked like spinach, have a slightly tart flavor. The crisp stem is sometimes pickled.

Q

QUAHOG *(kwô' hog, -hôg, kwuh hog', -hôg')*—Another name for the edible hard-shell clam. Quahog is an Indian word that is used primarily in the New England area. (See also *Clam.*)

QUAIL—A game bird that is highly esteemed for its culinary uses. The American quail belongs to the partridge family.

The elusive American quail, most commonly known as the bobwhite, is a non-migratory bird and is considered by many sportsmen to be the most cunning of all game birds. As an example of this natural cleverness, when quail group, they huddle in a circle, facing out, which serves two purposes: warmth and protection. And when "flushed" the birds scatter into many different directions to the dismay of the predator.

This type of quail nests on the ground, and it seems to perfer running rather than flying. The latter characteristic would ordinarily rule it out as a game bird, but the bobwhite's ability to conceal itself by means of a reddish brown coloring and its habit of "freezing" (remaining motionless when in danger of discovery) make it a challenging bird to hunt.

There are also varieties of quail common to Europe, Asia, and Africa. Many of these birds are migratory and were known to people of ancient lands. The Egyptians are said to have exported quail to other countries. Some Biblical scholars believe that the manna that was miraculously sent to the wandering Israelites consisted partially of migrating quail.

A quail should be properly handled after it is killed and should be cleaned immediately. When cooked, quail has a delicate flavor. This is due in part to the diet of the bird—berries, insects, and seeds. The meat is often dry and needs to be basted with butter or kept moist with fat during cooking. Broil or roast young birds.

Whole quail can be purchased frozen and canned. Smoked meat and quail eggs are considered gourmet items. (See also *Game.*)

Broiled Quail

> 4 4- to 6-ounce ready-to-cook quail,
> split in halves lengthwise
> ½ cup butter or margarine, melted
> Salt and pepper

Brush quail with melted butter or margarine; season with salt and pepper. Place, skin side up, on broiler pan (no rack). Broil about 5 minutes in a preheated broiler 4 to 5 inches from heat. Turn; broil 6 to 9 minutes. Brush frequently with melted butter or margarine during broiling. Remove to warm serving platter. Garnish with parsley and serve with currant jelly, if desired. Makes 4 servings.

How to roast quail

Salt inside of ready-to-cook 4- to 6-ounce quail. Stuff as desired; truss bird. Place, breast side up, on rack in shallow roasting pan. Place bacon slices over breast. Roast, uncovered, at 400° till tender, allowing 30 to 45 minutes. (Timing may vary, depending on age of the bird; young birds are the most suitable for roasting.) Baste occasionally with drippings. When necessary, place foil loosely over top of bird to prevent excess browning. Allow ½ to 1 pound quail for each serving.

QUANTITY COOKERY—A type of food preparation that is geared towards feeding a large number of people. Cooking for restaurants and other establishments as well as the cooking that homemakers do for church groups, large family gatherings, clubs, and organizations are included in this type of food preparation. However, restaurant cooking is a specialized business using quantity equipment and supplies not often available for home use.

Homemakers who cook for large groups know that it takes special planning to have everything ready at the designated serving time. Even if you're not the type of person who normally makes lists, your job will be easier if you write down deadlines and tasks to be completed.

The first step in planning for large-group entertaining is determining the guest list. This should help you decide whether to serve a buffet or a sit-down meal. You might also keep in mind friends you can call on for help. When you have some helpers, you can generally plan a more elaborate menu for your guests.

Next, plan what you'll want to serve, keeping in mind proper menu planning techniques. Be sure that the foods selected are varied in texture, temperature, flavor, color, size, and shape. Also consider the likes and dislikes of the group.

Another important consideration in planning for large groups is determining the amount of equipment that will be needed. If you don't have enough plates, flatware, or glasses on hand, paper or plastic items can be used for informal occasions. For more formal occasions, rent matching dishes. And don't overlook limitations in oven and refrigerator space as well as in the mixing and baking pans.

Keep the menu as uncomplicated as possible, but plan to have plenty of food on hand for seconds. Casseroles or one-dish meals are good choices for quantity serving. Both food preparation and serving are simplified with one main dish. To complete the meal, simply add a salad, bread, beverage, and dessert. Another advantage of casserole main dishes is that they can be prepared ahead of time and kept in the refrigerator. However, be sure to allow extra cooking time for the chilled casserole to heat through.

Although some recipes can be doubled or tripled successfully, others such as baked goods, which have balanced formulas, just don't adapt well to quantity cookery. Mixing and baking times as well as the seasoning balance can be affected by multiplying recipes. Therefore, unless the recipe is geared to quantity cookery, it is best to make several batches.

Many of the casserole recipes that follow are made in two 13x9x2-inch pans. However, you can substitute one 18x12x2½-inch baking pan if one is available. Be sure to allow two inches of space around the pan for even heat circulation.

When the final plans are completed and you know what you want to serve, make out a detailed market order including all cleanup supplies that will be needed. You may be able to purchase some food items in institution-sized containers from a wholesaler or restaurant supplier. If you're going to need any special items, be sure you know where they are available, and give advance notice so that you will be able to obtain the quantities you need.

When it comes time to prepare the food, do as much as possible ahead of time to eliminate last-minute work, especially if you are the only chef. You'll find that the freezer can be put to good use for make-ahead desserts, salads, and breads. Also have dishes used for food preparation washed so that there will be plenty of counter space for serving.

If you are fortunate enough to have some helpers, assign to each of them a specific task—making a batch of a specified recipe, helping with the table setting and decorations, or cleaning up the dining area after the meal has been served. Advance notice should be given to each helper so that she is informed of her task. well ahead of time. (See *Buffet, Meal Planning* for additional information.)

Hamburger-Noodle Bake

　4　pounds ground beef
　3　cups chopped onion

. . .

　16　ounces medium noodles, cooked and drained
　16　ounces sharp process American cheese, shredded (4 cups)
　3　10¾-ounce cans condensed tomato soup
　3　cups water
　¾　cup chopped green pepper
　½　cup chili sauce
　¼　cup chopped canned pimiento
　1½　teaspoons salt
　　　Dash pepper

. . .

　3　cups soft bread crumbs
　6　tablespoons butter or margarine, melted
　　　Green pepper rings

Divide beef and onion between 2 large skillets. Brown meat. Drain off fat. Combine meat and onion with cooked noodles, cheese, soup, water, green pepper, chili sauce, pimiento, salt, and pepper. Mix the ingredients well.

Turn ingredients into *two* 13x9x2-inch baking dishes. Combine soft bread crumbs and melted butter or margarine. Sprinkle atop casseroles. Bake, uncovered, at 350° till hot, about 40 to 45 minutes. Trim the casseroles with green pepper rings. Makes 25 to 30 servings.

For serving a crowd

← When it's your turn to bring a casserole for the church supper or family gathering, prepare the popular Hamburger-Noodle Bake.

Spanish Rice

　1　pound sliced bacon
　2　cups chopped onion
　2　cups chopped green pepper
　2　28-ounce cans tomatoes
　5　cups water
　1　pound uncooked packaged precooked rice (5 cups)
　1　cup chili sauce
　1　tablespoon salt
　¼　teaspoon pepper
　1　tablespoon brown sugar
　2　teaspoons Worcestershire sauce
　8　ounces sharp process American cheese, shredded (2 cups)

Cook bacon till crisp; drain. Pour off all but ½ cup bacon fat. In remaining fat, cook onion and green pepper till tender. Add remaining ingredients except cheese. Pour mixture into *two* 13x9x2-inch baking dishes. Cover; bake at 350° till rice is done, about 25 to 30 minutes. Crumble bacon; sprinkle each dish with *half* the bacon, then cheese. Return to oven to melt cheese. Makes 25 servings.

Macaroni and Cheese

　1¼　pounds elbow macaroni (6 cups)
　¾　cup butter or margarine
　½　cup sifted all-purpose flour
　2　teaspoons salt
　¼　teaspoon pepper
　10　cups milk
　1　cup chopped onion (optional)
　1½　pounds sharp process American cheese, cubed (6 cups)
　4　tomatoes, sliced

In two large kettles cook macaroni in large amount of boiling, salted water till tender; drain. In large kettle melt butter; blend in flour, salt, and pepper. Add milk; cook and stir the mixture till it is thickened and bubbly. Add onion and cheese; stir till cheese is melted. Spread macaroni in *two* 13x9x2-inch metal baking pans. Add *half* the sauce to each pan; mix with macaroni. Sprinkle tomato slices with salt; arrange them on top, pushing edge of each slice into macaroni. Bake at 350° till bubbly and hot in center, about 45 minutes. Makes 24 (about ¾ cup) servings.

Italian Meat Sauce

In two large kettles or Dutch ovens combine 4 pounds ground beef; 4 large onions, chopped; and 8 cloves garlic, minced. Brown the ingredients lightly. Drain off the excess fat. Divide the following ingredients evenly between the two kettles: six 30-ounce cans tomatoes, undrained and broken up; four 6-ounce cans tomato paste; 8 cups water; 1 cup snipped parsley; 1/4 cup brown sugar; 2 tablespoons ground oregano; 1 tablespoon salt; 1 teaspoon dried thyme leaves, crushed; and 4 bay leaves.

Simmer, uncovered, till sauce is thickened, about 3 hours; stir occasionally. Remove bay leaves. Cook 3 to 4 pounds spaghetti. Serve sauce over spaghetti. Pass shredded Parmesan cheese. Makes 25 (3/4 cup) servings.

Chili Con Carne

    4 pounds ground beef
    1 tablespoon salt
    4 large onions, chopped (4 cups)
    4 medium green peppers, chopped
    4 16-ounce cans kidney beans,
         drained
    2 29-ounce cans tomatoes
    2 15-ounce cans tomato sauce
 1 1/2 to 2 tablespoons chili powder
  1/2 teaspoon paprika
    3 bay leaves, finely crushed

Season ground beef with salt. Brown the meat in a 10-quart Dutch oven or kettle. Add onion and green pepper; cook till tender but not brown. Add the remaining ingredients. Cover and simmer for 2 hours, stirring occasionally. Add water if needed for desired consistency. Makes 25 (about 1 cup) servings.

Cabbage Slaw

Combine 2 1/4 pounds cabbage, shredded (15 cups); 3/4 pound carrots, shredded (3 cups); and 3/4 cup diced green pepper; chill. Blend together 3 cups mayonnaise or salad dressing, 1/3 cup sugar, 1/3 cup vinegar, 1 tablespoon prepared mustard, 3 teaspoons celery seed, and 2 teaspoons salt. Just before serving the slaw, toss the vegetables and the mayonnaise mixture lightly. Makes 25 (1/2 cup) servings.

Roaster Baked Beans

    8 31-ounce cans pork and beans
         in tomato sauce
    2 14-ounce bottles catsup
    1 large onion, chopped (1 cup)
  1/2 pound brown sugar (1 1/4 cups)
    2 tablespoons dry mustard
    1 pound bacon, cut in pieces

Empty cans of pork and beans into inset pan of electric roaster, preheated to 300°. Stir next 4 ingredients into beans. Sprinkle bacon pieces over. Cook, covered, at 300° for 2 hours. Uncover and continue cooking 2 hours, stirring occasionally. Makes 25 servings.

Punch for the Crowd

    3 quarts pineapple juice
 1 1/2 cups lemon juice
    3 cups orange juice
  1/3 cup lime juice
 2 1/2 cups sugar
    1 cup mint leaves
    4 28-ounce bottles ginger ale,
         chilled
    2 28-ounce bottles carbonated
         water, chilled
    1 pint fresh strawberries, sliced

Combine juices, sugar, and mint leaves; chill. Strain. Pour over large cake of ice in punch bowl. Carefully pour in ginger ale and carbonated water; add berries. Serves 75.

Tossed Green Salad

    3 heads iceberg lettuce
    1 bunch romaine
    2 bunches radishes, sliced
    2 large cucumbers, thinly sliced
    2 large green peppers, chopped
    1 large onion, chopped (optional)
    1 pint French dressing
  2/3 cup sweet pickle relish
  1/3 cup vinegar

Tear lettuce and romaine in pieces. Combine with next 4 ingredients. Chill. Combine remaining ingredients. Pour over salad before serving. Toss. Makes 25 (about 1 cup) servings.

Guide To Shopping For A Crowd

Use this table as a guide when planning and shopping for food for a large group. The size of one serving (Serving Unit) is listed for each item. For hearty eaters, plan about 1½ servings for each person.

Food	Servings	Serving Unit	Amount Needed
Beverages			
Coffee	25	1 cup	½ to ¾ pound
Tea, hot	25	1 cup	1 ounce
Tea, iced	25	1 glass	3 ounces
Cream, coffee	25	1 tablespoon	1 pint
Milk	24	1 8-ounce glass	1½ gallons
Breads and Cereals			
Biscuits	25	2 ounces	4½ dozen
Bread	25	1-ounce slice	1¼ pounds
Rice, long-grain	24	½ cup, cooked	1½ pounds, uncooked
Rolls	24	1	2 dozen
Spaghetti	25	¾ cup, cooked	2¼ pounds, uncooked
Desserts			
Cake	24	1/12 cake	2 9-inch layer cakes
	24	2½-inch square	1 15½x10½x1-inch sheet
Ice Cream	24	½ cup or 1 slice	3 quarts
Pie	30	1/6 pie	5 9-inch pies
Fruit			
Canned	24	½ cup	1 6½- to 7¼-pound can
Relishes			
Carrot strips	25	2 to 3 strips	1 to 1¼ pounds
Cauliflowerets	25	2 ounces sliced, raw	7 pounds
Celery	25	1 2- to 3-inch piece	1 medium stalk
Olives	25	3 to 4	1 quart
Pickles	25	1 ounce	1 quart
Radishes	25	2	5 bunches
Salads			
Side Dish:			
Cottage cheese	25	⅓ cup	5 pounds
Fruit	24	⅓ cup	2 quarts
Gelatin	25	½ cup liquid	3 quarts
Potato	24	½ cup	3 quarts
Tossed vegetable	25	¾ cup	5 quarts
Main Dish	25	1 cup	6¼ quarts
Soup	25	1 cup (main course)	2 50-ounce cans condensed
Vegetables			
Canned	25	½ cup	1 6½- to 7¼-pound can
Fresh:			
Potatoes	25	½ cup, mashed	6¾ pounds
	25	1 medium, baked	8½ pounds
Frozen:			
Beans	25	⅓ cup	5¼ pounds
Carrots, peas, or corn	25	⅓ cup	5 pounds
Potatoes, French-fried	25	10 pieces	3¼ pounds
Miscellaneous			
Butter	32	1 pat	½ pound
Jam or preserves	25	2 tablespoons	1½ pounds
Potato Chips	25	¾ to 1 ounce	1 to 1½ pounds

QUATRE-ÉPICES *(kä′ truh e′ pis)*—The name given to a French spice and herb mixture. Literally, it means four spices; however, more spices are usually used.

QUENELLE *(kuh nel′)*—Various-sized meat, poultry, or seafood dumplings popular in French cookery. The forcemeat, which is a very finely ground mixture, is formed into balls or ovals, poached, and then used as a garnish or served with a sauce.

QUICHE *(kēsh)*—An open-faced tart of French origin that is filled with an unsweetened custard filling and flavored with bacon, cheese, meat, or seafood. The well-known Quiche Lorraine contains bacon and sometimes cheese, onion, or seafood. This particular tart originated in the Lorraine province of France.

Quiches are baked in a pie plate or a special quiche pan with fluted, straight sides. The large, custard tarts are impressively served as a main dish, while miniature versions are found on the appetizer tray. (See also *French Cookery*.)

Quiche Lorraine

  1 9-inch *unbaked* pastry shell
     (See *Pastry*)
  8 slices bacon, diced
  8 ounces natural Swiss cheese,
     shredded (2 cups)

       • • •

  1 tablespoon all-purpose flour
½ teaspoon salt
    Dash ground nutmeg
  3 beaten eggs
1½ cup milk

Bake unpricked pastry shell at 450° only 5 minutes. Remove shell from oven. Reduce oven temperature to 325°.

Cook bacon till crisp; drain and crumble. Reserving 2 tablespoons crumbled bacon, place remaining bacon in partially baked pastry shell. Add shredded cheese. Combine flour, salt, nutmeg, eggs, and milk; pour over bacon and cheese in pastry shell. Trim with reserved bacon. Bake at 325° till knife inserted just off-center comes out clean, about 35 to 40 minutes. Let cool 10 minutes before serving. Serves 6.

Shrimp Quiche

Toss together 4 ounces process Swiss cheese, shredded (1 cup); 4 ounces Gruyère cheese, shredded; and 1 tablespoon all-purpose flour. Beat together 3 eggs, 1 cup light cream, ½ teaspoon prepared mustard, ¼ teaspoon salt, ¼ teaspoon Worcestershire sauce, dash bottled hot pepper sauce, and dash pepper. Prepare pastry for 1-crust 9-inch pie (See *Pastry*). Line 6 individual bakers with pastry. Divide about ¾ of the cheese mixture between the pastry-lined bakers. Add one 10-ounce package frozen, peeled, and cleaned shrimp, thawed and diced (about 1 cup). Add remaining cheese mixture. Pour into egg mixture.

Bake at 400° till knife inserted just off-center comes out clean, about 30 minutes. If desired, garnish with whole cooked shrimp and parsley. Makes 6 servings.

QUICK BREAD—Any one of several breads and breadlike foods that are made with quick-acting leavening, such as baking powder, baking soda, and steam. Biscuits, muffins, nut and fruit loaves, coffee cakes, pancakes, crêpes, fritters, and waffles fall into this group of quick-to-prepare breads. (See also *Breads*.)

Raisin-Nut Bread

In saucepan combine 1 cup raisins and 1 cup water; bring to boiling. Remove from heat; cool the mixture to room temperature.

Mix together 1 beaten egg, ¾ cup sugar, and ½ teaspoon vanilla; stir in raisin mixture. Sift together 1½ cups sifted all-purpose flour, 1 teaspoon baking powder, ¼ teaspoon baking soda, and ¼ teaspoon salt. Add to egg-raisin mixture, beating well. Stir in ¼ cup chopped walnuts. Pour into 2 greased and floured 16-ounce fruit cans. Bake at 350° till the bread tests done, about 50 to 60 minutes.

Variation of a classic

Serve Shrimp Quiche with refreshing iced →
tea and a green salad tossed with hearts of palm at an elegant luncheon for six.

QUICK COOKERY

Creative ways to quicker meals and menu plans for the busy, modern homemaker.

Homemakers have been searching for ways to speed up meal preparation ever since the first cavewoman decided that she was spending too much time slaving over a hot fire. Through the years many timesaving methods and products have been developed. However, the modern homemaker must evaluate expense in terms of money and time when using them. In the following recipes the cost of the food is more, but the meal is prepared in a jiffy.

Chicken and Biscuit Pie

  1 15¼-ounce can chicken in gravy
  1 10½-ounce can condensed cream
    of chicken soup
  1 tablespoon instant minced onion
  ½ teaspoon dried rosemary leaves,
    crushed
  1 8-ounce can peas, drained
  1 3-ounce can sliced
    mushrooms, drained
  1 5-ounce can boned chicken,
    diced
  1 tube refrigerated biscuits
    (10 biscuits)

Mix first 4 ingredients. Add peas, mushrooms, and chicken. Heat slowly, stirring occasionally, till boiling. Turn into 2-quart casserole. Snip each biscuit in 3 wedges; arrange, points up, atop *hot* chicken mixture. Bake at 450° till biscuits are done, 15 minutes. Serves 5.

Quick dinner with a German accent

← Prove that jiffy meals can be interesting. Feature Skillet Potato Salad with bologna rings and deviled eggs in a supper menu.

In Chicken and Biscuit Pie many convenience foods are used—canned chicken, canned gravy, instant onion, and refrigerated biscuits. If you stewed a chicken, made your own soup, chopped the onion, and made biscuits, the cost of the recipe would be much lower. However, if you do not have the time to do all of this work yourself, the savings in time are well worth the extra cost. It all depends on what you have more of—time or money.

Ways to save time

Basically, there are three things that make quick cookery possible—convenience food products, timesaving equipment, and efficient work habits.

Convenience food products: Today's homemakers have at their disposal a boundless array of canned, boxed, and frozen foods. Some of these products are handy ingredients to use in recipes; others are complete dishes in themselves. These complete dishes can also form the bases for an entirely different but still quick dish when other ingredients are added.

There are many reasons why you might want to have convenience foods on hand. They are good to have for emergency meals. They are easy to fix, so novice cooks can prepare meals easily and children can assist their mothers in the kitchen. They are helpful to the homemaker who is employed outside of the home or one who spends a great deal of time with either club or charity work. For instance, the busy woman can put a hot meal before her family in very little time by using convenience products to make Skillet Potato Salad to serve as the main dish for supper or Orange-Nut Ring for breakfast.

Skillet Potato Salad

5 slices bacon
1 10½-ounce can condensed cream
    of celery soup
2 tablespoons sweet pickle relish
1 tablespoon instant minced onion
2 tablespoons vinegar
½ teaspoon salt
1 tablespoon chopped canned
    pimiento
2 16-ounce cans sliced potatoes,
    drained
1 14-ounce bologna ring

Fry bacon till crisp; remove from skillet. Drain and crumble. Drain off bacon drippings and return 1 tablespoon to skillet. Blend in soup, relish, onion, vinegar, salt, and pimiento. Cook and stir till mixture comes to boiling.

Gently stir in sliced potatoes and all *but* 1 tablespoon crumbled bacon. Score bologna ring and lay on top of salad in skillet. Simmer, covered, till bologna is heated through, 10 minutes. Sprinkle remaining bacon over top. Garnish with snipped parsley, if desired. Serves 6.

Orange-Nut Ring

2 packages refrigerated orange or
    cinnamon Danish rolls with
    icing (16 rolls)
¼ cup chopped pecans

Separate rolls and arrange 1 package (8 rolls), flat side down, around the bottom of *ungreased* 6½-cup ring mold. Stagger the remaining package of rolls on top of the first layer, covering the seams of the rolls on bottom layer.

Bake at 375° for 20 to 25 minutes. Invert on serving plate while it is still warm. Spread top and sides with frosting included in packages. Decorate with nuts. Serve warm. Serves 8.

Timesaving equipment: Modern equipment is largely responsible for making quick cookery possible. The electric mixer, one of the first modern appliances, is often taken for granted. It shouldn't be. It saves you time and energy. It will speed up the thorough mixing so necessary for making a cake from a mix or standard recipe.

The electric blender, too, has many uses. Use it properly and you will speed up your techniques. Blenders chop, grate, purée, and blend in a matter of seconds.

Strawberry-Lemonade Slush

A blender-made thirst quencher—

2 cups strawberries
1 cup sugar
3 cups water
1 cup lemon juice
    Few drops red food coloring
    Crushed ice
    Strawberry and lemon slices

Purée strawberries in blender container. Combine sugar, *1 cup* water, and lemon juice; stir till sugar is dissolved. Add remaining water, the puréed berries, and food coloring. Serve over crushed ice with strawberry and lemon slice floaters. Makes 6 cups.

There are many other appliances that save you time and effort. For example, pressure pans cook foods in approximately a third of the regular time; electric knives slice quickly with little effort; electric skillets and griddles control the heat to eliminate pot-watching, and automatic timers on ovens and range outlets begin and stop the cooking automatically. Toasters, coffee makers, can openers, and microwave ovens are helpers, too.

Efficient work habits: One of the least expensive factors in quick cookery is your work habits. You save time and energy by constantly evaluating and improving. When you go to the refrigerator, get several items at one time instead of making several trips. Also line up foods when slicing so you can slice several with each stroke.

A great way to start the day

For a speedy meal, serve Canadian-style → bacon, Berry-Cereal Parfaits (see *Cereal* for recipe), and an Orange-Nut Ring.

Timesaving tips

- Eliminate wiping up crumbs. Crush cookies and crackers in a plastic bag with a rolling pin if you do not have a blender.
- Shake cookies in a bag to coat with sugar, as when coating meats with crumbs. This makes fast work of rolling hot cookies.
- Plan an entire meal that bakes in the oven. You will be free to do other things while dinner bakes without any watching.
- Make salad dressing in large quantities. Shake, store, and serve in the same bottle.
- Set the table the night before for a quick breakfast or for a large dinner party.
- Measure dry ingredients and set out utensils early when you have some extra time.
- Reduce dishwashing and cluttered work areas by washing up as you work and by mixing, baking, and serving in one dish.

Finding new ways of doing things will also speed up your work a great deal. Try using convenience products available on the market and ideas in cookbooks, magazines, or newspapers to see if they work well for you. Move your timesaving appliances to a handy place, and learn to use them to the fullest advantage.

Double up on your tasks to save time later on. When shredding cheese, make some extra to freeze for another time. Make two casseroles or dessert recipes as long as all the ingredients are out, and put the second one in the freezer for a quick meal later in the month.

Dovetail your jobs when cooking a meal. Overlap recipe steps so you are not waiting for one thing to finish before you begin another. Do all the chopping or measuring for the whole meal at the same time.

Quick menus

The art of quick cookery involves careful planning and carrying out the plan well. In the following menus for breakfasts, lunches, and dinners, note the suggestions for preparing these carefully selected menus in a minimum of time and with as little wasted effort as possible.

Breakfast: The morning meal is one of the most vital meals of the day, but unfortunately it is too often neglected. You can serve tasty breakfasts in a jiffy by incorporating quick-cooking foods, such as cereals, in the breakfast menus.

Butterscotch Oatmeal

Round out the menu with chilled apple juice, toast, and brown-and-serve sausage—

> 1 beaten egg
> 1¾ cups milk
> ½ cup brown sugar
> 1 cup quick-cooking rolled oats
> 2 tablespoons butter or margarine

In saucepan combine beaten egg, milk, and brown sugar. Cook and stir over medium heat till slightly thickened, about 5 minutes. Stir in oats; cook just till mixture begins to bubble, 3 minutes. (For creamier texture add oatmeal to *uncooked* egg mixture; cook and stir over medium heat till thickened, 8 to 10 minutes.) Add butter; cover and remove from heat. Let stand a few minutes, then stir to blend. Serve with light cream, if desired. Serves 2 or 3.

Other convenience products for breakfast include canned, fresh, and frozen berries, fruits, and juices. They are good in combinations as well as by themselves. There are also precooked sausages, dehydrated hashbrowns, and packaged, frozen refrigerated breads that take a minimum of work. Refrigerated rolls and biscuits are the bases of quick coffee cakes, such as Quick Apple Pinwheel and Orange-Nut Ring.

Another way to make a quick breakfast is to combine the main foods into one dish such as a soup and to do some of the work the evening before. In the following menu, dice the ham and boil the egg the day before. Also, place a package of frozen strawberries in the refrigerator to thaw and a can of pineapple in the refrigerator to chill. In the morning, start the coffee and make the ham soup first. While the soup is heating, drain the pineapple and mix it with icy strawberries. Make the toast and everything is ready to serve.

Cream of Ham Soup

2 tablespoons butter or margarine
2 tablespoons all-purpose flour
¼ teaspoon salt
Dash white pepper
2½ cups milk
1 cup diced fully cooked ham
1 hard-cooked egg, finely chopped
Toasted round oat cereal

In saucepan melt the butter. Blend in flour, salt, and pepper. Add milk all at once. Cook and stir till thickened and bubbly. Add ham and chopped egg; heat through. Top each serving with oat cereal. Makes 3 or 4 servings.

Lunch: Quick midday meals usually feature soups, sandwiches, or leftovers. Include relishes, chips, milk, cookies, fruit, and other prepared items to fill out the menu and to keep the work simple.

Sandwiches are a favorite that please the cook and the diners. You can simplify the preparation by letting everyone stack his own or by grilling hot sandwiches at the table on a portable appliance. To spark interest, add something different to old standards. For instance, Avocado Open-Facers combine avocado with the popular bacon, lettuce, and tomato sandwich.

Variation of bacon-lettuce-tomato

Avocado Open-Facers make a colorful lunch. Just add crisp chips, relishes, iced tea, and fruit for a quick, nourishing menu.

Hasten the setting of gelatin by placing the bowl in a larger bowl of ice and water till partially set. Then, fold in fruit.

Avocado Open-Facers

    3 tablespoons mayonnaise or salad
        dressing
    1 tablespoon lemon juice
    4 slices whole wheat bread,
        toasted
    1 avocado, peeled and sliced
        Leaf lettuce
    1 tomato, thinly sliced
        Salt and pepper
    8 slices bacon, crisp-cooked and
        drained
        Thousand Island salad dressing

Combine mayonnaise and *half* the lemon juice; spread on one side of each slice toast. Brush avocado with remaining lemon juice. Place leaf lettuce, tomato slices, and avocado slices on toast. Sprinkle with salt and pepper. Crisscross 2 bacon slices atop each. Spoon on Thousand Island dressing. Garnish plate with relishes, if desired. Makes 4 sandwiches.

Soup is another welcome lunch. You can use canned or packaged soups and add zest with seasonings, or make classics quickly with convenience products. Quick Clam Chowder, for example, made with frozen and canned products, is a hearty lunch. Make a cake ahead so that everything is ready when the gang arrives.

Quick Clam Chowder

    1 7½-ounce can minced clams
    ¼ cup chopped celery
    1 teaspoon instant minced onion
    1 tablespoon butter or margarine
    1 8-ounce package frozen green peas
        and potatoes with cream sauce
    1 13¾-ounce can condensed
        chicken broth
    1 6-ounce can evaporated milk
    ¼ teaspoon dried thyme leaves,
        crushed
        Dash salt
        Dash pepper

Drain clams, reserving liquid. Cook celery and onion in butter till tender but not brown. Stir in next 6 ingredients and clam liquid. Cook and stir till mixture is boiling. Reduce heat; cover and simmer 5 minutes. Stir in clams; heat to boiling. Garnish the chowder with paprika, if desired. Makes 4 to 6 servings.

Pink and White Marble Cake

    1 package angel cake mix
        Red food coloring
    ¼ teaspoon peppermint extract
    1 package fluffy white frosting
        mix

Prepare cake mix according to package directions. Tint a third of batter pink with few drops food coloring; add extract. Spoon red and white batter alternately into *ungreased* 10-inch tube pan. Bake as directed. Invert; cool. Prepare frosting according to package directions; tint pink. Frost cooled cake.

MENU

QUICK WEEKEND LUNCH
Quick Clam Chowder
Crackers
Pink and White Marble Cake
Milk   *Tea*

MENU

MEXICAN LUNCH

Enchilada Casserole

Celery Sticks   Carrot Sticks

Tortilla Chips

Milk   Tea

Lunch menus planned around casseroles, such an Enchilada Casserole, are quick because all the foods cook together. When preparing Mexican Lunch, make the casserole and put it in to bake. Clean the carrots and celery, set the table, fill the glasses, and you'll have a few minutes to spare before serving lunch.

Enchilada Casserole

- 1 6-ounce package corn chips
- 8 ounces sharp process American cheese, shredded (2 cups)
- 1 15-ounce can chili with beans
- 1 15-ounce can enchilada sauce
- 1 8-ounce can tomato sauce
- 1 tablespoon instant minced onion
- 1 cup dairy sour cream

Reserve 1 cup chips. Combine remaining chips with *1½ cups* cheese, chili with beans, enchilada sauce, tomato sauce, and instant onion. Pour into 11x7x1½-inch baking pan. Bake, uncovered, at 375° till hot, 30 minutes. Spread top of mixture with sour cream. Sprinkle with remaining cheese. Circle reserved chips around edge. Bake 5 minutes. Makes 6 servings.

Dinner: The largest meal of the day requires more dishes and, therefore, more planning in order to be quick. Canned and frozen meats and vegetables are outstanding time-savers. These convenience products make delicious meals when you use imaginative sauces and seasonings to dress them up. The following vegetable recipes illustrate how you can add interest.

Green Beans Plus

- 1 cup sliced celery
- 2 tablespoons butter or margarine
- 1 teaspoon sugar
- 2 16-ounce cans cut green beans

Cook celery in butter till crisp-tender; add sugar. Heat beans; drain. Toss with celery mixture. Season with salt and pepper. Serves 6 to 8.

Shrimp-Almond Sauce

- 1 3-ounce package cream cheese with chives
- ¼ cup milk
- 1 10-ounce can frozen condensed cream of shrimp soup
- 2 teaspoons lemon juice
- 2 tablespoon sliced almonds

Blend cheese and milk. Add soup. Heat and stir till hot. Add juice. Pour over hot vegetables. Toast nuts; sprinkle over sauce. Makes 1½ cups.

Gourmet vegetable dishes can be quick. Cook frozen broccoli spears or cauliflower while making a Shrimp-Almond Sauce.

MENU

OVEN MEAL
Luncheon Meat Dinner
Men's Favorite Salad
Bread   Butter
Busy-Day Cake
Caramel Sundae Topping
Coffee   Milk

Another way to make dinner quickly is to prepare oven meals. Arrange the menu, such as the following one so that everything bakes together at one temperature.

Luncheon Meat Dinner

    2 12-ounce cans luncheon meat
    ½ cup orange marmalade
    1 18-ounce can sweet potatoes, drained
    1 8½-ounce can sliced pineapple, halved
    ¼ cup butter or margarine, melted

Slice each piece of meat crosswise 3 times, slicing ¾ *of the way through.* Spread with marmalade. Place in an 11¾x7½x1¾-inch baking dish. Arrange potatoes around meat. Brush pineapple with butter. Insert in cuts in meat. Add remaining slices to dish with potatoes. Drizzle remaining butter over potatoes. Bake at 375° till browned, about 30 minutes. Baste the meat often. Makes 6 to 8 servings.

Men's Favorite Salad

    5 cups torn lettuce
    5 cups torn romaine
    ⅓ cup Italian salad dressing
    1 3½-ounce can French-fried onions
      Tomato wedges

Combine lettuce and romaine; add dressing and toss. Heat onions at 375° a few minutes to crisp. Toss warm onions gently with salad. Garnish with tomato. Serve at once. Serves 6.

Busy-Day Cake

    ⅓ cup shortening
    1¾ cups sifted cake flour
    ¾ cup sugar
    2½ teaspoons baking powder
    ½ teaspoon salt
    1 egg
    ¾ cup milk
    1½ teaspoons vanilla

Place shortening in mixing bowl. Sift in dry ingredients. Add egg and *half* the milk; mix till flour is moistened. Beat 2 minutes at medium speed on electric mixer. Add remaining milk and vanilla; beat 2 minutes longer. Bake in greased and floured 9x9x2-inch baking pan at 375° till done, about 25 minutes.

Creamy Pumpkin-Whip Pie

    1 6½-ounce package graham cracker crust mix
    1 3¾-ounce package vanilla whipped dessert mix
    1 cup cold milk
    1 cup canned pumpkin
    1½ teaspoons pumpkin pie spice
    1 2-ounce package dessert topping mix
    ½ teaspoon vanilla

Prepare crust mix according to directions for 9-inch pie. Whip dessert mix with ½ *cup* cold milk. Add pumpkin and spice; beat. Prepare topping with remaining milk and vanilla. Fold into pumpkin. Pour into crust. Chill.

MENU

JIFFY COMPANY DINNER
Fruit Juice Appetizer
Sweet-Sour Meatballs
Hot Rice   *Tomato Slices*
Creamy Pumpkin-Whip Pie
or *Butterscotch Torte Supreme*
Tea

Sweet-Sour Meatballs

  1 8¾-ounce can pineapple tidbits
  ¼ cup brown sugar
  2 tablespoons cornstarch
  ½ cup water
  ¼ cup cider vinegar
  1 teaspoon soy sauce
  1 5-ounce can water chestnuts
  1 16-ounce can meatballs in gravy
  1 green pepper, cut in strips

Drain pineapple, reserving syrup. In medium saucepan combine brown sugar and cornstarch. Blend in reserved syrup, water, vinegar, and soy sauce. Cook and stir over low heat till thickened and bubbly. Drain and thinly slice water chestnuts. Stir chestnuts, meatballs in gravy, green pepper, and pineapple into sauce mixture. Heat to boiling. Makes 4 servings.

Butterscotch Torte Supreme

  1 package 2-layer-size yellow
      cake mix
  1 3¾- or 4-ounce package *regular*
      butterscotch pudding mix
  1 8-ounce package pitted dates,
      snipped (1¼ cups)
    Dash salt
  ½ cup chopped walnuts
  2 tablespoons butter or margarine
        • • •
  1 package fluffy white frosting mix

Prepare cake mix according to package directions; bake in two 9-inch round pans. Cool thoroughly. Cut layers in half.

Meanwhile, prepare pudding according to directions, *using only 1½ cups milk and adding dates and salt.* When done, remove from heat; add nuts and butter. Place waxed paper directly on surface; cool to room temperature.

Spread pudding between cake layers and over top. Prepare frosting mix according to package directions. Spread on sides and add 1½-inch border of frosting on top of cake. Store any leftover cake in the refrigerator.

QUINCE *(kwins)*—A hard, yellow fruit resembling an apple or pear. Quinces have long been grown and enjoyed as food.

Identify quince by its golden yellow color and applelike shape. It has an acid-bitter pulp and seeds throughout the fruit.

At one time, quinces were considered sacred to the Goddess of Love and were given as a token of love. Luckily for today's women, fate interceded and replaced it with the diamond as an engagement symbol.

Quinces are usually grown locally and are available during the fall months. Ripe, desirable ones are pale yellow, firm, and free from blemishes. Quinces bruise quite easily, so be sure to handle them gently. Store them in a cool, dry place and they will keep very well.

When you are ready to use quinces, peel and core them and remove the hard seeds. Quinces must be cooked before eating or they will not be easily digested. You can make them into tart jellies, jams, and preserves. Or try stewing them for a dessert, a sauce, or an accompaniment to main dishes. One 3½-ounce quince contains 57 calories before it is cooked. It also contributes B vitamins, vitamin C, and carbohydrates to the diet. (See also *Fruit.*)

QUININE WATER *(kwī′ nīn)*—A carbonated beverage also called tonic or tonic water. Quinine water is made with the bitter-flavored quinine, lemon, and lime.

Quinine water mixes well with liquor and is used in many tall drinks. Gin and vodka are mixed with quinine water and lime juice for the popular summertime drink, gin and tonic or vodka and tonic. Thoroughly chilling the quinine water before making these drinks helps to keep the drinks cool and refreshing.

R

RABBIT—1. A long-eared animal related to the hare. **2.** Another name for Welsh Rabbit.

If you have a hunter in the family, chances are he will be bringing rabbit home since rabbit is the game most hunted in the United States. The entrails should be removed and the blood drained right after the animals are shot. The skin should be removed as soon as possible. Other than this, wild ones are prepared like the domestic rabbits you buy.

Plan to use fresh rabbit within two days. Cook rabbit as you would chicken, substituting it in your favorite poultry recipe if you like. Young rabbits are suitable to panfry, broil, and roast.

Fried Rabbit

      ¼ cup all-purpose flour
      ¾ teaspoon salt
         Dash pepper
      1 1- to 1½-pound ready-to-cook
         young rabbit, cut up
      2 tablespoons shortening

Combine flour, salt, and pepper. Coat rabbit with the flour mixture. In a skillet brown the meat slowly in hot shortening. Reduce heat; add 2 or 3 tablespoons water. Cover; simmer till tender, about 30 minutes, adding more water if necessary. Makes 2 servings.

Older rabbits should be braised or stewed, as in the famous hasenpfeffer and jugged hare. Rabbits are often soaked in brine, wine, or vinegar before cooking.

A 3½-ounce serving of raw wild rabbit contains 124 calories, while raw domestic rabbit has 159 calories. (See also *Game.*)

RACCOON—A small animal with a bushy, ringed tail. Raccoons, also called coons, are about 2½ to 3 feet long and weigh from 7 to 12 pounds. They were a source of food in pioneer days, and today they are hunted for food and sport during fall and winter.

The raccoon's dark flesh is tender and flavorful when prepared properly. Be sure to remove all the fat and the scent glands (small, round kernels). Raccoon is cooked like rabbit. Young ones are suitable for roasting whole; older raccoons are better braised and stewed. (See also *Game.*)

RACK OF LAMB—Another name for standing rib roast of lamb. (see also *Lamb.*)

RACLETTE *(rak let')*—A Swiss cheese dish that is related to fondue. As the cheese is melted, the softened parts are scraped off and eaten with bread or potatoes.

RADISH—An edible root vegetable belonging to the mustard family. The word is derived from the Latin word *radi* meaning root.

Although there is a distinct possibility that the radish originated in eastern Asia, varying forms of this vegetable have been cultivated for so many years that its origin is obscure. The Egyptians are known to have eaten radishes years before the pyramids were built, and the Greeks and Romans enjoyed them, too. These radishes, however, were much larger in size and were eaten in quantities like Americans eat corn and beans.

Various types of radishes are grown today—small and large; round and oblong; red, white, black, and purple. The small, round, red and the long, white icicle varieties are the most common at supermarkets. The large, white daikon or oriental radish, when available in the United States, is best known in its pickled form.

Nutritional value: Radishes contribute taste pleasure with their peppery flavor and crisp texture, but their nutritional offering is limited. They are quite low in calories (10 small radishes provide only 17 calories), and they contain vitamin C and other vitamins and minerals.

How to select and store: Radishes are marketed throughout the year, with the most plentiful supply appearing between May and July. Choose medium-sized radishes that are crisp and firm to the touch. Radishes that yield to pressure are more than likely overgrown, stale, and pithy. Avoid those that have cuts or any evidence of damage, too. Yellowed or decayed tops do not necessarily indicate poor quality.

At home, store radishes tightly covered in the refrigerator crisper. They will stay fresh in this way for about one week.

How to prepare and use: Before using radishes, wash them and remove the tops and root ends. Leave them whole for a relish tray or garnish. Slice them for use in salads, sandwiches, or vegetable dishes.

Although radishes are most often thought of as a relish food in this country, they are enjoyed in many different ways around the globe. In France, they are sliced, then buttered and salted. Mideastern cooks steam or boil the radish greens only. In Southeast Asia, one type of radish is highly valued for its fleshy, seed pots, which are eaten raw or pickled. In China and Japan, the daikon is commonly prepared this way. (See also *Vegetable.*)

Panama Radish Salad

 1½ cups sliced radishes
  1 cup finely diced tomato
 ¼ cup thinly sliced onion rings
  2 tablespoons salad oil
  2 tablespoons lemon juice
  2 teaspoons snipped parsley
 ½ teaspoon salt
 ⅛ teaspoon garlic salt
 ⅛ teaspoon black pepper

Combine radishes, tomato, and onion rings. In screw-top jar shake together remaining ingredients. Pour over radish mixture; toss. Chill for about 1 hour. Makes 4 to 5 servings.

RAGOUT (*ra gōo′*)—A highly seasoned French stew. Ragout is made with fish, meat, or poultry. The meat is browned and cooked like a typical stew. Vegetables may or may not be included in the stew.

French Ragout

 1½ cups sliced onion
  3 tablespoons butter or margarine
  1 beef bouillon cube
 1½ cups water
  2 cups cubed cooked beef
 ¾ cup leftover *or* canned gravy
  1 lemon slice
 1½ cups diced peeled potatoes
 1½ cups sliced carrots
 12 dried pitted prunes
 ¾ teaspoon salt
 ¼ cup cold water
  1 tablespoon cornstarch

Cook onion in butter just till tender. Add remaining ingredients *except* cornstarch. Bring to a boil. Simmer, covered, for about 25 minutes. Blend cold water with the cornstarch. Stir into the beef mixture. Bring to a boil, stirring constantly. Simmer the mixture, uncovered, 5 minutes longer. Makes 4 servings.

RAINBOW TROUT—A variety of fresh-water trout that is recognizable by its colorful markings—a pink stripe running the entire length of the body, and many dark spots on the fins, body, and head. The rainbow trout is a popular game fish and is found across the United States and in Canada. Some rainbow trout, known as steelheads, migrate to the ocean and then return to a freshwater stream.

The average weight of a rainbow trout is between two and eight pounds. The rainbow is a fat fish—a 3½-ounce portion of uncooked flesh equals 195 calories. It is a good source of high-quality protein and also contains the B vitamins.

Prepare rainbow trout by frying, baking, broiling, or poaching. (See also *Trout.*)

RAISIN—A grape that has been dried by natural or artificial methods. Not all grapes make good raisins, just as not all apples cook well. Only varieties that ripen to at least 18 percent sugar content and that have outstanding flavor, texture, and cooking characteristics when dried are used for raisins. Four pounds of fresh grapes will yield one pound of raisins.

More than likely, raisins are one of the oldest processed foods known to man. Prehistoric murals illustrate the very early use of raisins for jewelry and decoration, and religious and magical powers were attributed to these fruits, too.

There were also many functional uses for raisins. As food, they were often included in the menu at feasts of the Roman emperor Nero. Monetarily, they were used by the Israelites as tax payments to King David, and in Rome the value of a slave was indicated by the number of raisins placed into a narrow-necked vessel called an amphor. As medicine, they were suggested for the psychological relief of anger and sorrow by Egyptian doctors, and for the cure of dysentery, coughs, and certain poisons by Roman physicians.

Raisins were being produced long before the Christian Era. Four thousand years ago Armenia was the center of raisin production, and it remained so for 1,500 years. Greece and Spain provided only a small amount of the total poundage. Today, production is centered in California.

The early Spanish missionaries were largely responsible for the production of raisins in America. As they moved into California, they planted vineyards as sources for the missions' sacramental wines. By the 1850s, both the Sacramento and San Joaquin valleys were important production areas. Today, San Joaquin is the world's largest raisin-producing center.

Unforeseen weather conditions were responsible for changing the emphasis from grapes to raisins in the San Joaquin Valley. In 1873, summer and fall were so hot and dry that the grapes dried on the vines before they could be picked. In an effort to reduce the financial loss, one enterprising grower shipped the dried grapes to a grocer friend in San Francisco. A ship from Peru that had docked at the bay inspired the grocer to market the raisins as "Peruvian delicacies." The promotion was such a success that the foundations for the raisin industry were soon begun.

Nutritional value: Raisins contain the nutritive value of grapes in a concentrated form. The high sugar content is a good source of quick energy. One and one-half tablespoons of raisins contain 40 calories; 1 cup contains 408 calories. Raisins have all of the vitamins and minerals needed to convert raisin sugar to energy without borrowing from body stores.

Types of raisins: Raisins are often given the name of the grape variety from which they come, such as Muscat and Thompson Seedless. Dried Muscats were the first raisins marketed in the United States, but they are scarcely available now. Thompson Seedless have surpassed Muscats in availability. Zante currants (from the Black Corinthian grape variety) are also important.

Nearly all the California raisins marketed are of the Thompson Seedless variety. They are two forms of this variety, which vary in color and in the processing they undergo. Natural seedless raisins are medium brown in color and are naturally dried in the sun without any chemical additives. Golden raisins, with their rich yellow color, are dried artificially. The special drying procedures more nearly retain the natural color of the white grapes.

Small, dark Zante currants are a fourth the size of Thompson Seedless raisins. They are seedless and have a tart flavor. These currants are completely different from those used in currant jelly.

How raisins are produced: Practically all of the American-marketed raisins are produced and processed in the San Joaquin Valley of central California. In fact, almost half of the world's supply comes from a 100 mile area around Fresno. Except for golden raisins, the modern methods of raisin production still rely heavily on natural sun drying techniques without the use of chemical treatment.

In the traditional drying method, the grape bunches are picked from the vines in early September and placed on paper trays that lay between the vineyard rows. The grapes are arranged to give maximum sun exposure. For the next two weeks, hot dry weather is essential for the grapes to dry properly. The bunches are occasionally turned to ensure even dehydration.

When the moisture of the grapes has been reduced to about 15 percent, the raisins are rolled up in the paper trays for the journey to the grower's yard. There, they are put into sweat boxes or bins, which help to equalize the moisture in the raisins. The sweat boxes are stacked and tightly sealed in paper until they are sold.

The final stages of preparing the raisins for market are undertaken at the packing plant. The large grape stems are removed, and the raisins are carefully inspected, washed, and packed into an assortment of market-sized containers.

Golden raisins are produced by significantly different drying methods, but packing procedures remain essentially the same as for other raisins. After picking, the fresh grapes are transported immediately to the processing plant. There, they are treated in a special bath that readies the fruits for the drying operation. Next, the grapes go into ovens for sulfur dioxide treatment. This harmless chemical allows the grapes to retain their natural color. Prior to inspection and packing, the grapes are placed into the drying ovens where they must remain about 18 hours to achieve the proper moisture level.

How to select and store: Raisins are quite easy to purchase and store because of their versatility and stability.

You'll soon find the family congregating in the kitchen when the fragrant aroma of home-baked Raisin Loaves permeates the rest of the house. Serve the warm slices with butter pats.

Raisin varieties, in most cases, may be interchanged in recipes. The Thompson Seedless raisins are the most popular all-purpose variety. The brown one can be used for all dishes requiring raisins as well as for eating fresh as a snack food. Golden Thompson Seedless are used when special coloring is desired, such as in light fruitcakes and confections. Zante currants are traditionally used in hot cross buns and are ideal for rolls in which larger raisins would be less desirable.

The high sugar content of raisins acts as a natural preservative, thus, markedly improving their storage life as compared to the storage life of the fresh grapes. Store unopened boxes or bags of raisins at dry, room temperature conditions. Partially used boxes or bags of raisins should be sealed in a tightly covered container. Once opened, refrigeration prolongs freshness for extended storage.

How to prepare Plumping is a common cooking technique used in raisin preparation. For plumping, see the box below.

Contrary to popular belief, flouring (coating the fruit with flour) does not prevent raisins from sinking. The raisins sink because they are heavy with fruit sugar. Raisins must either be chopped or incorporated into a very stiff batter in order to keep them from sinking.

Ways to plump raisins

Plumped raisins are frequently used because of their added softness and moistness. Water is most often the liquid used, but fruit juice, coffee, brandy, or other liquid can be used to impart added flavor.

Plumping with water — Cover the raisins with very hot tap water and soak them 2 to 5 minutes, *or* cover the raisins with water in a saucepan and bring to boiling. Remove from heat; let stand 5 minutes.

Plumping with other liquid — Cover raisins with liquid. Soak raisins at room temperature for several hours or overnight.

How to knead and shape raisin bread

Knead raisin bread dough with heels of hands until the dough is smooth and satiny. This requires 8 to 10 minutes of kneading.

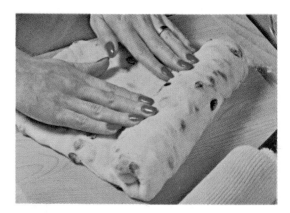

To shape the dough, flatten it with a rolling pin, making the width as long as the pan. Roll up dough from narrow end.

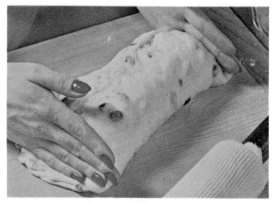

With edges of hands, seal ends of loaf. Fold the ends of dough under as the loaf is placed into the greased loaf pan.

How to use: Raisins possess worldwide popularity in a variety of different foods, such as side dishes, entrées, and desserts.

Raisin bread is popular in many different cuisines—in Ireland, it's called Irish soda bread; in Germany, raisin-filled *Stollen*. Americans love yeast-raised raisin bread drizzled with icing.

Raisin Loaves

In large mixer bowl combine 1 package active dry yeast and 2½ cups sifted all-purpose flour. In saucepan heat 2¼ cups milk, ⅓ cup sugar, ¼ cup shortening, and 2 teaspoons salt just till warm, stirring occasionally to melt shortening. Add warm liquid mixture to dry mixture.

Beat at low speed with electric mixer for ½ minute, scraping sides of bowl constantly. Beat 3 minutes at high speed. By hand, stir in 2 cups raisins and 3¼ to 3¾ cups sifted all-purpose flour to make moderately stiff dough. Turn out onto lightly floured surface; knead till smooth and satiny. Shape into a ball; place in lightly greased bowl, turning once. Cover; let dough rise in warm place till double.

Punch dough down. Cut in 2 portions.* Shape each into a smooth ball; cover and let rest for 10 minutes. Shape into loaves; place in 2 greased 9x5x3-inch loaf pans. Cover; let rise in warm place till double, 45 to 60 minutes. Bake at 400° for 35 minutes. While warm, drizzle with Confectioners' Icing, if desired (See *Confectioners' Sugar*). Makes 2 loaves.

*Or divide dough into 8 portions. Shape same as large loaves, placing in 4½x2¾x2¼-inch pans. Bake at 375° for 25 to 30 minutes.

Cinnamon Crescents

　　1 **package hot roll mix**
　　3 **eggs**
　　6 **tablespoons butter, softened**
　½ **cup all-purpose flour**
　　2 **tablespoons butter or margarine, melted**
　　1 **cup raisins**
　½ **cup sugar**
　½ **cup chopped walnuts**
　　1 **teaspoon ground cinnamon**
　　　Confectioners' Icing (See
　　　***Confectioners' Sugar*)**

Soften yeast from hot roll mix with ½ *cup water* following package directions. Beat eggs well in a large bowl. Add yeast, hot roll mix, and the 6 tablespoons softened butter or margarine. Blend the mixture well. Cover the dough; let it rise till double, about 1 hour.

Sprinkle the all-purpose flour on a board and knead it into the dough so that the dough is still very soft but not sticky. Divide dough in half. On a lightly floured surface roll *each half* of dough to a 12x10-inch rectangle. Brush with melted butter.

Combine raisins, sugar, nuts, and cinnamon; sprinkle *half* over each rectangle. Roll up in jelly-roll fashion, starting with long edge. Place, sealed sides down, on greased baking sheet, curving to form crescents and pinching ends to seal well. Cover and let rise till light, about ½ hour. Bake at 375° for 25 minutes. Frost with Confectioners' Icing. Top with additional nuts, if desired. Makes 2 crescents.

Australians, Indians, and Armenians as well as Americans like raisins in entrées and side dishes. In Australia, a well-seasoned stuffing with raisins is baked inside tender squabs. Raisins are a customary condiment for Indian curries. Raisins often are scattered throughout Armenian pilafs. Americans are well known for their baked ham with sweet raisin sauce and mayonnaise-dressed carrot-raisin salad.

Easy ways to chop and grind raisins

No matter which technique you choose, raisins are chopped and ground with stickless ease when you call on salad oil for help.

To chop raisins on a cutting board, coat each cup of raisins with about 1 teaspoon salad oil prior to chopping them.

For speed chopping, store the raisins in the freezer. At chopping time lightly oil blender container and blades with salad oil. Then chop ¼ to ½ cup raisins at a time.

To grind raisins, first oil the screw and blades of the food grinder.

Raisin Sauce

⅓ cup raisins
½ cup water
⅓ cup currant jelly
½ teaspoon grated orange peel
½ cup orange juice

· · ·

2 tablespoons brown sugar
1 tablespoon cornstarch
Dash ground allspice
Dash salt

Combine raisins, water, jelly, orange peel, and orange juice in saucepan; bring to boiling. Combine brown sugar, cornstarch, allspice, and salt; stir into raisin mixture. Cook and stir till thickened and bubbly. Serve warm with fully cooked ham. Makes about 1½ cups.

Gingery Macaroni Salad

½ 7-ounce package elbow macaroni, cooked and drained (about 2 cups)
¼ cup light raisins
¼ cup chopped celery

· · ·

½ cup mayonnaise or salad dressing
1 tablespoon chopped onion
1 teaspoon chopped candied ginger
¼ teaspoon salt
¼ teaspoon curry powder
Dash garlic salt
Dash pepper
2 tablespoons coarsely chopped peanuts

Combine macaroni, raisins, and celery. Blend together mayonnaise, onion, candied ginger, salt, curry powder, garlic salt, and pepper. Toss mayonnaise mixture lightly with macaroni mixture. Chill. Serve in lettuce cups; garnish with peanuts. Makes 4 to 6 servings.

Breakfast fanfare

← Alternate layers of coffee bread and moist raisin filling give nut- and icing-coated Cinnamon Crescents morningtime appeal.

Raisins are standouts in many international desserts, too. Italian fried cookies made with raisins are Christmas fare. In England, there's famed steamed puddings, once made with plums but now filled with currants and raisins. American versions of pies, cakes, puddings, and cookies, chock full of raisins, are unforgetably delicious, too. (See *Dried Fruit, Grape* for additional information.)

Raisin Pie

3 beaten eggs
1 cup sugar
½ teaspoon ground cinnamon
½ teaspoon ground nutmeg
¼ teaspoon salt
2½ tablespoons lemon juice
2 tablespoons butter or margarine, melted

· · ·

1 cup raisins
⅓ cup broken walnuts
1 8-inch *unbaked* pastry shell (See *Pastry*)

Combine eggs, sugar, cinnamon, nutmeg, salt, lemon juice, and butter. Stir in raisins and the ⅓ cup broken walnuts. Pour the mixture into a pastry shell. Bake at 375° till filling is set in center, 35 to 40 minutes. Cool.

Old-Fashioned Raisin Bars

A spicy classic—

Combine 1 cup raisins and 1 cup water in a saucepan; bring to boiling. Remove the mixture from heat. Stir in ½ cup shortening *or* salad oil; cool mixture to lukewarm. Stir in 1 cup sugar and 1 slightly beaten egg.

Sift together 1¾ cups sifted all-purpose flour, 1 teaspoon baking soda, 1 teaspoon ground cinnamon, ½ teaspoon ground nutmeg, ½ teaspoon ground allspice, ¼ teaspoon salt, and ¼ teaspoon ground cloves; beat into raisin mixture. Stir in ½ cup chopped walnuts. Pour into a greased 15½x10½x1-inch baking pan. Bake at 375° for 12 minutes. When cool, cut in bars. Dust lightly with confectioners' sugar, or frost while warm. Makes about 4 dozen bars.

RAMEKIN *(ram' uh kin)*—1. A baked dish, usually based on cheese, that is prepared in individual serving dishes. 2. A small baking container that holds an individual portion. Usually straight-sided, ramekins look like miniature soufflé dishes. The dishes are most often used for baking individual soufflés or casseroles.

RAMPION *(ram' pē uhn)*—A vegetable with a long, white root that resembles a large radish. Native to Europe, rampions are eaten raw or cooked. Europeans enjoy the roots and young leaves in salads.

RANCID—A word that describes the unpleasant aroma and flavor of fats and oils that have deteriorated or spoiled.

Although most common to foods high in fat, rancidity can occur theoretically in any food containing fat. Exposure to air, heat, light, and moisture hastens this reaction. Many of the commercial fats and oils contain antioxidants, which help retard this change. (See also *Fat.*)

RAPE—1. Grape stems and skins that remain after the juice has been pressed out in the winemaking process. The rape is sometimes used as a filter in vinegar production. 2. A vegetable of the cabbage family that has edible leaves and a fleshy stem. Rape is little used for food in the United States, but abroad its warm, aromatic flavor is enjoyed in salads or as a cooked green. An edible oil is also extracted from rape seeds.

RAREBIT—Another name often used for the famous cheese dish, Welsh Rabbit. (See also *Welsh Rabbit.*)

RASPBERRY—A small, thimble-shaped fruit belonging to the rose family.

Whether red, black, purple, or amber, raspberries are, in the scientific sense, aggregate fruits rather than berries. According to the botanical definition, a berry consists of many seeds scattered throughout the pulp of a fruit, as in currants or grapes. Like all aggregate fruits, on the other hand, a raspberry is a cluster of fruits each of which contains one seed surrounded by pulp.

Early historical references to the existence of wild or cultivated raspberries are scattered throughout Europe. Raspberry seeds were excavated from both Swiss and Glastonbury lake dwellings, which existed during the Neolithic and Iron ages respectively. In the first century A.D. the Roman naturalist Pliny recorded the belief that raspberries came from Mt. Ida, Greece, an area of mythological importance. The first reference to raspberries in England appeared in an orchard book published in 1629 in which an entire chapter was devoted to red and white (amber-type) raspberries. By the 1800s, many good raspberry varieties were being cultivated in northern Europe.

By the time America was settled, Europeans were quite familiar with red raspberries. They found similar wild varieties growing in this country as well as the unfamiliar black raspberries, which were called "black caps." At first, only the wild berries were used, but as more territories were settled, raspberry cultivation became necessary to satisfy the demand. European plants were imported and for many years were more popular than the American raspberry varieties.

How raspberries are produced: Raspberry plants have a unique growth cycle. Although the roots of raspberry bushes are perennial, the thorny canes grow biennially. Fruits are produced during the second year of the cane's growth. Each year two-year-old canes are replaced by new canes. In addition to canes, the plants send out suckers. Both root cuttings and suckers are used to propagate new plants.

What are "black caps?"

Unfamiliar with the black raspberries that grew wild when America was settled, our forefathers nicknamed the berries "black caps" to distinguish them from blackberries. Like other raspberries, black raspberries separate from their stem caps and white cores when picked. Blackberries, on the other hand, do not separate from their cores and leave only the stem caps on the canes.

The colors purple (left front), black (right front), and red (rear) identify the three most popular raspberry varieties.

Raspberry cultivation requires careful training of the thorny canes to achieve greatest yield and to make the berries easily accessible for picking. The canes are either staked, trellised, or topped (tops pruned to promote branching). Pruning is carried out during spring or fall, depending on the raspberry variety.

Raspberry plants also need cool, moist climatic conditions. Because of these factors, the major raspberry-producing areas in the United States are in the north.

Nutritional value: Raspberries supply varying caloric, vitamin, and mineral values, depending on the variety. Black raspberries are higher in calories than red ones: 100 calories per cup of black raspberries; 70 calories per cup of red raspberries. Small amounts of the B vitamin thiamine, vitamin C, and minerals such as calcium, phosphorous, potassium, and iron are also present in raspberries.

Types of raspberries: The varieties presently important from a commercial standpoint have been adapted from the wild American species or from hybrid crossings of the American and European varieties. Red and black raspberries are the most popular. Purple (a cross of red and black) and amber ones are less well-known and are of less importance.

Raspberries have played a part in the hybridizing of new berry types, too. Loganberries are a cross between blackberries and red raspberries, and boysenberries are a blend of a raspberry, loganberry, and three blackberry varieties.

How to select: These very perishable fruit usually are marketed in the areas in which they are grown. Fresh raspberries are a summer luxury, but for year-round pleasure there are frozen and canned berries available in most supermarkets.

When selecting fresh raspberries, the appearance of the berries is of utmost importance. They should look clean, have bright, uniform color, and be plump. Avoid berries that are dirty, mashed, or wet, and those that have caps that are still fastened to the cores (underripe). Overripe raspberries are usually dull in color, soft, and leak excess juice.

How to store: Raspberries are one of the most delicate fresh fruits. Thus, they must be handled gently to ensure taste and appearance satisfaction when served.

The berries can be washed prior to storage if they are drained thoroughly on paper toweling. However, some homemakers prefer to wash the berries just before they are used. In either case, cover the dry berries lightly and refrigerate.

Because raspberries stay fresh for only a few days, use them as soon as possible after purchasing. Red raspberries are more perishable than are the black ones.

Freezing and canning can be employed when raspberries are in plenteous supply. The berries can be frozen unsweetened, mixed with sugar, or mixed with a sugar syrup, depending on whether they will be used for special dietary purposes, for cooking, or for eating right from the package. Canned preserves and jellies made from fresh raspberries provide fruit flavor during the off-seasons, too.

How to use: Raspberries are a family favorite whether served plain or fancy.

Raspberries are sandwiched between a crumb crust-meringue base and whipped dessert topping for Raspberry-Meringue Squares.

Fresh raspberries add color and flavor to morning cereal bowls and to midday salads. Raspberries with cream hit the spot as a morning appetizer or an evening dessert. Raspberries with or without other fruits take on gourmet dessert appeal simply with the addition of a flaming liqueur.

Red Raspberry Ring

Ice cream adds richness—

> 1 10-ounce package frozen raspberries, thawed
> 2 3-ounce packages red raspberry-flavored gelatin
> 2 cups boiling water
> 1 pint vanilla ice cream
> 1 6-ounce can frozen pink lemonade concentrate, thawed (¾ cup)
> ¼ cup chopped pecans

Drain raspberries, reserving syrup. Dissolve gelatin in boiling water. Add ice cream by spoonfuls, stirring till melted. Stir in lemonade concentrate and the reserved syrup. Chill till partially set. Fold in raspberries and pecans. Turn into a 6½-cup ring mold. Chill till firm. Makes 8 to 10 servings.

Gingery Fruit Salad

> 2 cups sliced, peeled fresh peaches *or* nectarines
> ¼ cup sugar
> 1 teaspoon lemon juice
> 1 3-ounce package cream cheese, softened
> ½ teaspoon ground ginger
> 1 to 2 tablespoons milk
> 3 cups torn mixed salad greens
> 1 cup fresh raspberries, chilled
> 1 cup fresh blueberries, chilled

Place peach slices in bowl; toss with sugar and lemon juice. Cover and refrigerate about 1 hour. Drain peaches, reserving syrup. Cover peach slices and refrigerate. To prepare dressing, add cream cheese and ginger to reserved syrup; beat till smooth. Stir in milk till dressing is desired consistency. Chill.

Place greens in salad bowl. Arrange fruit atop. Serve with dressing. Makes 6 servings.

For more fanciful eating, use raspberries in your baking or in cold dishes. Let the aroma of freshly baked raspberry pie, cake, or shortbread permeate throughout the house. Versatile raspberry syrup or jam spruces up bread products as well as ice cream and sherbet. (See also *Berry*.)

Raspberry-Cream Cheese Coffee Cake

> 1 3-ounce package cream cheese
> ¼ cup butter or margarine
> 2 cups packaged biscuit mix
> ⅓ cup milk
> ½ cup raspberry preserves
> 1 cup sifted confectioners' sugar
> 1 to 2 tablespoons milk
> ½ teaspoon vanilla

Cut cream cheese and butter into biscuit mix till crumbly. Blend in the ⅓ cup milk. Turn onto floured surface; knead 8 to 10 strokes.

On waxed paper, roll dough to 12x8 inches. Turn onto greased baking sheet; remove paper. Spread preserves down center. Cut 2½x1-inch strips on long sides. Fold strips over filling. Bake at 425° for 12 to 15 minutes. Combine remaining ingredients; drizzle atop.

Raspberry-Meringue Squares

- 1½ cups vanilla wafer crumbs
  (about 30 small wafers)
- ¼ cup butter, melted
- 2 tablespoons sugar
- 4 egg whites
- ½ cup sugar
- 1 pint red raspberries, slightly
  sweetened
- 1 2-ounce package dessert topping
  mix
- 1 tablespoon lemon juice

Combine crumbs, butter, and the 2 tablespoons sugar; mix well. Press firmly in bottom of 9x 9x2-inch baking pan. Beat egg whites till soft peaks form; gradually add the ½ cup sugar, beating to stiff peaks. Swirl meringue over crust; bake at 325° for 12 to 15 minutes. Cool.

Spread raspberries over meringue. Prepare dessert topping mix according to package directions; gently stir in lemon juice. Spread over berries; chill. Cut in squares to serve. Top with additional berries, if desired. Serves 9.

Cherry-Raspberry Pie

Thaw one 10-ounce package frozen red raspberries and one 20-ounce can frozen pitted, tart red cherries. Drain, reserving syrups. Add enough cherry syrup to raspberry syrup to make 1 cup. Blend ¾ cup sugar, 3 tablespoons cornstarch, and ¼ teaspoon salt in saucepan; stir in raspberry syrup and a few drops red food coloring. Add cherries. Cook and stir over low heat till thick. Stir in raspberries.

Prepare Plain Pastry for 2-crust 9-inch pie (See *Pastry*). Line 9-inch pie plate with half of pastry. Add filling. Adjust top crust, cutting slits for escape of steam; seal. Bake at 425° for 30 to 35 minutes.

Note: Two cups pitted fresh tart red cherries may be substituted for the frozen cherries. Add water to raspberry syrup to make 1 cup.

Summer salad special

Brighten a luncheon menu by using perky greens, fresh fruits, and ginger-spiked cream cheese dressing for Gingery Fruit Salad.

Red Raspberry Salad

> 2 10-ounce packages frozen
>   raspberries, thawed
> 2 3-ounce packages red raspberry-
>   flavored gelatin
> 1 16-ounce can applesauce

Drain raspberries, reserving 1 cup syrup. Dissolve gelatin in 2 cups boiling water; stir in reserved syrup and applesauce. Chill till partially set; fold in raspberries. Pour into 6-cup ring mold; chill till firm. Serve 6 to 8.

RASPBERRY VINEGAR—A product made by steeping ripe raspberries in cider or in wine vinegar, then straining out the raspberries and sweetening the liquid to taste. It is used as a base for fruit beverages.

RATAFIA *(rat' uh fe' uh)*—1. General name for liqueurs flavored with fruit and/or fruit kernels. Ratafia once meant any liqueur drunk at the ratification of a treaty. 2. An almond-flavored sweet biscuit.

RATATOUILLE *(râ tâ' tuy)*—A well-seasoned vegetable stew or casserole that originated in Provence, France. Eggplant, squash, green pepper, tomatoes, garlic, and olive oil are traditional ingredients.

Eggplant Ratatouille

> 2 medium onions, sliced (1½ cups)
> 1 clove garlic, minced
> 3 tablespoons olive oil
> 2 small zucchini, cut in ½-inch
>   slices
> 2 tomatoes, peeled and diced
> 1 small eggplant, chopped
> 1 large green pepper, chopped
> 1 bay leaf
> 3 slices bacon

In Dutch oven cook onion and garlic in hot oil till tender but not brown. Add next 5 ingredients, 2 teaspoons salt, and dash pepper. Bring to boil; cover and simmer 30 minutes, stirring occasionally. Fry bacon till crisp; drain and crumble. Add to vegetables; simmer, uncovered, 10 minutes. Remove bay leaf. Serves 6.

RAVIGOTE BUTTER *(ra vē gôt')*—Softened butter mixed with finely chopped green herbs, particularly tarragon, parsley, and chervil. Ravigote butter, sometimes called green butter, is usually served as an accompaniment to broiled meat.

RAVIGOTE SAUCE—1. A cold sauce made of mayonnaise, chopped chives, parsley, wine vinegar, and lemon juice, or an oil and vinegar mixture with hard-cooked egg yolks, mustard, and chopped herbs added. Cold ravigote sauce is usually served with seafood. **2.** A warm sauce made of wine, vinegar, green onion, white sauce, and crushed herbs. This piquant sauce is usually served with poultry, fish, or egg dishes.

Ravigote Sauce

Try this with broiled fish—

> ¼ cup snipped green onion
> 1 tablespoon butter or margarine
> 3 tablespoons dry white wine
> 1 tablespoon vinegar
> 1 tablespoon butter or margarine
> 1 tablespoon all-purpose flour
> 1 cup light cream
> ¼ teaspoon salt
> ¼ teaspoon dried tarragon leaves,
>   crushed

In saucepan cook snipped green onion in 1 tablespoon butter or margarine till tender. Add dry white wine and vinegar. Simmer till liquid is reduced by half. Melt 1 tablespoon butter or margarine; blend in flour. Add light cream. Cook, stirring constantly, till mixture bubbles. Remove from heat; stir in salt and crushed tarragon. Return to low heat; *gradually* stir in onion mixture. Do not boil. Makes 1 cup.

RAVIOLI *(rav' ē ō' le, rä' vē-)*—An Italian dish made of pasta dough cases filled with a meat or vegetable mixture. These Italian dumplings are boiled, then covered with a tomato sauce. Ravioli makes a delicious appetizer or a satisfying main dish. Although homemade ravioli is more authentic, canned or frozen ravioli can be used for those quick-to-prepare meals.

Chicken and Spinach-Filled Ravioli

A homemade dish with real Italian flavor that guests and family alike are sure to appreciate—

> 4 well-beaten eggs
> ¾ cup water
> 3¾ cups sifted all-purpose flour
> 1½ teaspoons salt
>
> • • •
>
> 1 cup ground cooked chicken
> 1 8-ounce can spinach, well
>   drained and chopped
> 3 tablespoons butter or margarine,
>   melted
> 3 tablespoons grated Parmesan
>   cheese
> ¼ teaspoon salt
> ⅛ teaspoon ground nutmeg
>   Dash pepper
>   Spicy Tomato Sauce

To make ravioli dough, combine well-beaten eggs and water in large bowl. Add *2 cups* flour and the 1½ teaspoons salt; beat well. Gradually stir in enough of remaining flour to make moderately stiff dough. Turn out on lightly floured surface and knead till smooth and elastic, about 8 to 10 minutes. Divide dough into two parts. Cover and let rest 10 minutes. Roll each part of dough out to a 16x12-inch rectangle. Cut each rectangle into 2-inch squares.

Combine ground chicken, chopped spinach, and melted butter or margarine. Stir in Parmesan cheese, ¼ teaspoon salt, ground nutmeg, and pepper. Place a teaspoon of filling on one two-inch square of dough. Moisten edges of dough with water and top with second square; seal well with tines of fork. Repeat with remaining filling and ravioli dough. Set aside to dry for 1 hour, turning once.

Cook ravioli in large kettle of rapidly boiling, salted water till tender, about 7 to 8 minutes. Rinse in cold water and drain well. Place in a 13½x8¾x1¾-inch baking dish. Pour Spicy Tomato Sauce over. Bake, covered, at 350° for 30 minutes. Makes 6 to 8 servings.

Spicy Tomato Sauce: In saucepan combine 1 cup water; one 15-ounce can tomato sauce (2 cups); one 7½-ounce can tomatoes (1 cup), cut up; 2 tablespoons snipped parsley; 2 teaspoons sugar; 1 teaspoon dried oregano leaves, crushed; and 1 teaspoon salt. Simmer, uncovered, for 30 minutes, stirring occasionally.

Inside-Out Ravioli

> 1 pound ground beef
> ½ cup chopped onion
> 1 clove garlic, minced
> 1 10-ounce package frozen chopped
>   spinach
>   Water
> 1 16-ounce can spaghetti sauce
>   with mushrooms
> 1 8-ounce can tomato sauce
> 1 6-ounce can tomato paste
> ½ teaspoon salt
>   Dash pepper
>
> • • •
>
> 1 7-ounce package shell or elbow
>   macaroni (2 cups), cooked
>   and drained
> 4 ounces sharp process American
>   cheese, shredded (1 cup)
> ½ cup soft bread crumbs
> 2 well-beaten eggs
> ¼ cup salad oil

In large skillet brown ground beef, chopped onion, and minced garlic. Cook chopped spinach according to package directions. Drain spinach, reserving liquid; add water to make 1 cup. Add spinach liquid, spaghetti sauce, tomato sauce, tomato paste, salt, and pepper to meat mixture. Simmer 10 minutes.

In mixing bowl combine drained spinach with cooked macaroni, shredded process American cheese, soft bread crumbs, well-beaten eggs, and salad oil; spread in 13x9x2-inch baking dish. Top with meat sauce. Bake at 350° for 30 minutes. Let stand 10 minutes before serving. Makes 8 to 10 servings.

REAMER *(rē' muhr)*—A utensil that is used for extracting the juice from oranges, lemons, and limes. It consists of a shallow dish with a ribbed, inverted cone in the center. The juice is squeezed out of citrus fruit by inverting the fruit half over the center of the reamer and pressing the fruit against the cone. As the juice is extracted, it accumulates in the dish part of the reamer. In electric juicers of this type, the ribbed center revolves.

RÉCHAUFFÉ *(rā shō fā')*—The French word for a reheated food or leftover.

RECIPE—A detailed guide to the preparation of ingredients and the cooking of a dish. A recipe includes the proportions of ingredients needed and the method in which these ingredients are to be put together. The yield is usually given, too.

To ensure success in the preparation and serving of a recipe, two preliminary steps are recommended. First, read through the entire recipe to get the complete picture of what the food is intended to be. Secondly, get all of the necessary ingredients out of storage to make sure that you have all that is called for.

If the dish is to be served at mealtime with several other foods, preparation will necessitate dovetailing work from one recipe to another. In this way, the dishes can be served at the planned time and in the proper sequence.

For the new cook, greatest success in preparing recipes is achieved by following recipe directions explicitly. In time, however, experienced homemakers become familiar with cooking principles and techniques, and thus, can take some liberties in making desired recipe alterations and ingredient substitutions.

RED BEAN—A dark red type of kidney bean. Although red beans are similar in flavor to the dark reddish purple kidney beans, their flavor is less intense. For this reason, they are frequently used to replace kidney beans when a milder flavor is desired. They are of great importance in Mexican cookery. (See also *Kidney Bean*.)

Red Bean Toss

      1 16-ounce can red beans, drained
      1 cup thinly sliced celery
    ⅓ cup chopped sweet pickle
    ¼ cup finely chopped onion
      4 ounces sharp process American
          cheese, diced (1 cup)
    ½ teaspoon chili powder
    ½ teaspoon salt
    ½ teaspoon Worcestershire sauce
          Few drops bottled hot pepper
          sauce
    ½ cup mayonnaise or salad dressing
      1 cup coarsely crushed corn chips

Combine red beans, celery, sweet pickle, onion, and process American cheese. Blend chili powder, salt, Worcestershire sauce, and hot pepper sauce with mayonnaise; add this mixture to the bean mixture and toss lightly.

Spoon bean mixture into a 1-quart shallow baking dish; sprinkle with corn chips. Bake at 450° about 10 minutes. Garnish with green pepper rings, if desired. Makes 4 servings.

Bean and Cheese Patties

      2 beaten eggs
    ¼ cup catsup
    ¼ cup finely crushed saltine
          crackers (7 crackers)
      2 tablespoons chopped onion
      2 teaspoons Worcestershire sauce
          . . .
      1 pound ground beef
      1 tablespoon salad oil
      1 10½-ounce can condensed cream
          of mushroom soup
          . . .
      1 16-ounce can red beans
    ⅓ cup chopped green pepper
      4 ounces sharp process American
          cheese, shredded (1 cup)

Mix first 5 ingredients, ¼ teaspoon salt, and dash pepper. Add beef; mix well. Shape into 4 or 5 patties. Brown in hot oil; spoon soup over. Drain beans; sprinkle vegetables and cheese atop patties. Cook slowly, covered, 10 to 15 minutes. Makes 4 to 5 servings.

RED CABBAGE—A purplish red cabbage. The flavor and texture of red cabbage are identical to the green varieties. Thus, preparation and cooking techniques are the same for both types. To retain the color of the red cabbage during cooking, add an acidic food such as vinegar, lemon juice, or sliced apple to the cooking water. (See also *Cabbage*.)

RED CINNAMON CANDY—A small, round, red sugar candy flavored with cinnamon. Many people refer to them as "red hots." They may be eaten as a snack food or used in assorted fruit salad, dessert, and accompaniment recipes such as cinnamon apples.

Cinnamon-Apple Salad

Dissolve two 3-ounce packages lemon-flavored gelatin and $\frac{1}{2}$ cup red cinnamon candies in 3 cups boiling water. Stir in 2 cups unsweetened applesauce, 1 tablespoon lemon juice, and dash salt. Chill till partially set. Add $\frac{1}{2}$ cup broken walnuts. Pour into an 8x8x2-inch pan. Blend two 3-ounce packages softened cream cheese, $\frac{1}{4}$ cup milk, and 2 tablespoons mayonnaise; spoon atop gelatin. Swirl the gelatin mixture to marble. Chill till the apple salad is firm. Makes 9 servings.

Cinnamon Popcorn Balls

    3 quarts popped corn
      Butter or margarine
    1 cup sugar
    $\frac{2}{3}$ cup red cinnamon candies
    1 tablespoon vinegar
    $\frac{1}{4}$ teaspoon salt
    1 or 2 drops oil of cinnamon

Keep popped corn hot in very slow oven (200° to 250°). Rub butter on sides of a medium saucepan; in it combine sugar, cinnamon candies, $\frac{2}{3}$ cup water, vinegar, and salt. Cook to hard-ball stage (250°), stirring till sugar and candies dissolve. Add oil of cinnamon.

Pour syrup slowly over hot popped corn, mixing well. Butter hands. Press coated popcorn lightly into $2\frac{1}{2}$-inch balls.

RECONSTITUTE—To restore a concentrated liquid to its original proportions. For example, frozen orange juice or frozen grape juice is reconstituted to its natural concentration by the addition of a specified amount of water.

RED PEPPER—1. A spice that is ground from red *Capsicum* peppers. 2. Any sweet or hot, red-colored vegetable pepper that is of the *Capsicum* family.

The seasoning called red pepper is often labeled "cayenne pepper" as well as "red pepper," even though originally they were two distinct spices. When first manufactured, red pepper was made from milder-flavored peppers than cayenne. Now, the terms and the spices are interchangeable.

The vegetables referred to as red peppers are more often considered to be hot varieties—cayenne, chili, Tabasco, and bird peppers—rather than sweet varieties. If allowed to fully ripen, however, some sweet ones turn red and are thus called red peppers. These include the red bell and paprika peppers. Because of this broad terminology, red peppers may be very small or large, and mild or extremely hot.

The hot red peppers are a characteristic food used in the cooking of Central and South America, the Caribbean islands, India, Africa, Indonesia, and Korea. Sweet red peppers are a brilliant color substitute for sweet green peppers and taste much the same. (See also *Cayenne Pepper, Pepper* for additional information.)

Jellied Potato Salad

    5 cups diced, peeled, cooked
        potatoes
    1 tablespoon vinegar
    1 cup chopped onion
    $1\frac{1}{2}$ cups mayonnaise or salad dressing
    1 tablespoon celery seed
            · · ·
    2 3-ounce packages lemon-flavored
        gelatin
    $\frac{1}{4}$ cup vinegar
    9 green pepper rings
    9 red pepper rings *or* pimiento
        strips
    1 cup diced cucumber

Sprinkle potatoes with the 1 tablespoon vinegar and 2 teaspoons salt. Toss with onion, mayonnaise, and celery seed; chill. Dissolve gelatin in $2\frac{1}{2}$ cups boiling water; stir in the $\frac{1}{4}$ cup vinegar. To *half* the gelatin mixture add $\frac{1}{4}$ cup cold water. Pour into a 9x9x2-inch pan. Chill till partially set; arrange peppers atop gelatin. Chill till *almost* firm.

Meanwhile, chill remaining gelatin till partially set; beat till soft peaks form. Fold in potato mixture and cucumber. Spoon over gelatin in pan; chill till firm. Invert to unmold. Cut in squares. Makes 9 servings.

RED PERCH—Another name for the freshwater yellow perch. (See also *Perch.*)

RED SNAPPER—A bright red, lean fish with a juicy, delicate flavor. These fish, weighing as much as 30 pounds and measuring up to 2 feet long, are commonly found in the Gulf of Mexico and around Florida.

Red snappers, usually weighing ½ to 5 pounds, are available in food and fish stores in fresh and frozen forms, including whole or dressed fish, fillets, and portions Any of these forms can be fried, boiled, steamed, or made into soup. With the addition of butter or shortening, they can also be baked or broiled. Baked red snapper is considered a choice entrée as are snapper throats.' The flavor of these throats is similar to that of the white meat around the breast bone in a chicken.

Since the red snapper is available all year and is shipped to all parts of the country, this fish can be included in menus during any season and in any place.

Red snapper is a rich source of protein. It also supplies some minerals and the B vitamins thiamine and riboflavin. A 3½-ounce serving of uncooked red snapper yields about 95 calories. (See also *Fish.*)

Snapper with Cashews

  2 pounds fresh or frozen red snapper
     steaks or other fish steaks
  2 tablespoons butter or margarine,
     melted
  2 cups soft bread crumbs (3 slices)
  ¼ cup chopped cashew nuts
  ½ teaspoon seasoned salt
     Dash pepper
  ¼ cup butter or margarine, melted

Thaw frozen fish. Cut fish into 6 portions. Sprinkle with salt and arrange in a greased 9x9x2-inch baking pan. Drizzle 2 tablespoons butter over fish. Combine crumbs, nuts, seasoned salt, and pepper; add remaining ¼ cup melted butter. Sprinkle crumb mixture over fish. Bake at 350° till fish flakes easily when tested with a fork, 25 to 30 minutes. Serves 6.

REDUCE—To boil down a broth of other liquid to decrease the amount and to concentrate the flavor. This process is used in making sauces to yield a richer flavor.

RED WINE—A wine made from red or black grapes and fermented with the grape skins, which provide the color and other characteristic constituents. Burgundy and Claret are examples of red wines.

As red wine ferments, the grape skins and pulp float on top and form a layer called a "cap" over the wine. In order to distribute the flavor contained in this cap throughout the wine, the wine usually is pumped over the cap or the mixture is punched down or stirred. At the completion of fermentation, the wine is drained off, leaving the pulp and skins behind. Then, the wine is aged, bottled, and labeled before it reaches the consumer.

Although some red wines are used as appetizer and dessert wines, most red wines are used as a main course table wine. Since these table wines, as a class, are generally dry and full-flavored, they most often are served with hearty meats such as beef, pork, veal, and game. Besides their use as a beverage, red wines also add a delightful flavor to a variety of dishes. (See also *Wines and Spirits.*)

Spicy Rump Roast

  1 3- to 4-pound beef rump roast
  2 tablespoons shortening
  ½ teaspoon dried marjoram leaves,
     crushed
  1 8-ounce can tomatoes
  ½ cup dry red wine
  ½ cup chopped onion
  ¼ cup chopped green pepper
  1 clove garlic, crushed
  1 tablespoon sugar
  ⅛ teaspoon ground cinnamon
     Dash ground cloves
  ¼ cup all-purpose flour

In Dutch oven slowly brown roast in hot shortening. Season with 1 teaspoon salt and marjoram. Add remaining ingredients except flour. Cover tightly; cook slowly till tender, 2¼ to 2½ hours. Remove the roast to platter.

To make gravy, pour pan juices into large measuring cup; skim off excess fat. Return 1½ cups juices to pan. Blend ½ cup cold water with flour; add to juices. Cook and stir till thickened and bubbly. Makes 8 servings.

Rotisserie Rib Roast Barbecue

½ cup red Burgundy
½ cup vinegar
½ cup salad oil
¼ cup finely chopped onion
2 tablespoons sugar
1 tablespoon Worcestershire sauce
½ teaspoon dry mustard
¼ teaspoon chili powder
⅛ teaspoon dried thyme leaves,
    crushed
1 clove garlic, minced
5 drops bottled hot pepper sauce
1 5- to 6-pound rolled beef
    rib roast

Combine all ingredients *except* roast with 1½ teaspoons salt and ½ teaspoon pepper; marinate roast for 2 hours at room temperature or overnight in refrigerator. Drain, reserving marinade. Insert spit rod through center of roast and adjust holding forks; test balance. Insert meat thermometer. Attach spit and turn on motor (have medium coals at rear of firebox and a drip pan under meat). Lower hood; roast for 2½ to 3 hours for medium-rare doneness, brushing with marinade last ½ hour. Thermometer should register 140° for rare, 160° for medium, 170° for well-done.

Meatballs à la Burgundy

1 beaten egg
½ cup milk
⅓ cup quick-cooking rolled oats
¼ cup finely chopped onion
1 pound ground beef
2 tablespoons shortening
¼ cup all-purpose flour
½ cup red Burgundy
2 beef bouillon cubes
1 teaspoon sugar
1 teaspoon Kitchen Bouquet

Combine first 4 ingredients and ½ teaspoon salt. Add beef; mix well. Shape into 24 balls; brown in hot shortening in skillet. Remove balls; reserve drippings. Stir flour into reserved drippings. Add 2 cups water, wine, and bouillon cubes; cook and stir till bubbly. Stir in remaining ingredients; add meatballs. Cover; simmer 20 minutes. Serves 6.

REFLECTOR OVEN—A portable oven used in campfire cookery for baking breads, pies, and cookies. The most common design for a reflector oven features one shelf set horizontally between two inclined, shiny, metal surfaces. Heat is obtained by setting the open front of the oven so that it faces a flaming campfire. The shiny, metal interior of the oven reflects and intensifies the heat, which provides heat for baking.

To make these ovens more efficient, focus more heat into the oven by building the fire against a ledge or backdrop of green sticks. (See also *Campfire Cookery*.)

REFRIED BEANS—Another name for frijoles refritos. (See also *Frijoles Refritos*.)

REFRIGERATED BISCUITS AND ROLLS—Commercially prepared bread products, usually sold in a tube, that are ready for baking as purchased. These convenience products include plain biscuits, sweet rolls flavored with cinnamon, butterscotch, or orange, and at least one type designed for shaping into crescent rolls. Besides being used separately as dinner rolls or sweet rolls, refrigerated biscuits and rolls are also shortcuts for casserole toppers, coffee cakes, desserts, and other quick bread fix-ups. (See also *Bread*.)

Caramel-Apple Whirls

Start with refrigerated caramel nut rolls—

1 21-ounce can apple pie filling
½ cup fruit juice (orange, pineapple,
    or other)
2 tablespoons butter or margarine
⅓ cup chopped pecans
1 package refrigerated caramel
    nut rolls (8 rolls)
Dairy sour cream

In saucepan combine apple pie filling, fruit juice, butter or margarine, chopped pecans, and topping mix from the caramel rolls. Bring to boiling. Pour into an 11x7x1½-inch baking pan. Top with caramel rolls. Bake at 375° till done, about 20 to 25 minutes. Serve warm topped with dairy sour cream. Makes 8 servings.

Pizza Pronto

2 8-ounce packages refrigerated
   biscuits
1 8-ounce can tomato sauce
1 teaspoon instant minced onion
1/4 teaspoon ground oregano
1/4 teaspoon garlic salt
1 4-ounce package shredded sharp
   Cheddar cheese (1 cup)
2 slices mozzarella cheese, torn
   in pieces
1 6-ounce can mushroom crowns,
   drained *optional*
1/2 cup pitted ripe olives, halved
   lengthwise (optional)

With palms of hands, flatten refrigerated biscuits into 4½x2-inch ovals. On greased baking sheet, stagger 10 biscuits in 2 rows so that narrow ends fit between space left between biscuits in other row. Press adjoining ends together securely. Repeat with remaining biscuits.

Combine tomato sauce, instant minced onion, ground oregano, and garlic salt; spread mixture evenly over biscuits to within ½ inch of edges. Sprinkle with shredded sharp Cheddar cheese; top with mozzarella cheese pieces. Arrange mushroom crowns atop the cheese.

Bake at 450° till edges of crusts are brown, about 8 to 10 minutes. If desired, garnish with ripe olive halves. Makes 2 pizzas.

Quick Apple Dumplings

1 21-ounce can apple pie filling
2½ cups water
1/2 cup raisins
1/3 cup red cinnamon candies
1/3 cup sugar
1/4 cup chopped nuts
2 tablespoons butter or margarine
1 tablespoon lemon juice
1 package refrigerated cinnamon
   rolls with icing (8 rolls)

In electric skillet combine all ingredients *except* rolls. Cook and stir till butter melts and mixture is bubbly. Arrange rolls atop filling. Cover; with lid vent open cook at 250° till rolls are done, 20 to 25 minutes. Spread icing from package over rolls. Serve warm with cream, if desired. Makes 8 servings.

Quicky Crullers

Unroll one tube refrigerated crescent rolls (8 rolls). Pinch together diagonal perforations of each 2 crescents, making 4 rectangles. Cut in thirds lengthwise. Tie each strip in knot. Fry in deep hot fat (375°) till browned. Drain. While warm, brush with confectioners' sugar frosting (see *Confectioners' Sugar*).

Parmesan Biscuits

1/4 cup butter or margarine, melted
2 tablespoons snipped parsley
1 clove garlic, minced

. . .

2 packages refrigerated biscuits
   (20 biscuits)
1/4 cup grated Parmesan cheese

Mix melted butter or margarine, snipped parsley, and minced garlic. Dip biscuits in butter mixture. Overlap 15 biscuits around edge and **rest of** biscuits in center of well-greased 9x1½-inch round pan. Top with remaining butter mixture and Parmesan cheese. Bake at 425° for 15 minutes. Remove from pan at once.

REFRIGERATOR CAKE—A chilled dessert that is made with pieces of cake or cookies and a puddinglike mixture. As the dessert chills, the cake or cookies absorb the pudding mixture until the two parts are blended into a moist, flavorful whole.

Cherry-Angel Dessert

A delicious make-ahead dessert—

8 cups ½-inch cubes angel cake
1 21-ounce can cherry pie filling
1 3¾- or 3⅝-ounce package
   instant vanilla pudding mix
1½ cups milk
1 cup dairy sour cream

Place *half* the angel cake cubes in 9x9x2-inch pan. Spoon pie filling over cake. Top with remaining cake. Combine pudding mix, milk, and sour cream; beat smooth. Spoon over cake. Chill 5 hours. Makes 9 servings.

Chocolate-Angel Delight

Mold this rich, delicious refrigerator cake in a decorative mold for an extra-special dessert—

  1 envelope unflavored gelatin
     (1 tablespoon)
  ½ cup cold water
  1 package fluffy chocolate
     frosting mix
  1 cup whipping cream
  4 cups angel cake cubes
  ¼ cup chopped peanuts
     Chopped peanuts

Soften unflavored gelatin in cold water; dissolve over hot water. Remove from heat and set aside. Prepare fluffy chocolate frosting mix according to package directions; blend in dissolved gelatin. Chill, stirring constantly, till mixture mounds when spooned.

Whip cream; fold into chocolate mixture with angel cake cubes. Sprinkle ¼ cup chopped peanuts in bottom of oiled 5½- to 6-cup mold. Spoon in chilled chocolate mixture. Chill till firm, at least 5 hours or overnight. Carefully unmold on serving plate; top with additional chopped peanuts. Makes 8 servings.

REFRIGERATOR COOKIES—Crisp cookies made from dough that is shaped in rolls and chilled thoroughly before it is thinly sliced and baked. (See also *Cookies.*)

Flossie the Fish

The kids will love these—

Cut eighteen ¼-inch slices from roll of refrigerated slice-and-bake sugar cookie dough. For body of fish, make a slit in 12 of the cookie slices, *cutting just from edge to center.* Place cookies, 2 inches apart, on *ungreased* cookie sheet, spreading slits apart slightly to make mouths. Cut remaining cookie slices in sixths. Arrange these wedges around body of fish to make tails and fins; don't crowd various pieces together—barely touching is close enough. Press on silver decorettes for eyes. Bake as directed on package. Cool 1 minute; remove to rack. Repeat the process with the remaining dough. Makes about 3 dozen cookies.

Chocolate Pinwheels

One cookie with two colors and flavors—

  ½ cup butter or margarine
  ¾ cup sugar
  2 teaspoons vanilla
  1 egg
        . . .
  1¾ cups sifted all-purpose flour
  ½ teaspoon baking powder
  ½ teaspoon salt
  1 1-ounce square unsweetened
     chocolate, melted
     Milk

In mixing bowl cream butter or margarine, sugar, and vanilla till light and fluffy; beat in egg. Sift together dry ingredients; mix into creamed mixture. Divide dough in half; mix melted chocolate into one part.

On waxed paper, roll each half of dough into a 12x10-inch rectangle. (Piece dough together, if necessary, to make rectangle.) Brush one layer with milk; place other layer on top. Peel off waxed paper. Roll as for jelly roll. Wrap in waxed paper. Chill thoroughly. Slice thin; bake on *ungreased* cookie sheet at 375° for 8 to 10 minutes. Makes 4 to 6 dozen.

Slice Orange Refrigerator Cookies thinly so they will be crisp. Fresh orange juice and peel give the cookies a refreshing flavor.

Orange Refrigerator Cookies

Nuts add texture—

    1 cup butter or margarine
    ½ cup granulated sugar
    ½ cup brown sugar
    1 egg
    1 tablespoon grated orange peel
    ¼ cup orange juice
    1 teaspoon vanilla
        • • •
    3 cups sifted all-purpose flour
    ½ teaspoon salt
    ¼ teaspoon baking soda
    ½ cup chopped walnuts

In mixing bowl thoroughly cream butter, granulated sugar, and brown sugar; add egg, grated orange peel, orange juice, and vanilla. Beat well. Sift together all-purpose flour, salt, and baking soda; add to creamed mixture, mixing well. Stir in chopped nuts. Shape into rolls 2 inches in diameter. Wrap in waxed paper and chill thoroughly. Slice thinly; about ⅛ inch thick. Bake on *ungreased* cookie sheet at 375° for 12 to 15 minutes. Makes 8 dozen.

Orange-Ginger Cookies

Serve these with hot tea—

    1 cup butter or margarine
    1½ cups sugar
    1 egg
    2 tablespoons light corn syrup
    3 cups sifted all-purpose flour
    2 teaspoons baking soda
    2 teaspoons ground cinnamon
    2 teaspoons ground ginger
    ½ teaspoon ground cloves
    1 tablespoon shredded orange peel

In mixing bowl thoroughly cream together butter and sugar. Add egg and syrup; beat well. Sift together flour, baking soda, cinnamon, ginger, and cloves; mix into creamed mixture along with orange peel. Shape into two 9-inch rolls about 2 inches in diameter. Wrap in waxed paper; chill several hours or overnight. Slice about ⅛ inch thick. Place 2 inches apart on *ungreased* cookie sheet. Bake at 400° till done, about 5 to 6 minutes. Makes about 8 dozen.

REFRIGERATOR DESSERT—Any of several types of desserts that require chilling in the refrigerator. Whipped cream and gelatin are ingredients frequently used in this kind of dessert. Refrigerator desserts, particularly appealing to the hurried hostess, can be prepared ahead and then refrigerated until serving time. (See also *Dessert.*)

Chilled Banana Cheesecake

    1 cup graham cracker crumbs
    ¼ cup sugar
    ¼ teaspoon ground cinnamon
    ¼ cup butter or margarine, melted
    ¾ cup sugar
    2 envelopes unflavored gelatin
        (2 tablespoons)
    ¼ teaspoon salt
    2 beaten egg yolks
    1 6-ounce can evaporated milk
        (⅔ cup)
    1 teaspoon grated lemon peel
    2 13-ounce cartons cream-style
        cottage cheese, sieved
    1½ teaspoons vanilla
    1 cup mashed banana
    1 tablespoon lemon juice
    2 egg whites
    ¼ cup sugar
    1 cup whipping cream

For crust, combine graham cracker crumbs, ¼ cup sugar, and cinnamon. Blend in melted butter. Lightly butter sides of an 8-inch springform pan; reserve ¼ of the crumb mixture and firmly press the remaining crumb mixture onto bottom and sides of the springform pan.

For filling, combine ¾ cup sugar, gelatin, and salt in heavy saucepan. Stir in egg yolks and milk. Cook and stir till gelatin dissolves and mixture thickens slightly, 5 to 10 minutes. Remove from heat. Add lemon peel; cool.

Stir in cottage cheese and vanilla. Chill, stirring occasionally, till partially set. Combine mashed banana and lemon juice; fold into gelatin mixture. Beat egg whites to soft peaks. Slowly add the ¼ cup sugar, beating to stiff peaks; fold into gelatin mixture. Whip cream; fold cream into gelatin mixture.

Pour filling into crumb-lined pan. Sprinkle with reserved crumbs. Chill till firm, 6 to 8 hours or overnight. Makes 12 servings.

Strawberry Swirl

A dessert that can be made ahead of time—

   1 cup graham cracker crumbs
   1 tablespoon sugar
   ¼ cup butter or margarine, melted

      . . .

   1 3-ounce package strawberry-
      flavored gelatin
   1 cup boiling water
   1 cup cold water
   8 ounces marshmallows
   ½ cup milk
   1 cup whipping cream
   2 cups sliced fresh strawberries

Mix crumbs, sugar, and melted butter. Press mixture firmly over the bottom of a 9x9x2-inch baking pan. Chill till crumbs are set.

Dissolve strawberry-flavored gelatin in the 1 cup boiling water. Add the cold water. Chill till gelatin mixture is partially set.

Meanwhile, in saucepan combine marshmallows and milk; heat and stir till marshmallows melt. Cool thoroughly. Whip cream just till peaks begin to form; fold into cooled marshmallow mixture. Add berries to gelatin, then swirl in marshmallow mixture to marble. Pour into crust and chill till set in refrigerator. Cut into squares to serve. Garnish with additional whipped cream, if desired. Serves 9 to 12.

Choco-Date Dessert

  12 packaged, cream-filled chocolate
      cookies, crushed
   ¼ cup butter or margarine, melted
   1 cup pitted dates, cut up
   ¼ teaspoon salt
   2 cups miniature marshmallows
   ½ cup chopped walnuts
   1 cup whipping cream
   ½ teaspoon vanilla

Combine cookie crumbs and butter; spread all but ¼ *cup* in 10x6x1¾-inch dish. In saucepan mix dates, ¾ cup water, and salt; bring to boil. Reduce heat; simmer 3 minutes. Remove from heat. Add marshmallows; stir to melt. Cool. Add nuts; spread in dish. Whip cream with vanilla; swirl over dates. Top with remaining cookie crumbs. Chill. Makes 8 servings.

Flapper Pudding

   1 cup fine vanilla wafer crumbs
   ¾ cup butter or margarine
   2 cups sifted confectioners'
      sugar
   2 egg yolks
   2 stiffly beaten egg whites
   1 8½-ounce can crushed pineapple,
      well drained
   ½ cup chopped walnuts

Spread *half* of vanilla wafer crumbs in bottom of a 10x6x1¾-inch baking dish. In small bowl cream butter; gradually add confectioners' sugar, beating till light and fluffy. Add egg yolks, one at a time, beating well after each addition. Beat 1 minute more.

Fold in egg whites (mixture may look curdled); beat at medium speed for a few *seconds* or till smooth. Fold in pineapple and nuts. Carefully spread mixture over crumbs. Top with remaining vanilla wafer crumbs. Chill till firm, 5 hours or overnight. Cut in squares. Garnish with maraschino cherries, if desired. Serves 10.

Serve Strawberry Swirl for a delicious meal ending. Give each serving the finishing touch by garnishing it with a fresh mint sprig.

REGIONAL COOKERY

"As American as apple pie" is a phrase often used to describe something that is considered typical of all the United States. Although apple pie is served throughout this country, many other dishes are considered specialties of specific areas. In fact, a close examination reveals that just about every village and town has a food specialty. However, there are common characteristics and foods that tend to divide the United States into four general culinary regions—Northeast, South, Midwest, and Southwest-West.

Describe your favorite dishes, and you more than likely give a clue to which part of the nation you are from. For example, a fondness for slow-cooked baked beans indicates that you are from New England, while a craving for scrapple comes from a Pennsylvania Dutch background. If sweet potato pie is high on your list of favorites, no doubt you're from the South. A longing for a grilled beef steak denotes that you were brought up in the Midwest, while a love of barbecue feasts places you with other Texans. Natives of the states that border Mexico undoubtedly will express a preference for foods that show a Mexican influence. And if you were raised on the West Coast, Dungeness crab and abalone are probably favorites of yours.

These examples, however, are only a few of the many foods and dishes that typify the four regions of this country. A more extensive culinary journey will uncover many other regional characteristics.

Steak southwestern style

← Tender Ranch House Round Steak served with cornbread and Texas-Style Beans (see *Pinto Bean* for recipe) make a hearty meal.

Northeastern

This region extends from the northern east coast, with its bountiful fish and seafood, inland to Pennsylvania where the food of the Pennsylvania Dutch is at home. Although fine food is plentiful in this region, the foods of three distinctive cuisines—New England, Shaker, and Pennsylvania Dutch—best illustrate northeastern cookery.

New England: The mention of New England's food invariably brings to mind baked beans. Rich with a flavor acquired through hours of baking, Boston baked beans are indeed a classic. However, New England cooks are also noted for numerous other good foods.

The close proximity of the Atlantic Ocean has resulted in a large number of New England fish and seafood dishes. Saltwater fish are deliciously cooked in many ways, and lobsters are boiled, broiled, or baked and made into bisque, chowder, stew, and pie. There are all types of fish and seafood chowders, but the most famous of these is clam chowder. This dish is made with milk everywhere in New England except in Rhode Island where Manhattan-style chowder with tomato is preferred.

New England is also noted for its cranberry bogs. These bogs produce thousands of pounds of berries yearly. Although this crop is shipped throughout the United States, New Englanders keep part of the berries for use in pies, cakes, breads, ice creams, sherbets, and sauces.

The New Englanders' traditional thriftiness is exemplified by their boiled dinner of corned beef and root vegetables, which is served fresh. Later, the leftovers become red flannel hash. Thrifty and good, too, are a salt fish dinner of cod, and crisp, fried salt pork in milk gravy.

Other specialties of this area include molasses doughnuts spiced with cinnamon and ginger, anadama bread flavored with molasses and cornmeal, and squash muffins and biscuits. And don't forget gingerbread, Hartford election cake, and old-fashioned Indian pudding with ice cream on top.

Shaker: During the mid-1700s, a band of religious people called Shakers established several colonies in the New England area. Although these colonies are no longer active, Shaker recipes have survived as part of the cuisine typical of this region.

The relatively simple foods of these people were prepared almost entirely from their farm crops and foods found in the woodlands. During the growing season, fruits and vegetables were used fresh and large quantities of these were also canned for use during the long winter. Milk, cream, butter, and lard were used extensively as ingredients as were a wide variety of herbs grown in large herb gardens.

The Shakers were excellent bakers, too. White and whole wheat bread, salt-rising bread, potato bread, and muffins were a common part of the Shaker diet. Cakes and pies, sometimes sweetened with maple sugar, honey, or molasses, where also frequently prepared. Rosewater and herbs were favorite flavorings for cakes and cookies.

Pennsylvania Dutch: Down the coast and inland a bit from New England, Pennsylvania Dutch cooks set lavish tables with hearty German-style foods. For breakfast there is scrapple, fried liver pudding, or any of a number of sausages as a change from eggs. Buckwheat grows well in Pennsylvania, so a jug of starter for buckwheat batter is kept from October to May for winter pancakes. Some of the soups these cooks make from noodles and an abundance of vegetables, are hearty enough to be the supper main dish. Creamed or buttered vegetables with a touch of herb, coleslaw, or wilted lettuce, and, maybe a bowl of cottage cheese also help tame the appetite. A selection of sweets such as jams, jellies, or preserves, and sours ranging from mustard pickles to pickled cherries is always there to "make things taste good." In this area, all the food for a meal, soup through dessert (often shoofly pie), is placed on the table at once so that each person can see what's there and tailor his servings to the size of his appetite.

New England Dinner

    1 small clove garlic
    1 bay leaf
 2½ pounds corned beef
    6 small potatoes, peeled and
      halved
    1 small rutabaga *or* turnip,
      cut in chunks
    6 medium carrots, peeled and
      halved
    1 small head cabbage, quartered
    4 peppercorns

Place 1 cup water, garlic, and bay leaf in a 6-quart pressure pan with rack. Place meat on rack. Close cover securely. Cook 45 minutes at 15 pounds pressure. Let pressure drop of its own accord. Open pan and add potatoes, rutabaga, carrots, cabbage, and peppercorns. Close cover securely and return pan to heat. Cook 6 to 7 minutes at 15 pounds pressure. Reduce pressure quickly by placing under cold running water. Makes 6 servings.

Rosewater and Caraway Cookies

    1 cup butter or margarine
    1 cup sugar
    2 beaten eggs
 2¾ cups sifted all-purpose flour
    1 teaspoon baking soda
   ½ teaspoon cream of tartar
   ½ cup mixed, chopped, candied
      fruits and peels
   ½ cup light raisins
    2 tablespoons caraway seed
    2 tablespoons rosewater

Cream first 3 ingredients till light and fluffy. Sift together flour, soda, cream of tartar, and dash salt; add to creamed mixture. Stir in remaining ingredients. Drop from teaspoon onto *ungreased* cookie sheet. Flatten with glass dipped in flour; center each with a light raisin. Bake at 375° till lightly browned, 8 to 10 minutes. Cool on rack. Makes about 4½ dozen.

Mennonite Chicken with Sour Cream

¼ cup butter or margarine
¼ cup all-purpose flour
1 teaspoon salt
1 2-pound ready-to-cook broiler-
   fryer chicken, split in half
   Paprika

• • •

3 tablespoons water
1 tablespoon all-purpose flour
¼ teaspoon salt
   Dash pepper
   Dash paprika
½ cup dairy sour cream

Place butter in shallow baking pan or oven-going skillet; heat to melt butter. Combine ¼ cup flour, salt, and dash pepper; roll chicken in mixture till coated. Dip coated chicken in melted butter and arrange, skin side up, in the baking pan. Sprinkle with paprika. Bake at 325° till the chicken is tender and nicely browned, about 1¼ hours. Remove the chicken from the baking pan; keep the chicken warm.

Add water to pan drippings; mix well. Blend in remaining ingredients. Bring just to boiling, stirring constantly. Remove from heat and serve over chicken. Makes 2 servings.

Southern

The area known as the South extends down the Atlantic coast from Maryland to Florida and then westward through Louisiana. Seafood is plentiful and southern cooks excel in preparing it. Other specialties include fried chicken and baked goods.

One of the outstanding characteristics of the cookery of this area is the great influence exerted by immigrants. For example, English influence is evident in Maryland and Virginia, while Louisiana shows both French and Spanish influences.

All through the South there is evidence of the influence of Afro-American cooks who created specialties from the foods of the region. These cooks are credited with developing many of the southern dishes using sweet potatoes and peanuts as well as dishes such as gumbo and chitterlings.

Since the majority of southern states border the ocean, fish and seafood are important in this cuisine. Crab is fixed in numerous ways in Maryland and the Carolinas, from plain, boiled hard-shells to delicate crab timbales. Oysters are scalloped in Virginia, baked with spinach in New Orleans, and fried, broiled, or made into soups everywhere. There are okra-flavored gumbos of shrimp, crab, or lobster, and shrimp is also found in pilaf, with corn in a pie, or crumb-coated and fried.

Southern fried chicken is popularly prepared throughout the South. Although some cooks flour the chicken for frying, others prefer crumbing. Still others like to coat it with a batter dip. But, no matter which technique is used, the chicken typically turns out moist and delicious. Another meat favorite in this area is smoked ham, which is served with "red-eye" gravy.

Southern cooks are great bakers, too. Tiny baking powder biscuits, all flaky crust with almost no "innards," melt like snowflakes when eaten. By contrast, southern cornbread is plain, unsweetened, and unleavened, and beaten biscuits are reminiscent of thick, though tender, crackers. Other hot bread favorites include spoon bread, buttermilk batter bread, and crackling bread. Regional sweet baked specialties include sweet potato pie, pecan pie, and the elegant Lady Baltimore cake.

The favorite vegetables of this region include rice and hominy grits. The ever-popular sweet potato is served baked, boiled, fried, mashed, and candied. Turnip, mustard, and collard greens as well as spinach and green beans are usually cooked with a piece of salt pork or ham.

In the Gulf states, particularly southeastern Louisiana, the descendants of French and Spanish settlers, called Creoles, have developed a distinctive cuisine. The frequent use of fish, shellfish, game, rice, and vegetables such as okra and tomatoes typifies the foods of the Creoles. One of the most important parts of this cuisine is the *roux*. This cooked flour-shortening mixture is the basis for many thickened soups, sauces, and seafood dishes.

Most of the flavorful Creole dishes are highly seasoned with a combination of herbs and spices. The seasoning that is most distinctively Creole is filé (powdered sassafras leaves), which is popularly used in seafood dishes and gumbos.

Bacon Spoon Bread

  ¾ cup cornmeal
1½ cups cold water
  8 ounces sharp natural Cheddar
      cheese, shredded (2 cups)
  ¼ cup butter, softened
  2 cloves garlic, crushed
  ½ teaspoon salt
  1 cup milk
  4 well-beaten egg yolks
  8 ounces sliced bacon, crisp-
      cooked and drained
  4 stiffly beaten egg whites

Combine cornmeal and water; cook, stirring constantly, till the mixture is consistency of mush. Remove from heat. Add cheese, butter, garlic, and salt; stir to melt cheese. Gradually add milk. Stir in egg yolks.

Crumble bacon, reserving some for garnish; add to cornmeal mixture. Fold in egg whites. Pour into greased 2-quart soufflé dish. Bake at 325° till done, about 65 minutes. Spoon into warm dishes; top with butter. Serves 6.

Oysters Bienville

Open 18 oysters in shells. With knife, remove oysters. Wash shells. Place each oyster in deep half of the shell. Arrange shells on bed of rock salt in a shallow pan; set aside.

Cook ½ cup chopped green onion and 1 clove garlic, minced, in 2 tablespoons butter or margarine till tender but not brown. Blend in 2 tablespoons all-purpose flour and ¼ teaspoon salt. Add ⅔ cup chicken broth all at once. Cook and stir till mixture thickens and bubbles.

Beat 1 egg yolk and ⅓ cup dry white wine together. Add a little of hot mixture to egg and wine; return to hot mixture. Stir in one 3-ounce can sliced mushrooms, drained; 2 tablespoons snipped parsley; and dash bottled hot pepper sauce. Cook and stir till almost boiling.

In small saucepan melt ½ tablespoon butter; add ½ cup soft bread crumbs (1 slice) and toss to coat. Stir in 2 tablespoons grated Parmesan cheese. Heat oysters at 400° for 5 minutes. Top each oyster with 1 tablespoon of the sauce mixture. Sprinkle 1 teaspoon bread-Parmesan mixture atop each oyster. Bake till heated through and crumbs are lightly browned, about 10 to 12 minutes longer. Makes 6 servings.

Pecan Pralines

  3 cups sugar
  1 teaspoon baking soda
  1 cup buttermilk
  ¾ cup light corn syrup
  2 tablespoons butter or margarine
  2 cups pecan halves

In large saucepan or Dutch oven combine sugar, baking soda, and ⅛ teaspoon salt. Stir in buttermilk and corn syrup. Bring to boiling over medium heat, stirring constantly. Cook and stir to soft-ball stage (234°). Remove from heat; add butter. Stir in pecans; beat till mixture is thick enough to drop from spoon, 5 to 6 minutes. Quickly drop from tablespoon onto waxed paper. If candy becomes too stiff, add 1 teaspoon hot water. Makes about 45.

Midwestern

The large area called the Midwest extends from Ohio to California and from Canada to Oklahoma. Like all of the other regions, this area is very diverse. However, the cuisine of the Midwest is banded together by the use of the crops and livestock that thrive on the farms and ranches of this area. Another quality of the Midwest that is often overlooked is the retention of immigrant cuisines in settlements scattered throughout this region. For example, the Germans and Scandinavians in the northern states, the Dutch in Michigan, and the polyglot of nationalities in Chicago have not only retained many of their native foods but have also introduced many dishes into the general cuisine of this region.

The Midwest is corn country, with roasting ears aplenty, custardy corn pudding, corn fried with onions and green peppers, and even corn chowder. It is wheat country, too, with tables plenteously supplied with breads and coffee cakes reminiscent of the baking of many lands. There are dumplings both hearty and sweet, numerous dishes that make use of the dairy products of the Midwest, pasta made of locally grown hard wheat, and numerous delicious pies, cakes, cookies, and other baked goods.

Midwestern cooks who know how to cook the beef of Kansas, Nebraska, and Iowa do equally well with a New York-style sirloin or an economical chicken-fried steak. They roast the pork of Iowa to succulent perfection, and they are only slightly fazed by the prospect of cooking a bear or buffalo pot roast, elkburgers, or antelope chops. The lakes and rivers of the area abound with fish, which are baked, broiled, or panbroiled. This in an area of hearty food, which is prepared simply to bring out the food's basic good quality.

Fresh Peach Ice Cream

  1¼ **cups sugar**
  1½ **teaspoons unflavored gelatin**
   4 **cups light cream**
   1 **slightly beaten egg**
   1 **teaspoon vanilla**
  ¼ **teaspoon almond extract**
   6 **peaches, peeled, seeded, and mashed (3 cups)**

In saucepan combine ½ *cup* sugar and gelatin. Stir in *half* the cream. Stir over low heat till gelatin dissolves. Slowly blend small amount of hot mixture into beaten egg; return to hot mixture. Cook and stir till slightly thickened, about 1 minute. Chill. Add remaining cream, vanilla, almond extract, and dash salt. Combine mashed peaches and the remaining sugar; add to chilled gelatin-cream mixture.

Pour into ice cream freezer can. (Fill can only ⅔ full to allow for expansion during freezing.) Fit can into freezer. Adjust dasher and cover. Pack crushed ice and rock salt around can, using proportions of 6 parts ice to 1 part salt. (Pack ice and salt up to—but not over—lid of can.) *Turn handle slowly till ice melts and forms brine; add more ice and salt throughout freezing to maintain ice level. Turn handle at constant speed till crank becomes difficult to turn. Remove ice to a level below the lid of freezer can; thoroughly wipe cover and top of freezer can. Remove lid; pull out and scrape dasher. Makes about 2 quarts.

To ripen ice cream: Plug opening in lid. Pack more ice and salt (using proportion of 4 parts ice to 1 part rock salt) around freezer can to fill freezer. Cover with heavy cloth or newspapers. Let ripen for at least 4 hours to improve and mellow the flavor.

*If using electric ice cream freezer, follow manufacturer's directions.

Six-Layer Dinner

Layer the following in a 3-quart casserole, seasoning each layer with salt and pepper: 3 cups sliced, peeled, raw potatoes; one 17-ounce can whole kernel corn, drained; 1 medium onion, sliced; 1 pound ground beef; and 1 cup sliced raw carrots. Pour one 16-ounce can tomatoes, cut up, over casserole. Cover and bake at 350° about 1¾ hours. Serves 6.

Quick Corn Chowder

In large saucepan cook 5 slices bacon till crisp. Remove bacon; crumble and set aside. Reserve 3 tablespoons drippings in saucepan; discard remainder. Add 1 medium onion, sliced and separated into rings; cook till lightly browned. Add 2 medium potatoes, peeled and diced, and ½ cup water; cook over medium heat till potato is tender, 10 to 15 minutes.

Add one 17-ounce can cream-style corn, 2 cups milk, 1 teaspoon salt, and dash pepper; cook till heated through. Pour into warmed bowls; top each serving with crumbled bacon and a pat of butter or margarine. Serve with crackers, if desired. Makes 4 or 5 servings.

Southwestern and Western

This region of the United States includes eight states—Texas, New Mexico, Arizona, California, Oregon, Washington, Alaska, and Hawaii. Since this region includes so many different types of cookery, it is further divided into the southwestern states, the Pacific coast states, Alaska, and Hawaii.

Southwest: The cookery of the southwestern states is influenced by Mexican and Indian foods. Tortillas, tamales, and tacos are as much at home here as south of the border. Corn, the basic grain, is used in the all-purpose corn flour dough. Hot chili peppers, hung to dry in the sun, are used to season corn, bean, and meat dishes. Chili powder mixtures, too, are used for pungent seasoning. From the Indians come sage-flavored honey for sweetening, pine nuts to add flavor and texture, and cookery with cornmeal as an Apache bread. Other Indian contributions are acorn soup, fried bread dough, and jerky stew.

Texas is barbecue country, with anything from a whole steer to a hamburger skillfully grilled and sauced. However, Texas cookery also includes typical southern dishes and many Mexican dishes. Frijoles and candied yams are as much at home here as are ranch house beans. And, backing up the Texan's claim that everything is richer in Texas, pecan pie is made there with more butter and eggs than elsewhere.

Pacific coast: This area has several foods that deserve special mention. Seafood is king—crabs, clams, oysters, and fish. Crab Louis originated in Seattle, and both Dungeness and king crabs are cooked and served in dozens of other ways. Special taste treats of this area include barbecued salmon up north, cioppino (fish stew) in San Francisco, and grilled abalone from southern California. Throughout the area, oriental foods are popular. And sourdough bread has had a revival in California.

Alaska and Hawaii: Both of these states are separated from the other states by such great distances that they are not really tied to the cuisine typical of the western region. Alaskans enjoy dishes that are not available in other parts of the country, such as mooseburgers, reindeer steaks, and ptarmigan stew. Fish, seafood, and native berries and vegetables are also commonly used by Alaskan cooks. Unlike the cold of Alaska, the climate of Hawaii is tropical. As a result, tropical friuts are used extensively by the Islanders. Hawaiian cookery is also noted for its adoption of dishes brought in by Oriental, Portuguese, and other immigrants to the Islands.

Grilled Abalone

Use 1 pound fresh or frozen abalone steaks (thaw if frozen). Combine 1/3 cup all-purpose flour, 1 teaspoon salt, and 1/4 teaspoon pepper. Combine 1 beaten egg and 1 tablespoon milk. Dip abalone steaks in flour mixture and then in egg mixture. Coat steaks with 1 1/2 cups fine saltine cracker crumbs. Melt 1/4 cup butter or margarine in skillet; cook steaks 1 minute on each side. *Do not overcook.* Drain on paper toweling. Serve piping hot. Makes 4 servings.

Western Salad

Seed, peel, and slice 2 avocados. Prepare 2 cups cantaloupe balls. Cook 6 slices bacon till crisp; drain and crumble. In large salad bowl toss 4 cups shredded lettuce with *half* the avocado, melon, and bacon. Arrange remaining avocado and melon atop; add remaining bacon. Pass sweet French salad dressing. Serves 8.

Ranch House Round Steak

Cut 3 pounds 1/2-inch thick round steak into serving-sized pieces; trim off excess fat and slash edges of meat. Combine 1/4 cup all-purpose flour, 2 teaspoons dry mustard, 1 1/2 teaspoons salt, and 1/8 teaspoon pepper; coat meat with mixture. (Set aside any remaining mixture.)

In heavy skillet brown meat on both sides in 1/4 cup hot salad oil. Add reserved flour mixture to skillet. Combine 1/2 cup water and 1 tablespoon Worcestershire sauce; stir into mixture in skillet. Cover tightly; cook over low heat till meat is tender, 1 to 1 1/4 hours. Remove meat to platter. Skim fat from pan juices; drizzle juices over meat. Serves 8.

Today, it is often difficult to define what typifies a region because of the speed of transportation of fresh foods and the population mobility. As people move, they take their food favorites of one region with them to their next home. Yet, because of the regional availability of some ingredients and the retention of traditions, certain foods are still distinctively regional. It is these foods along with regional differences in the people and countryside that give each area of the United States a separate charm.

REHYDRATE—To replace fluid lost during dehydration. Instant nonfat dry milk must be rehydrated before it is drunk.

REINDEER—A deer with branched antlers that lives in the cold, northern parts of the world. The inhabitants of these areas raise reindeer for its pelt amd meat. The delicate, sweet reindeer meat can be prepared similarly to beef or venison, and it is delicious marinated, then braised.